THE ELECTION OF 1980

THE ELECTION OF 1980

Reports and Interpretations

GERALD M. POMPER

ROSS K. BAKER

KATHLEEN A. FRANKOVIC

CHARLES E. JACOB

WILSON CAREY MCWILLIAMS

HENRY A. PLOTKIN

MARLENE MICHELS POMPER
editor

CHATHAM HOUSE PUBLISHERS, INC.
Chatham, New Jersey

THE ELECTION OF 1980
Reports and Interpretations

CHATHAM HOUSE PUBLISHERS, INC.
Box One, Chatham, New Jersey 07928

Publisher: Edward Artinian
Book Design: Quentin Fiore
Cover Design: Lawrence Ratzkin
Composition: Chatham Composer
Printing and Binding: Hamilton Printing Company

LIBRARY OF CONGRESS CATALOGING IN PUBLICATION DATA

Main entry under title:

The Election of 1980.
    Includes bibliographical references and index.
    1. Presidents--United States--Election--1980--Adresses, essays, lectures. I. Pomper, Gerald M.
JK526 1980.E43   324.973'0926   81-598
ISBN 0-934540-10-1   AACR2
ISBN 0-934540-09-8 (pbk.)

Manufactured in the United States of America

10 9 8 7 6 5 4 3 2 1

Contents

Preface

Men and women often live their lives seeking a perfect time, a brief moment that will provide a matchless experience. This was the quest of Faust, who dreamt of a point in his existence when he could say, "Tarry a while, you are so beautiful."

With these words, we began our examination of the election of 1976. That seemed to be a time of new opportunities. Four years later, we recall it as a period of brief satisfaction but incomplete fulfillment. Writing now of the election of 1980 we, like other voters, have mixed feelings — of nostalgia for the bittersweet past, of acceptance of the ambiguous present, of hope for the uncertain future.

In the following essays, six political scientists report and interpret the 1980 election results. The political year saw much innovation and much conflict. A conservative faction won full control of the Republican party, while the incumbent Democratic President faced a major challenge. Issues ranged from economic policy to women's rights. Public opinion, uncertain through much of the campaign, eventually turned decisively toward the Republicans. As the twentieth century waned, America inaugurated its oldest elected President. These events require years of analysis. We hope to contribute to that effort.

The authors of this work — Ross K. Baker, Kathleen A. Frankovic, Charles E. Jacob, Wilson Carey McWilliams, Henry A. Plotkin, and Gerald M. Pomper — are associates of the political science program of Rutgers University. The book represents a collaborative effort of this group, consisting of five Rutgers faculty members and a distinguished alumna. We agree in many of our conclusions — most notably in interpreting the 1980 results as a negative reaction to the Carter administration rather than a victory for conservative ideology. We differ on some other interpretations and hope that our diverse arguments will provoke further discussion.

A note on the authors should mention the following:

Ross K. Baker is a professor and the author of *Friend and Foe in the United States Senate;*

Kathleen A. Frankovic, a Rutgers Ph.D., is Manager of Surveys, CBS News;

Charles E. Jacob is a professor and the author of *Policy and Bureaucracy*;

Wilson Carey McWilliams is a professor and the author of *The Idea of Fraternity in America*;

Henry A. Plotkin is an assistant professor and the author of the forthcoming *The Corporation in America*;

Gerald M. Pomper is a professor and the author of *Elections in America.*

We are grateful to the many people who enabled us to produce this early interpretation of the 1980 elections. Edith Saks, of Rutgers' Eagleton Institute of Politics, prepared most of the final draft and supervised its completion. Janet Aktabowski, Lyn Stroock, and Nadine Varca aided us in typing. Helpful criticism was provided by Emmet J. Hughes, Maureen Moakley, Stephen Salmore, and Nancy Schwartz. Staff members at CBS, particularly Elda Vale, Wayne Reedy, Solomon Barr, and Patrice LoCicero, provided rapid data analyses. Myung Chung of the Rutgers University Library was most helpful. Edward Artinian, our publisher who is also a friend, conceived the project and steadfastly saw it through all stages. Our greatest debt, as in 1976, is to our editor, Marlene Michels Pomper. She again provided whatever coherence, stylistic grace, and clarity is evident in these essays. Ours is the responsiblity for the hasty and ill-considered thoughts.

We dedicate this book to our mothers. Their care and concern have enabled us to learn and to pass on whatever knowledge we have to our own children, our friends, and our students. With these words, we express our thanks — to Augusta Baker, Olga Frankovic, Thelma Jacob, Dorothy McWilliams, Lillian Michels, Sarah Plotkin, and Celia Pomper.

January 1981   GERALD M. POMPER

1

The Nominating Contests

GERALD M. POMPER

It was a year of political paradox.

Jimmy Carter, first nominated and elected in 1976 as an "outsider," used the traditional techniques of the "insider" to win renomination. His major opponent, Edward M. Kennedy, was the leading choice for President among the Democrats — until he became a candidate. The Republicans had established a quadrennial custom of bloodletting between their conservative and moderate wings, but early chose Ronald Reagan as their standard-bearer and united in his cause. Although Gerald Ford was more popular than any potential Republican candidate, the former President won no open support in his party. America entered the new decade facing an electoral choice among Carter, regarded less favorably by the voters than any President since 1952; Reagan, achieving nomination only after a twelve-year quest; and John B. Anderson, a Republican turned Independent and repudiated by his Republican colleagues.

The major parties' nominations reversed past patterns and contemporary expectations. Contests for the presidential designation typically occur in the party out of power, while the party holding the Presidency is expected to confirm its leadership ritualistically. Although they held the White House in 1980, the Democrats engaged in a vigorous contest that continued in one form or another until the convention balloting. For their part, after surveying an initially crowded field, the Republicans gave Reagan the consensual suport commonly granted an incumbent President. Parties are expected to nominate the candidate most likely to win the November election, but the opinion polls frequently showed Carter likely to lose, unless Reagan became the Republican nominee. Yet the parties, with some apparent perversity, selected two potential losers for a race they wanted to win. In another anomaly, the major parties' nominations were closed early in the year. Yet much effort had been spent in writing statutes and revising party rules in order to "open" the election process to new groups, new candidates, and new sources of money.

1

The ultimate paradox is that the choices, despite their deficiencies, were probably the most appropriate ones available to the two major parties. The Democrats selected their incumbent President and thereby accepted their most popular candidate and, for good or ill, the record he had established in their name. The Republicans named the aspirant with the most widespread support among party members and the one who represented best the ideological bent of the party. Many voters would be dissatisfied with the principal alternatives available in the November election, but the parties had somehow presented an honest choice.

To explain these paradoxes, we need to examine the changing setting of presidential nominations. We will then proceed to analyze the major party contests. In this chapter, we consider John Anderson only as a Republican contender, reserving fuller discussion of his independent candidacy for later in the book.

THE CHANGING SETTING

The nominations of 1980 were the culmination of trends in presidential politics that had been developing for twelve years. In the recent past, nominations had been made by the leaders of the political parties, who gave considerable attention to public opinion polls, mass media, and state primaries. By 1980, a new system was established, in which individual candidates were the major actors who sought to influence the polls, the media, and the primaries, while paying little notice to party leaders.

In form, the presidential nominations of 1980 were made at the Republican convention in Detroit and the Democratic meeting in New York. The procedures followed there were similar to those used for the past 150 years in America. In substance, the conventions had been reduced to rituals by major rule changes.

Most delegates to these conventions were chosen in popular primaries. In 1968, this method had been employed in only 17 states, resulting in popular selection of little more than a third of the delegates. By 1980, primaries were used in 37 states and territories, and determined three-fourths of the delegates. Aspirants to the White House no longer needed to win the favor of party leaders; they could take their case directly to the voters in these primaries (even if only a minority of those eligible actually voted). Because the delegates chosen also were pledged to particular candidates, the opportunities for any convention bargaining among uncommitted blocs were limited.

A second major change was in the means by which delegates were chosen in the individual states. Particularly in the Democratic party, the new rules required division of the delegates in proportion to the support each candidate demonstrated in the state primary or in local caucuses, selection meetings open to all members of the party. Moreover, the Democrats required that the principle of proportional division be used even at the local level so that minority candidate preferences would be represented within every congressional district. (Illinois was the major exception.) Although they were also affected, the Republicans did not follow the principle as completely as the Democrats did in 1980. In total, 91 percent of the Democrats and 31 percent of the Republicans chosen in primaries were selected by strict proportional representation.[1]

Primaries and proportional representation worked to the advantage of candidates who had diffuse support, who could do reasonably well throughout the nation even if they did not have overwhelming strength in any single area. This encouraged candidates to invade one another's home turf, and reduced the advantage of regional loyalties.[2] It benefited candidates who had the time and resources to develop organizations in many states so that they could win some share, even if not the majority, of the delegates over the long period of selection; but it created problems for candidates who started later, who concentrated their attention in a few places, who lacked widespread contacts. The presidential race now favored turtles rather than hares.

Beyond these particular changes, a fundamental shift had occurred in the nature of the nation's political parties. It had once been a cliché of American politics that there were no national parties, that we had one hundred parties, two in each state. By 1980, there were national Democratic and Republican parties, but they were quite different in their character.[3] The Democrats had been transforming themselves into an organization based on mass membership in which the individual party member had a direct effect on national decisions, most prominently on the selection of the presidential candidate. This was the philosophic basis for new rules on the apportionment, selection, and demographic characteristics of delegates. The Republicans took a different tack, creating a strong organization built on techniques of business management and modern campaign technology. In that party, the effort was to create an efficient bureaucracy that could effectively pursue the basic party goal of winning elections.

Common to both major parties was a lack of attention to the selection of party leadership. Neither Democrats nor Republicans provided for a regular means within the revitalized party for the designation of the presidential candidate. The party would be either a mass movement or an efficient vote-gatherer, but not a recruiter of top leadership. That decision would be left to the unorganized voters. Once the candidate was selected, the new party would be available for his use.

But politics is never unorganized. If the choice of a President was no longer to be channeled by state parties or elected officials acting in the party's name, others would take up the task. The initiative had passed by 1980 to the individual candidates. They now make the basic choices — whether to run, what to emphasize, how to use resources. Their decisions are, of course, limited by formal rules and other participants, but they take the first steps and thereby blaze the trail. A candidate must organize his or her own effort, and need give little attention to the erstwhile "power brokers" within the party. If successful, the candidate becomes the leader of the party, possessing its name and machinery, with few obligations toward other party leaders — but also with few claims on their loyalty.

The focus on candidates favored a special breed. A long campaign would be needed, one requiring physical stamina, an enormous tolerance for travel, and the ability to repeat in earnest the same "spontaneous" plea to thousands of small groups. Because an open and direct effort was required, there was almost no chance for a candidate to be drafted or to appear as a last-minute "dark horse" at the convention. The nominee was more likely to be selected from what Woodrow Wilson described as the "small group of middle-aged athletes." Furthermore, public officials were at a disadvantage, for the new nominating system required a long period of full-time activity with no allowances for other, distracting responsibilities. Two years of open campaigning, preceded by years of preparation, had become normal. Presidential nominations were for the active, the ambitious, and the unemployed.

In the new nominating system, candidates are particularly concerned with their relationship to mass media, notably television. The media are important not only as transmitters of the candidates' messages to millions of voters; they are also critical as screening devices, presenting some men (but no women or blacks) as possible nominees and giving scant attention to others. The press and television create "a consensus on the characteristics and qualifications of candidates and potential candidates." Campaign events are then interpreted in the light of this consensus.[4]

Given the media's importance, candidates direct their efforts to influencing media content. "Accordingly, the attitudes, beliefs, and behavior of the journalist corps become a milieu for political competition." Those seeking the nomination become concerned with issues the media are emphasizing; they offer exclusive interviews or inside information; they search for ways to gain special attention. In turn, they are affected by the media and "accommodate their political strategies to the expected nature of the campaign reporting."[5]

A major concern of the media in a nominating campaign is identifying the winner. In fact, this "horse race" aspect of an election is commonly given more attention than any other feature.[6] Candidates attempt to take advantage of this media emphasis, and to obtain favorable interpretations of their own standing. Throughout the race, "the press informs the public how the candidates are faring: who is winning? who is losing? who is still 'viable'? who is the front-runner? who can no longer be taken seriously?"[7] The candidates attempt to influence these media judgments — a leader in a state primary finds it evidence of momentum; a close runner-up sees a moral victory; a loser minimizes the outcome. These interpretations are especially important in regard to public opinion polls, which have become one of the major influences on presidential nominations.[8] Amid their deluge of information, it becomes simple to see which way the wind is blowing. The result is a rapid "winnowing" of the candidates to a small number — possibly only one.[9]

A final background factor is money. Conducting a presidential campaign is an expensive process, particularly with the new stress on direct contact with the public through mass media and in state primaries. In 1980, finance had an even greater influence because of changes in legislation and in the economy.

The federal government both subsidized candidates and limited their spending. By providing money to candidates directly, the law furthered the trend toward individual campaigning, since candidates no longer needed to rely on party organizations to raise funds. Government support also created problems, however. To receive funds, a candidate was required to limit his spending to $17.6 million. The total was not very large, given the size of the electorate, amounting to about 50 cents for each voter in the primaries. Moreover, federal funds were provided on a shared basis, with the government matching up to $250 of each private contribution. To receive a full allotment, therefore, a candidate needed to devote considerable time and some funds to raising small contributions from a large number of persons.

There were few alternatives to this method of financing a campaign. A candidate could seek larger individual contributions, but the law provided for a maximum donation of $1,000 from any individual. Moreover, the value of even a maximum contribution had been further reduced by inflation. Since the law's first use in 1976, the purchasing power of $1,000 had decreased to $740, but the limitation remained unchanged. Campaign costs had been particularly affected by economic trends. While prices generally rose 35 percent, the cost of chartering an airplane had increased 143 percent in the four-year period, the cost of a one-minute television commercial had gone up 63 percent (to $7,400), and the cost of postage was half again as great in 1980 as in 1976. "This year's Presidential hopefuls," one journalist observed early in the year, "will have less opportunity . . . to tell how they are qualified . . . to curb inflation . . . because of inflation itself."[10]

The financial pinch facing all candidates further promoted early closure of the nominating battles. A candidate who did not do well quickly found it difficult to raise funds, and there were no means to run a campaign on a small budget, given the increased costs. A faltering candidate also faced a new legal hurdle: if he did not win 10 percent of the vote in two consecutive primaries, all federal funds were cut off, accelerating his decline. In contrast, a successful candidate would get not only more attention from the media and more prominence in the polls but would also double any new funds received because of federal matching funds. Those rich in votes would also get richer in money.

The new political setting of 1980 worked to the advantage of a distinct political type. Successful candidates would be those who had long prepared their campaigns, who had diffuse strength and extensive political organizations, who could achieve attention from media and the polls, and who could stimulate early primary victories and contributions. Who were these men?

THE   POLITICS   OF   1980

As the incumbent President, Jimmy Carter would inevitably be the focus of the 1980 election. By the summer of 1979, a year before the nominating conventions, the Georgian appeared headed for defeat. Fewer than 30 percent of the electorate believed that he was doing a good or excellent job as President, a lower approval rating than any chief executive had received with the exception of Harry Truman in the midst of the Korean war and Richard Nixon at the depths of the Watergate scandal.[11] Despite such foreign policy victories as the Panama Canal treaty and peace between Israel and Egypt, Carter was seen as a weak leader.

The President was widely regarded with suspicion by power holders in Washington whom he had denounced during his successful campaign as an "outsider" in 1976. By his third year in office, he was under attack even from friends. A principal speechwriter concluded ruefully, "Carter's willful ignorance, his blissful tabula rasa could — to me — be explained only by a combination of arrogance, complacency and — dread the thought — insecurity at the core of his mind and soul."[12]

The wide circle of critics was then joined by the President himself. For ten days, Carter conducted a "national retreat" at the presidential lodge at Camp David, Maryland. Isolated from normal business and public appearances, he met with hundreds of persons from all groups. On July 15, amid much anticipation, and having gained the country's attention, the President spoke of a national "crisis of confidence." Remarkably, Carter also accepted some of the responsibility for this despair, admitting that his concerns had "become increasingly narrow, focused more and more on what the isolated world of Washington thinks is important."[13] To deal with the crisis, he called for a major national effort to resolve the energy problem.

The President's stern sermon and the admission of his own failings did not dramatically improve his political standing. Critics said that the national problem was not a "crisis in confidence" but a lack of competence within the administration. A reshuffling of the Cabinet, including some forced resignations, brought further criticism. The President's energy program remained stalled in Congress for another year. Three months after his dramatic speech, the President still trailed Senator Edward Kennedy 2–1 among Democrats, and ran even with Reagan and behind Ford in "trial heats."[14]

On November 4, 1979, exactly one year before the presidential election, the President was rescued. Armed revolutionaries seized the American Embassy in Teheran, Iran, and took hostage more than sixty American diplomats, clerks, and guards. The militants, presenting themselves as students, justified the seizure as a reaction to American support of the former Shah of Iran, deposed in the February revolution.

The coming months would see many attempts to recover the American hostages. Diplomatic channels were sounded; the International Court of Justice called for the captives' release; the United States imposed economic sanctions on Iran and broke diplomatic relations, while also indicating a readiness to meet some Iranian demands; missions were sent of private individuals and a UN commission; a U.S. naval task force was moved near the Persian Gulf; and an attempt to rescue the hostages by armed helicopters failed, resulting in the death of eight Americans. All these efforts to induce or compel the release of the captives were frustrated by the revolutionary ferment in Iran, except for the freeing of blacks, women, and one sick hostage.

The foreign policy crisis deepened two months later when the Soviet Union invaded Afghanistan, a nation that borders on Iran. The Carter administration, and most of the nation, saw this action as a major threat to world peace. Strong reactions followed, including a substantial increase in the military budget, the reinstitution of registration for the draft, the halting of sales of grain and advanced technology to the Soviet Union, a deferral of Senate action on a new arms control treaty, and a boycott of the Olympic games scheduled to be held in Moscow in July.

Diplomatically, these measures did not succeed. At the time of the presidential election, the hostages remained prisoners, the Soviet armies kept control of Afghanistan, and the Olympic Games had been held. (The hostages would not be freed until their 444th day of captivity, on the very morning of the new President's inauguration, January 20, 1981.) The impact of the measures on the presidential nominations, however, was great. These crises had underlined the President's role as the nation's leader in foreign policy, a role in which his power is least subject to challenge. They had enabled Carter to present himself as a strong leader, reacting calmly and forcefully. Unable to control or even to anticipate events, his opponents were restricted to ceremonial expressions of support for the chief executive. If they attempted tentative criticisms, as Senator Kennedy did, they were attacked for undermining national unity.

The President became the willing beneficiary of a surge of patriotic fervor in late 1979. Flags were flown daily, Christmas ceremonies were curtailed, prayer vigils and marches were held, and thousands of messages were sent to Teheran to demonstrate support for the hostages. The President both symbolized and stimulated these feelings of national solidarity. He referred to the problems abroad at almost every opportunity. Because of his concentration on the nation's problems, Carter declared that he would not conduct an active campaign, but would remain at work in the White House:

> I, as President, have got to maintain the accurate image that we do have a crisis, which I will not ignore until those hostages are released. I want the American people to know it. I want the Iranians to know it. I want the hostages' families and the hostages to know it. I want the world to know that I am not going to resume business-as-usual as a partisan campaigner out on the campaign trail until our hostages are back here — free and at home.[15]

Whatever its diplomatic impact, the "rose garden" strategy had the political merit of further identifying the President as the obvious leader of the nation in the year it was again deciding on its leadership.

Earlier in 1979, President Carter's political weakness had stimulated challenges within his own party. Although an incumbent President has traditionally been assured of renomination, this tradition has been weakened considerably in the past decade, and three of the last four White House residents have faced strong opposition. This change is related to the attenuated relationship between Presidents and their parties. Since nominations are no longer achieved principally through the party, there is less basis for party loyalty to the individual nominee.

The first Democratic challenger of the President was Governor Jerry Brown of California. Brown had entered the 1976 campaign at a late date and had shown impressive strength, defeating Carter in primaries from coast to coast. As governor of California, Brown had favored programs that combined typically conservative goals (e.g., limitations on government spending), established liberal purposes (e.g., aid to minorities), and new liberal causes (e.g., elimination of nuclear power plants and women's equality). Brown personally had gained attention through his philosophic musings, ascetic life style, and romantic involvement with rock star Linda Ronstadt. After an overwhelming reelection victory as California's governor in 1978, he began preparing for a full-scale effort to win the presidential nomination.

Potentially the most serious Democratic challenge to Carter came from Massachusetts Senator Edward (Ted) Kennedy. As the youngest brother of both an assassinated former President and an assassinated presidential candidate, Kennedy possessed almost a prescriptive right to party leadership. In three successive election years, 1968, 1972, and 1976, efforts had been made to draft him as the Democratic candidate. Polls repeatedly showed him to be the most popular Democrat and the man most likely to win, a conclusion reinforced by sophisticated academic research.[16] Kennedy was seen as the standard-bearer for the traditional economic liberalism of the party and as a candidate whose personal appeal cut across ideological divisions.

His greatest liability was personal. In the summer of 1969, Kennedy had caused an automobile accident on Chappaquiddick Island in Massachusetts that resulted in the death of a young woman, and he had failed to report the event until the following day. The death on Chappaquiddick had raised questions about Kennedy's sexual morality, his honesty in explaining the matter, and his reaction to the pressure of personal crisis. Nevertheless, a decade after the accident, Kennedy's popularity was high, and he was urged to run for President by Democrats who saw a second Carter candidacy as involving electoral disaster for the party.

After months of deliberation, Kennedy announced his candidacy. He did so only four days after the seizure of the American Embassy in Teheran. The Iranian crisis damaged his campaign from the start. It focused attention on Carter and limited the opportunity for adverse criticism. The President's calm behavior under pressure was emphasized in his advertisements, and implicitly contrasted with Kennedy's conduct at Chappaquiddick. The problems created by unanticipated events were compounded by a national televised interview with Roger Mudd of CBS, in which Kennedy appeared unsure of himself and unprepared. The audience did not know, nor were they informed by CBS, that the interview had actually been taped in August, when Kennedy was still undecided about the race.

The principal challenge to President Carter would come from the Republican party. As election year neared, a large number of potential candidates were suggested, as is typical in the party out of power. Seven men survived the early winnowing. Only one, Representative John Anderson of Illinois, third-ranking Republican in the House, could be considered a liberal. Two candidates presented themselves as moderates within the party: Howard Baker of Tennessee, the leader of the Senate Republicans; and George Bush of Texas, former national party chairman and former American ambassador to China. The others were ideologically conservative, including Representative Philip Crane of Illinois, chairman of the American Conservative Union; Kansas Senator Robert Dole, the party's 1976 vice-presidential candidate; and John Connally, former secretary of the navy for Lyndon Johnson and former secretary of the treasury for Richard Nixon.

The leading conservative candidate was Ronald Reagan. After serving two terms as governor of California, Reagan left public office in 1975, first to campaign for President (for the second time) in 1976, then to organize conservatives in the nation in an independent organization, Citizens for the Republic. His extensive tours and contacts with party and interest groups around the nation made him the first choice of Republican voters by the fall of 1978. Reagan did not need to win the nomination; he needed only to avoid losing it. Despite some setbacks, and deficiencies in his effort, the ex-governor was able to persevere.

The large and divided Republican field worked to the advantage of Reagan. Although other conservatives were in the race, he had long been the leader of this faction of the party. Barring some campaign slip, there was no reason for conservatives to divide their support among these other right-wing aspirants. Reagan's freedom from official responsiblities allowed him to travel extensively and keep contact with the network he had established in two previous attempts.

Moderate and liberal aspirants began with the disadvantage of having a minority position among Republicans. Since the nomination of Barry Goldwater in 1964, the party had become clearly dominated by conservatives. Those who were active in the party, and the top stratum of convention delegates, evidenced a relatively coherent conservative ideology.[17] This position was strengthened by a shift of population away from the more liberal sections of the nation, the Northeast and Midwest, and was further aided by the allocation of delegates among the states, which gave an edge to the less industrialized and less urbanized states.[18]

In this strategic environment, a nonconservative candidate needed to consolidate all possible support. With the advantage of incumbency, Gerald Ford was barely able to defeat Reagan in 1976. In 1980, there was no single candidate to rally moderate Republicans, and very few liberal Republicans. Anderson, Baker, and Bush competed with one another for the leadership of their faction, while Ford remained an outside possiblity for a last-minute draft. By the time this competition was resolved, the Reagan candidacy was unbeatable.

The changing position of the candidates can be seen in the pattern of public opinion polls. Over the course of the campaign, the aspirants tried both to become well-known and to be well-treated. Candidates want, first, to be known. Initially, this desire for recognition may be more important than the reasons for recognition. As the old saw has it, a politician "doesn't care what they say about me, as long as they spell my name right." Yet they must be concerned also about content — favorable notice obviously is more likely to lead to votes than detrimental publicity.

These two aspects are combined in table 1.1 in a measure called a "reputation index." It gives equal weight to the degree to which a candidate is known and to the relatively favorable position he holds. The course of this index during the nominating campaigns helps explain the fates of the various hopefuls. Kennedy was always recognized by most voters, but their later unfavorable impressions lowered his reputation index. Moderate Republican aspirants generally did not become both widely known and favorably received. Governor

TABLE 1.1
REPUTATION INDEX OF 1980
PRESIDENTIAL CANDIDATES*

	June 1979	Nov. 1979	Jan. 1980	Feb. 1980	March 1980	April 1980	June 1980
Carter	.49	.50	.75	.84	.80	.75	.64
Brown	.55	.52	.48	.48	.36		
Kennedy	.85	.83	.73	.59	.64	.65	.60
Anderson	.26	.23	.28	.22	.46	.49	.47
Dole	.41	.32	.33	.33			
Baker	.57	.58	.56	.56			
Crane	.42	.35	.22	.28			
Reagan	.80	.74	.77	.72	.73	.78	.65
Bush	.26	.37	.46	.64	.56	.54	.50
Connally	.57	.58	.61	.50			
Ford					.75		

*The table shows all candidates included in the CBS News/*New York Times* polls in the designated months. Interviews were concluded on June 6 and November 3, 1979 (the day before the American Embassy seizure in Teheran),and on January 13, February 17, March 15, April 14, and June 22, 1980.

Brown suffered from low recognition and also from a low estimate of his abilities, even among those who claimed to know him.

Carter and Reagan were able to establish high, generally positive profiles at critical times. Carter's rating was at the neutral point of 50 before the campaign began. It jumped enormously in the three months at the beginning of the year, when delegates were being elected. It later declined, but too late to hurt his renomination. Reagan's position was more constant. His vulnerability was shown by the greater reputation of Ford during March, when the former President was considering a race, and by his own decline in June. The objective situation did not enable his opponents to exploit these potential weaknesses.[19]

THE NOMINATIONS OF 1980:
THE REPUBLICANS

Ronald Reagan's basic strategy was to maintain the front-runner position he had established in earlier years. For each of the other candidates, the goal was to establish himself as the major alternative to Reagan and to remove all other possibilities. The first formal step toward the nomination came in the Iowa caucuses. Reagan remained out of the state, presenting a pose of party healer. Having devoted himself to the state over a period of months, George Bush was able to lead the pack in a straw poll of participants in the Republican meetings, winning a third of the vote to Reagan's 27 percent. With turnout in these caucuses three times the level of 1976, and with the news media emphasizing the results, Bush was suddenly seen as the new leader in the GOP.

In this analysis, commentators reverted to the favorite cliché of 1976, "momentum." Bush himself claimed the backing of "the big Mo." "We're right on target," his manager added. "We're not changing anything in our basic plan that we laid out."[20] Soon, however, a new cliché would become dominant: "volatility." In the coming weeks, attention would shift rapidly among Bush, Reagan, Anderson, and former President Gerald Ford. Voters seemed to be behaving as if they were seeking a "new romance."[21] Not fully satisfied with the most evident choice, they restlessly sought the excitement of a new face, a new political affair. As they learned more about the new object of their affection, however, their ardor cooled, and the search for a better electoral mate resumed.

The romance with Bush was short-lived. The New Hampshire primary became the focus of all Republicans' efforts, and Bush was handicapped by the need to maintain his strong position. Reagan, reversing his previous aloof stance, campaigned vigorously, while Anderson and Baker competed for the moderate vote with Bush. The former ambassador's campaign was harmed when he refused to allow the other candidates to participate in a two-man debate between himself and Reagan. Maintaining his position as one above personal battles, the former California governor genially invited them in.

The results restored Reagan to his front-runner position, as he won half the votes cast in New Hampshire. Although Bush came in second, he was seen as severely damaged. Even more serious was the effect on the other Republican contenders. Weak showings soon brought the formal or tacit withdrawals of four contenders: Dole the next day, Baker and Crane a week later (after another setback in Massachusetts), and Connally three days later (when he lost to Reagan in South Carolina).

In a week and a half, the grim reaper of the winnowing process had done its work. Only 6 percent of the primary electors had voted, and only states bordering the Atlantic Ocean had held contests. Despite this sectional bias, the hasty process had eliminated from further consideration candidates of apparent distinction: the party's Senate leader, its past vice-presidential candidate, an articulate spokesman of its conservative philosophy, and a former Cabinet member in two administrations. These results showed the problems of the new system. By creating pressure for early decision, the system did not permit a satisfactory second choice, such as Baker, to remain in contention. Moreover, success was heavily dependent on continuing financial support. Each of the withdrawing candidates cited the lack of funding as a partial explanation of his elimination. Even Connally was affected. The Texan had spent nearly $12 million, all in private contributions. The political gain was a single committed delegate — surely the most expensive investment in American political history.

These defeated candidates could easily have echoed the complaint of another loser, Democrat Morris Udall in 1976:

> After three of those primaries I'm convinced it was all over. The die was cast. . . . It's like a football game, in which you say to the first team that makes a first down with ten yards, "Hereafter your team has a special rule. Your first downs are five yards. And if you make three of those you get a two-yard first down. And we're going to let your first touchdown count twenty-one points. Now the rest of you bastards play catch-up under the regular rules."[22]

At this point, conservative ranks were limited to Reagan alone, while the moderates still lacked a single leader. The next to court the Republican party was John Anderson. Previously disparaged as a minor aspirant, the Illinois congressman deliberately emphasized the differences between himself and the other Republicans and took liberal positions likely to be unpopular in his party, such as support of abortion and opposition to enlarged military spending. These distinctive positions brought him considerable media attention, fervent backing by a minority of Republicans, and the votes of Democrats and Independents crossing over to vote in the Republican contest. Non-Republicans provided two-fifths of the vote in the Massachusetts primary, making that contest a virtual three-way tie between Anderson, Bush, and Reagan, and made Anderson a close second to Reagan in the Vermont primary held the same day.[23] The Republican contest became a three-man race, one conservative against two moderates or liberals. With no opposition from ideological conservatives, Reagan began to accumulate support in other regions, winning decisively in four southern primaries.

The impact of the division among the moderate candidates can be glimpsed by an analysis of a survey of voters in the New Hampshire primary in which they were asked to designate their second choice for President. Only a third of the voters would have chosen a conservative — Reagan, Crane, Connally, or Dole — as their alternate choice. Twice as many would have switched to Anderson, Baker, or Bush, and these candidates even would have attracted a substantial majority of Reagan voters. A single moderate condidate would certainly have run a closer, and perhaps a successful, race.[24]

As the Reagan movement was developing, a new threat to his progress, and a new division among his opponents, appeared. Former President Gerald Ford openly invited a draft by his party. Agreeing that Reagan was well in the lead for the nomination, he also predicted the Californian's defeat because "a very conservative Republican can't win in a national election." Ford declared his willingness to campaign if the "broad base" of the party wanted him. One such indication soon came in a national opinion poll, when Ford led Reagan overwhelmingly as the presidential preference of Republicans (52 to 27 percent); Ford also was the only Republican preferred by all voters over Carter (47 to 42 percent).[25]

A political party interested only in winning the Presidency might have given Ford more consideration. The nature of the new nominating system, however, precluded this consideration. Opportunities to enter state primaries were ending rapidly, but most delegates would be selected in these primaries. While Reagan had an organization working throughout the nation, Ford had no campaign staff in the field. There were no party "bosses" to control delegations and no feasible means to delay a decision until the convention met. Ford received no support from the remaining moderates, Bush and Anderson, who still hoped for their own victories; no support from the defeated conservatives, who preferred Reagan; and no support from state governors, who might have influenced their delegations. "The politicians he hoped would come forward and urge him to run responded with a deafening, if occasionally solicitous, silence."[26] Two weeks after floating his trial balloon, the former President punctured it with a definitive statement of withdrawal.

The Illinois primary on March 18 was critical for the Republicans. Anderson, running in his home state, with large numbers of Democrats crossing over to the Republican primary and with Ford eliminated, had the opportunity to become Reagan's leading opponent. Anderson did lead Bush considerably, but lost to Reagan by a 4–3 margin. Reagan was very strong among Republican voters and also showed an ability to draw 28 percent of the non-Republicans, particularly conservative Democrats, thereby rebutting the argument that he would be a weak candidate in the November election. The news media began to concede the nomination, finding that "the staunch loyalty of Mr. Reagan's supporters in state after state made him appear virtually impossible to beat, barring some major error."[27]

Anderson's position within the Republican party was further undercut when he ran third in both Connecticut, a traditionally liberal state, and Wisconsin, a liberal state in which Democrats could vote freely in the opposition primary. Anderson, defeated in his home region and without favorable prospects within the party, abandoned the Republican race and began his independent candidacy.

Finally, for the Republicans, it was Bush alone against Reagan. The front-runner held a steady course, winning a majority of votes and capturing most states. The former ambassador scored some successes, including primary victories in Connecticut, Pennsylvania, and Michigan. Yet, aside from a strong second-place finish in his adopted state of Texas, Bush's strength was confined to the Northeast and the traditionally liberal factions of the party.[28] These results, presented in table 1.2, were unsatisfactory in a party that had been shifting its geographical base to the South and West, and its ideological center toward conservatism. Reagan better represented the views of Republicans, as shown by the results in table 1.3.[29]

Reagan's support was broadly based but not evenly distributed. He showed the ability to draw support from some persons in traditionally Democratic constituencies, such as union members, Catholics, and those who expected a worsening of their economic position. Voters unhappy with Carter policies were more likely to choose Reagan than were the smaller number who approved of the present administration. The bedrock of Reagan's support came from those who favored a conservative ideology, who were traditional Republicans, and who decided their ballot on the bases of policy rather than personal considerations. Reagan thus was the true embodiment of the ideological and partisan challenge to Carter.

Bush's success was not only limited but was less meaningful in the context of rules that prescribed proportional division of delegates in some states, winner-take-all in Reagan bailiwicks in the South and West, and separate election of delegates in other areas. In Pennsylvania, for example, the Bush victory

TABLE 1.2, THE REPUBLICAN PRIMARIES

Date	State*	State Total Vote	Reagan Vote	Reagan %	Total Vote	Cumulative Reagan Vote	Reagan %
February 26	New Hampshire*	147,157	72,990	49.6	147,157	72,990	49.6
March 4	Massachusetts	400,826	115,438	28.8			
	Vermont*	65,611	19,749	30.1	613,594	208,177	33.9
March 8	South Carolina*	145,501	79,589	54.7			
March 11	Alabama*	211,353	147,313	69.7	759,095	287,766	37.9
	Florida*	614,995	345,627	56.2			
	Georgia*	200,171	146,525	73.2			
March 18	Illinois*	1,130,181	547,008	48.4	1,785,614	927,231	51.9
March 25	Connecticut	182,284	61,794	33.9	2,915,795	1,474,239	50.6
April 1	Kansas*	285,398	179,801	63.0	3,098,075	1,536,033	49.6
	Wisconsin*	907,853	364,957	40.2	4,291,330	2,080,791	48.5
April 5	Louisiana*	41,683	31,220	74.9	4,333,013	2,112,011	48.7
April 22	Pennsylvania	1,241,002	527,426	42.5	5,574,015	2,639,437	47.4
May 3	Texas*	526,769	268,652	51.0	6,100,784	2,908,089	47.7
May 6	Indiana*	568,315	418,848	73.7			
	North Carolina*	168,391	113,832	67.6			
	Tennessee*	195,210	144,651	74.1	7,032,700	3,585,420	51.0
May 13	Maryland*	167,303	80,640	48.2			
	Nebraska*	205,203	155,954	76.4	7,405,206	3,822,014	51.6
May 20	Michigan	595,176	189,266	31.8			
	Oregon*	304,647	166,033	54.5	8,305,029	4,177,313	50.3
May 27	Idaho*	134,879	111,815	82.9			
	Kentucky*	94,795	78,111	82.4			
	Nevada*	47,395	39,338	83.0	8,582,098	4,406,577	51.3
June 3	California*	2,512,994	2,015,421	80.2			
	Montana*	76,716	66,973	87.3			
	New Jersey*	277,977	225,995	81.3			
	New Mexico*	59,101	37,647	63.7			
	Ohio*	854,967	690,813	80.8			
	Rhode Island*	5,335	3,841	72.0			
	South Dakota*	88,325	72,515	82.1			
	West Virginia*	133,871	114,593	85.6	12,591,384	7,634,375	60.6

*Primaries in Puerto Rico and the District of Columbia, which Reagan did not enter, are omitted. The asterisks in this column designate states in which Reagan led the preference poll.

in the primary did not pay off in delegates. There, because the Reagan forces had organized more extensively for the separate choice of delegates, Reagan won a plurality of the convention-goers. By the end of May, Reagan was assured of a convention majority and had become the leading choice of Republican voters as well. Although a Republican defeat in November still seemed likely, Bush declined to continue his financially limited campaign through the final primaries and withdrew to leave Reagan a clear path to the nomination.

TABLE 1.3
REAGAN'S VOTING SUPPORT IN THE REPUBLICAN PRIMARIES*

	N.H.	Mass.	Fla.	Ill.	Wisc.	Penn.
Emphasize personal qualities	39	23	53	37	36	40
Emphasize policy qualities	51	31	64	50	46	50
Republican identification	47	33	59	59	51	48
Non-Republican	34	22	54	28	33	32
Conservatives	63	43	68	61	57	53
Moderates, liberals	31	34	47	33	33	38
Approve Carter foreign policy	28	18	55	−	37	45
Disapprove	51	32	58	−	43	44
Approve Carter economic policy	26	25	−	32	35	47
Disapprove	46	29	−	47	41	42
Favorable financial situation	31	21	60	30	38	27
Unfavorable	50	33	60	48	41	44
Protestant	42	28	57	51	42	46
Catholic	56	36	56	51	38	36
Precollege	59	51	66	55	48	50
College	37	20	52	33	34	33
Union member	−	−	−	42	35	47
Nonmember	−	−	−	43	43	41

*See chapter note 29 for explanation of table entries.

On the formal roll call of the Republican convention, Reagan was officially nominated as the Republican candidate, receiving 1,939 of the 1,994 votes. The last echoes of the spring campaign were heard in 37 votes for Anderson and 13 for Bush. The roll call did not reflect earlier divisions. To better record the factions within the party, table 1.4 presents the candidate preferences in each state at the time the delegates were chosen. Reagan's strength is exaggerated even in this table, but it is more valid than the data from the night of his party coronation.

Unlike 1964, when Barry Goldwater had called for a right-wing direction for the party, the newly dominant conservative faction was not strident in its ideology. Cheered by polls predicting electoral success, the party attempted to present itself and its candidate as pragmatic and patriotic. Some platform language was modified to assuage moderates, and special sections were included to appeal to blacks, urban residents, and blue-collar workers — the traditional Democratic base. Respectful attention was given to established figures in the moderate wing of the party, such as Gerald Ford and Henry Kissinger. A study of future rules was undertaken to consider more representation for the industrial and liberal states. The moderate and effective national chairman, Bill Brock, was kept in office.

TABLE 1.4
REPUBLICAN PRECONVENTION NOMINATION SUPPORT

State	Votes	Reagan	Bush	Anderson	Other
Alabama	27	18	9		
Alaska	19	19			
Arizona	28	28			
Arkansas	19	7	2		10
California	168	168			
Colorado	31	31			
Connecticut	35	14	15	6	
Delaware	12	4	6		2
D. C.	14		14		
Florida	51	51			
Georgia	36	36			
Hawaii	14	3			11
Idaho	21	19			2
Illinois	102	50	2	26	24
Indiana	54	54			
Iowa	37	21	16		
Kansas	32	20	4	5	3
Kentucky	27	27			
Louisiana	31	29			2
Maine	21		17		4
Maryland	30	18	12		
Massachusetts	42	13	14	13	2
Michigan	82	29	53		
Minnesota	34	26	8		
Mississippi	22	22			
Missouri	37	34			3
Montana	20	20			
Nebraska	25	25			
Nevada	17	14	1		2
New Hampshire	22	15	5		2
New Jersey	66	64			2
New Mexico	22	22			
New York	123	105	6		12
North Carolina	40	30	10		
North Dakota	17	12	1		4
Ohio	77	77			
Oklahoma	34	34			
Oregon	29	18	11		
Pennsylvania	83	34	17		32
Rhode Island	13	12	1		

TABLE 1.4(*Continued*)

State	Votes	Reagan	Bush	Anderson	Other
South Carolina	25	25			
South Dakota	22	22			
Tennessee	32	24	8		
Texas	80	61	19		
Utah	21	21			
Vermont	19	16		1	2
Virginia	51	51			
Washington	37	34	2	1	
West Virginia	18	15			3
Wisconsin	34	28		6	
Wyoming	19	16			3
Puerto Rico	14		14		
Guam	4	4			
Virgin Islands	4				4
Total	1994	1540	267	58	129
		(77.2%)	(13.4%)	(2.9%)	(6.5%)

SOURCE: *Congressional Quarterly Weekly Report* 38 (12 July 1980): 1928-37.

The most obvious effort to unify the party came in the vice-presidential nomination. Following recent practice, there was a general agreement that the convention should refer this decision to Reagan as the prerogative of the presidential candidate. He listed a number of persons suitable to the position, discussed the choice widely with party leaders, and conducted a poll of the delegates. By the middle of the convention, it was widely believed that George Bush would be selected, as a means of adding electoral strength to the ticket in the Northeast and consolidating the support of the moderate faction. While not enthusiastic about this choice, the ideological conservatives were prepared to accept it.

Then, dramatically, on the third day of the convention, as Reagan himself was being formally ratified, rumors became widespread that former President Ford would join Reagan on the ballot. The prospect was opened of a "dream ticket," combining the two most prominent Republicans and adding the popularity and experience of Ford to the partisan and ideological appeal of Reagan. In televised interviews, Ford established conditions that he be assured of significant power as vice-president, reportedly amounting to a "co-Presidency." Prominent party leaders, including the national chairman and the convention chairman, stated that an arrangement had in fact been concluded. At the last moment, however, the "deal" unraveled as Ford's conditions became too great for Reagan to accept. To still the speculation and uneasiness, he made an unscheduled post-midnight appearance to announce his support of George Bush. The following day the selection was ceremoniously confirmed.

The tentative selection of Ford for vice-president was one of the strangest incidents in recent conventions. If consummated, it would have surely complicated the conduct of American government. The potential alliance was certainly affected greatly by the ubiquitous television reporters. Seeking some excitement to enliven a dull convention, they found an exciting story in the unprecedented possibility of a former President running for the position of "superfluous excellency."

By speculating on the possibility, television helped make it more of a probability. At the same time, television might have made it more difficult to make the "dream ticket" a reality. Establishing a working arrangement in power between Reagan and Ford required delicate negotiations, perhaps even a written agreement. As diplomats have long known, negotiations cannot be conducted in the glare of publicity. By their insistent questioning, television reporters both stimulated dealings between Reagan and Ford and contributed to their ultimate failure. The incident demonstrated the difficulty of decision making in the contemporary nominating convention. The time, privacy, and multiple alliances necessary for meaningful decisions no longer exist at these publicized mass meetings.[30]

The convention concluded with the candidates' acceptance speeches, which continued the effort to broaden the appeal of the Republican ticket. Conservative slogans were balanced with assertions of social concern. A film biography of Reagan emphasized his union membership and administrative ability while passing over his long-time corporate activity. Dwight Eisenhower's Republican record was invoked, but not that of Barry Goldwater or Richard Nixon. In the final speech, candidate Reagan twice identified himself with Franklin Roosevelt and made deliberate appeals to Democratic voters, including blacks and union members. Reagan would not wage a conservative crusade but a unifying campaign, directed to the national "community of shared values" and based on the "unprecedented calamity" created by Jimmy Carter and the Democratic Congress.[31] As Republicans happily left Detroit, they foresaw victory.

THE NOMINATIONS OF 1980:
THE DEMOCRATS

President Carter's strategy was based on his position as the incumbent. He emphasized the experience he had gained as the nation's chief executive, an asset unavailable to any Democratic contender. Without any special effort, he could be assured of daily news coverage and could request network time for "nonpolitical" events at any time. Every visit of a foreign dignitary, every signing of legislation, and every speech to Congress or news conference was a reminder that Jimmy Carter was the President, while others only hoped for the job. The Carter campaign demonstrated the truth of another cliché, "The Presidency is the best place to campaign for President."

Events added to the inherent advantage of incumbency. When the President ordered naval forces toward Iran, he reminded the public of his role as the commander-in-chief. When he drafted an antiinflation program, he underlined his position as the national economic manager. When he offered Christmas prayers for the hostages, he invoked the reverence accorded the chief of state.

By no means was the President the passive beneficiary of events. By refusing to leave Washington to campaign, he removed himself as a personal target of campaign criticism. By declining televised debates with Governor Brown and Senator Kennedy, he deprived his rivals of free exposure and an equal forum. By calling attention to foreign crises, he limited the media's attention to his rivals.

The year's foreign policy crises, in political terms, were a lucky break for the President. While he did not initiate and was unable to control them, he did make effective political use of these problems. Presidential responses were closely associated with the electoral calendar. The Olympic boycott was formally proposed the Sunday before the Iowa caucuses, first in the nation. The UN commission was dispatched to Teheran the weekend before the primary in New Hampshire. Two days before the critical Illinois contest, the President emphasized his strong stand on Afghanistan by hinting that he would renounce the strategic arms treaty. On the day before the final important primary, in Wisconsin, the United States set a deadline for the transfer of the hostages. As the polls opened in that state at 7:00 A.M., the President gave a televised address to announce an apparent breakthrough in negotiations with Iran. These actions were not necessarily manipulative, but their favorable effects on his prestige were convenient for the President.

There were practical benefits from the incumbency as well. The White House used the accustomed methods of an "insider" candidate. State and local officials and party leaders needed the support of the executive for their own goals, from appointments of federal judges to funds for local highways or job-training programs. While the connection between support of Carter and federal largesse was not always direct, a presidential assistant made the point: "We will not punish the people of any city. But having said that, when there is discretion in the use of Federal funds on how the President can help the people, we will go to our friends."[32]

The timing of federal grants showed the advantages of holding power. As Maine conducted its caucuses in January, $75 million in federal grants were distributed to the state, an increase from $15 million in November and $25 million in December. As New Hampshire voted in the first primary in the nation, it received twice as many grants as in the two previous months.[33] An organizer of the Carter campaign in one critical state reported, tongue in cheek, that he had a budget of "$4.75 for expenses, and $200 million in federal grants."

The personal prestige of the Presidency was also invoked. Although he avoided the hustings, the President did campaign, personally telephoning about twenty persons a day in states holding primaries, meeting with community delegations and the U.S. Olympic hockey team in the White House, providing exclusive interviews with reporters from contested states, and using the unchallengeable forums of news conferences and speeches to promote his cause and attack his opponents. While members of his family, members of the Cabinet and Vice-President Walter Mondale traveled the country, the President conducted a modern version of the nineteenth-century "front-porch" campaign. Only in May, after the rescue mission to Teheran failed, did he campaign openly, and then only for one full day.

The "rose garden" strategy worked. The day before the American Embassy in Teheran was captured, only 30 percent approved of Carter's performance as President, and only 28 percent supported his handling of foreign policy. By February 1980, as the primaries began, a 53 percent majority approved of his general performance, while 48 percent supported his foreign policy and 63 percent endorsed his actions in Iran. Among Democrats, who would principally decide the President's renomination, his approval rating went from 37 percent in November to an overwhelming 62 percent in February. The figures later would drop to their previous levels. By June, Carter won only 30 percent approval from the general electorate and 36 percent from Democrats. But, by June, Carter had been assured of a second bid for the White House.[34]

Senator Kennedy began with widespread recognition and apparent popularity. He hoped to convert these personal assets into a revived coalition of traditional Democratic voters such as union workers, urban residents, Catholics, and blacks. He won only one early success, when he received the endorsement of Chicago's Mayor Jane Byrne. When party leaders were critical in presidential nominations, this endorsement might have begun a swing toward the senator. In the new selection system, however, the crucial elements were direct appeals to the voters and extensive organization to take advantage of the rules of proportionality. Having waited to announce his candidacy until late 1979, Senator Kennedy had ready support only in a small number of states. He would find his personal popularity slipping badly as he made the transition from cult figure to potential President. The issues of personal character summarized by Chappaquiddick, which seemed forgotten and irrelevant when he was a senator, received new emphasis as he sought the most powerful office in the nation.

The Democratic campaign became tangible with the first selection of delegates in Iowa. Tramping through snow-covered fields and streets, Democrats met in neighborhood caucuses to choose delegates to later meetings in congressional districts and the state convention. Because these initial delegates were required to announce their candidate preference, it was possible to project the final outcome of the state. The early preparations of the Carter campaign paid off; 59 percent of the local delegates supported Carter and only 30 percent Kennedy, with the remainder either favorable to Brown or uncommitted. Eager for any news on the presidential contest, the television networks had devoted hours to the campaign in this single state and had stimulated an incredibly high turnout of 20 percent of the voters. The consensual interpretation of the media was that the President had demonstrated and solidified his position as front-runner.

The first direct electoral test came, as had become habitual, in New Hampshire. Still riding the crest of his popularity, the President came in first, winning slightly less than a majority of the total vote. At the same time, he was winning delegates in state caucuses in Maine and other states. An immediate effect of this primary was virtually to eliminate Governor Brown from the race soon after its start. With only a tenth of the New Hampshire vote, Brown found himself short of funds and limited himself to one more try — in Wisconsin. His low standing soon eliminated his federal financing as well. When he ran a poor third in Wisconsin, he left the race.

The critical test for Kennedy came in the Illinois primary. The state exemplified the constituency to which the Senator was appealing: urban, industrial, heavily ethnic, and Catholic in population. Kennedy had the endorsement of the vaunted Chicago "machine," and he had extensive personal contacts. Despite these advantages, the result was an overwhelming victory for the President, who won not only by 2–1 in the expressed preference of the Democratic voters but by a 165–14 margin in the separate election of delegates. The Illinois results led the press virtually to declare the nomination decided. As even the cautious *New York Times* reported, "The prevailing view of neutral politicians, as well as the private estimate of underdog camps, was that Mr. Carter's overwhelming victory in Illinois had all but eliminated Senator Edward M. Kennedy's hopes of blocking the President's renomination."[35]

Kennedy's defeat in Illinois *was* substantial, but its effect was exaggerated by a quirk in the rules. The state was the only significant area in which Democratic delegates were not divided proportionately. Instead, they were chosen in congressional districts, with the leading candidate winning all the delegates from that district. The effect of this rule was to convert a 2–1 Carter majority in the popular vote to a 12–1 margin in delegates.

The Illinois primary was the decisive moment of the Democratic campaign. In one day, it gave Carter a tenth of the delegates needed for nomination. It showed that Senator Kennedy had not revived the traditional Democratic coalition on which he had based his hopes. It led the media to conclude that the race was virtually over, and this discouragement further decreased the chances of an upset. Illinois established a momentum that would carry the President to victory in his party. Carter staffers felt sufficiently relaxed to take vacations.

The dynamics of a campaign are such that "once the competitive balance is substantially tipped, candidates with momentum have an increasing probability of attaining the nomination."[36] With his victory in Illinois, Carter had accumulated almost a quarter of the votes needed for nomination. From that point, his bandwagon rolled, and even accelerated every week. The objective reality of primary victories was magnified by the press. The media generally counted and reported not only delegates won by the candidates but totals that could be projected from the local-level caucuses. A further handicap for Kennedy was his press coverage, which gave more attention to his campaign's predicted early demise than to any other aspect.[37]

The rest of the nominating campaign can be divided into two phases: the inexorable collection of delegates and the culmination of the national convention. During the next three months of primaries, Senator Kennedy improved his personal position and President Carter's standing declined. The challenger won upset victories in New York and Connecticut following his defeat in Illinois, but their impact was lost one week later when Carter bested Kennedy in the Wisconsin primary. Ultimately, Kennedy assembled part of his anticipated coalition of industrial states. A narrow success in the Pennsylvania primary was followed by a similarly close win in Michigan caucuses. On the final day of primary contests, 5 million Democrats voted, 52 percent of them for Kennedy, giving him victory in 5 of 8 contests, including the large states of California and New Jersey

These victories were too little and too late. Kennedy, even when he won, won narrowly, and the proportional division of delegates in these states resulted in few gains relative to the President. Kennedy's Pennsylvania "victory," for example, gave him only one more delegate than Carter. Kennedy was unable to establish an appeal that extended significantly beyond the industrial northeastern quadrant of the nation and California, and his appeal was not overwhelming even in those areas. Carter, by contrast, was dominant in his own southern region, showed strength in the Midwest by large victories in industrial Indiana and liberal Wisconsin, and captured most states in the West. The President had lost popularity over the course of the campaign. After Illinois, as seen in table 1.5, his percentage of the primary vote fell somewhat and then stabilized. Still, he retained enough strength to continue to add to his delegate totals. Even on the last day, he could win three primaries, including Ohio, and thereby bring his pledged delegate count above the majority needed for nomination.

The delegate selection process also showed the advantages the President now held as an "insider" in the party. Although he had been an advocate of further reform of the nominating process, Carter did particularly well in states with more traditional means of selecting delegates. He won 64 percent of those chosen in party caucuses, where organizational strength was critical, and 86 percent in states (particularly Illinois) where delegates were awarded "winner-take-all" for the leader in each legislative district. In primaries where the rule of proportional division fully applied, the President won a bare 52 percent majority of the votes cast. He carried the popular vote in two of the nation's four regions, the South and Midwest, but lost the East and West.[38]

Senator Kennedy was no longer a candidate with a realistic chance of success. He had become the political object through which Democratic voters expressed their discontent with the administration. He did best when the electorate wanted to "send a message" of complaint to the President. An anti-Israel vote in the United Nations by the American delegate thus contributed to a protest vote in New York, as high inflation and rising unemployment led to anti-Carter ballots in the industrial states. As a candidate in his own right, however, Kennedy was not popular enough, not trusted enough, and not favored enough on the issues.

Kennedy's deficiencies become apparent if we examine the attitudes of voters interviewed after voting in eight of the most significant primaries, as presented in table 1.6.[39] They show a lack of consistently high support by the senator's expected constituency: liberals; those in unfavorable financial circumstances; critics of the administration; or such demographic groups as Catholics, those with or without college education, blacks, and union members. It is true that Kennedy generally won among self-identified liberals or critics of Carter's foreign and economic policies. Nevertheless, his margin of victory was generally far less than Carter's edge among the more numerous moderates and conservatives or among those approving the President's actions. The opposition candidate did not unify the opposition to the administration.

TABLE 1.5, THE DEMOCRATIC PRIMARIES

Date	State*	State Total Vote	Carter Vote	Carter %	Total Vote	Cumulative Carter Vote	Carter %
February 26	New Hampshire*	111,930	52,719	47.1	111,930	52,719	47.1
March 4	Massachusetts	907,332	260,404	28.7			
	Vermont*	39,703	29,023	73.1	1,058,965	342,146	32.3
March 11	Alabama*	237,464	193,771	81.6			
	Florida*	1,098,003	666,488	60.7			
	Georgia*	384,780	338,606	88.0	2,779,212	1,541,011	55.4
March 16	Puerto Rico*	870,235	449,911	51.7			
March 18	Illinois*	1,201,067	780,694	65.0	4,850,514	2,771,616	57.1
March 25	Connecticut	210,275	87,264	41.5			
	New York	989,062	406,504	41.1	6,049,851	3,265,384	54.0
April 1	Kansas*	193,918	109,757	56.6			
	Wisconsin*	629,619	353,846	56.2	6,873,388	3,728,987	54.2
April 5	Louisiana*	358,741	199,819	55.7	7,232,129	3,928,806	54.3
April 22	Pennsylvania	1,613,223	732,403	45.4	8,845,352	4,661,209	52.7
May 3	Texas*	1,377,354	769,941	55.9	10,333,706	5,431,150	53.1
May 6	D.C.	64,150	23,671	36.9			
	Indiana*	589,441	399,052	67.7			
	North Carolina*	737,262	516,821	70.1			
	Tennessee	294,680	221,599	75.2	11,908,239	6,592,293	55.4
May 13	Maryland*	477,090	226,618	47.5			
	Nebraska*	153,881	72,170	46.9	12,539,210	6,891,081	55.0
May 20	Oregon*	343,050	199,655	58.2	12,882,260	7,090,736	55.0
May 27	Arkansas*	448,290	269,442	60.1			
	Idaho*	50,482	31,400	62.2			
	Kentucky*	240,331	160,781	66.9			
	Nevada*	66,948	25,172	37.6	13,688,311	7,577,531	55.4
June 3	California	3,323,812	1,489,068	37.7			
	Montana*	125,002	64,501	51.6			
	New Jersey	560,908	212,584	37.9			
	New Mexico	157,499	65,992	41.9			
	Ohio*	1,183,499	603,584	51.0			
	Rhode Island	38,327	9,888	25.8			
	South Dakota	67,671	31,061	45.9			
	West Virginia*	314,985	194,976	61.9	19,460,014	10,249,185	52.7

*Michigan's nonbinding primary, which neither Carter nor Kennedy entered, is omitted. The asterisks in the column designate states in which Carter led the preference poll.

The source of this weakness is indicated in the last two rows of table 1.6. These percentages compare those voters who said they cast their ballots on the basis of candidate honesty, integrity, and judgment, to those voters who decided on the basis of candidate policy orientations. When the voters stressed policy, Kennedy was preferred, usually by a considerable margin. When they stressed personal characteristics, however, Carter won overwhelmingly. In the end, Kennedy did not make the nominating contest a referendum on the administration's record. Instead, he suffered from a comparison of the character and individual qualities of the contestants. The tides of Chappaquiddick continued to flow.

A final phase was that leading up to and including the convention. Arithmetically defeated, Senator Kennedy attempted to reopen the contest by having delegates released from candidate pledges made during the primaries. He emphasized the declining position of Carter in the polls and the need for the party to find a more popular candidate for the November election. He offered to release his own delegates, following a public debate, if the President would do likewise, and sought inclusion of his liberal programs in the party platform.

As the convention neared, the Kennedy effort revived, resuscitated by polls showing a commanding Reagan lead and by revelations of a possible scandal involving the President's brother, Billy Carter. As many as fifty congressmen joined in an effort to release delegates from their previous pledges and create an "open," or uninstructed convention. In turn, the President again employed the resources of an incumbent, reiterating promises of federal aid to cities, inviting delegates to group meetings in the White House, and paying individuals the compliment of a personal phone call; in addition, he defended his conduct toward his brother in an hour-long televised press conference.

The battle was directly joined on the first day of the convention when the Democrats debated a new rule that would require delegates to vote, at least for one ballot, for the candidate they had originally supported. Supporters of the rule, such as Senator Abraham Ribicoff, defended it as an implementation of popular sovereignty, a means by which the party would keep its commitment to the "nineteen million Democrats who went to the polls expecting their votes to mean something." Those arguing for a reconsideration of these commitments, such as Edward Bennett Williams, sought to make the delegates "free to vote their will, free to vote their consciences, free to vote their minds." In the end, candidate loyalty rather than political philosophy determined the result, as the convention adopted the new rule in a roll-call vote closely paralleling the later balloting for President (see table 1.7).

The call for an "open" convention was partially political and partially philosophical, but considerably irrelevant. Justifications for the opposing posi-

TABLE 1.6
VOTING PATTERNS IN THE DEMOCRATIC PRIMARIES

	New Hampshire		Massachusetts		Illinois		New York	
	Carter	Kennedy	Carter	Kennedy	Carter	Kennedy	Carter	Kennedy
Democratic identification	46	38	27	66	66	32	43	57
Non-Democratic	47	30	27	66	59	32	39	61
Liberals	26	45	16	76	60	35	32	68
Moderates, conservatives	54	34	31	62	65	30	45	55
Approve Carter foreign policy	76	11	69	28	88	10	84	16
Disapprove	13	66	8	84	28	65	15	85
Approve Carter economic policy	89	6	77	19	90	8	93	7
Disapprove	26	52	15	78	40	53	24	76
Favorable financial situation	54	29	31	61	76	20	64	36
Unfavorable	27	55	22	71	51	44	32	68
Protestant	53	31	49	46	64	30	52	48
Catholic	46	41	24	70	64	32	47	53
Precollege	55	32	29	65	63	33	48	52
College	38	42	26	66	62	33	36	64
White	46	38	26	67	66	29	40	60
Black	53	26	46	50	57	39	47	53
Union member	—	—	22	73	63	33	36	64
Nonmember	—	—	31	61	62	32	48	52
Emphasize personal qualities	70	13	56	36	86	11	75	25
Emphasize policy qualities	18	65	8	88	37	52	23	77

	Wisconsin		New Jersey		Ohio		California	
	Carter	Kennedy	Carter	Kennedy	Carter	Kennedy	Carter	Kennedy
Democratic identification	56	31	40	55	49	49	—	—
Non-Democratic	55	23	38	50	55	43	—	—
Liberals	38	39	29	64	42	55	33	52
Moderates, conservatives	59	26	43	51	53	45	44	43
Approve Carter foreign policy	86	7	80	14	85	13	75	21
Disapprove	17	56	19	73	24	73	22	61
Approve Carter economic policy	90	4	88	9	92	7	86	10
Disapprove	30	45	24	67	32	65	25	60
Favorable financial situation	65	23	62	36	62	34	48	39
Unfavorable	40	40	31	60	40	57	28	58
Protestant	60	25	44	46	58	39	48	38
Catholic	53	32	39	55	45	53	38	53
Precollege	55	29	44	50	51	47	43	46
College	54	28	33	60	46	51	40	46
White	56	29	38	55	50	47	44	42
Black	—	—	45	46	55	43	32	63
Union member	59	27	41	53	47	49	34	52
Nonmember	53	29	39	53	52	47	45	43
Emphasize personal qualities	82	7	78	20	77	22	70	22
Emphasize policy qualities	35	42	29	69	27	72	23	71

TABLE 1.7
DEMOCRATIC CONVENTION ROLL CALLS

State	Total Votes	Open Convention Vote For	Open Convention Vote Against	Presidential Nomination* Carter	Presidential Nomination* Kennedy
Alabama	45	3	42	43	2
Alaska	11	6.1	4.9	8.4	2.6
Arizona	29	16	13	13	16
Arkansas	33	9	24	25	6
California	306	171	132	140	166
Colorado	40	24	16	27	10
Connecticut	54	28	26	26	28
Delaware	14	6.5	7.5	14	
D. C.	19	12	7	12	5
Florida	100	25	75	75	25
Georgia	63	1	62	62	
Hawaii	19	4	15	16	2
Idaho	17	9	8	9	7
Illinois	179	26	153	163	16
Indiana	80	27	53	53	27
Iowa	50	21	29	33	17
Kansas	37	17	20	23	14
Kentucky	50	12	38	45	5
Louisiana	51	15	36	50	1
Maine	22	12	10	11	11
Maryland	59	27	32	34	24
Massachusetts	111	81	30	34	74
Michigan	141	71	70	102	38
Minnesota	75	30	45	41	14
Mississippi	32		32	32	
Missouri	77	20	57	58	19
Montana	19	9	10	13	6
Nebraska	24	11	13	14	10
Nevada	12	6.5	5.5	8.1	3.9
New Hampshire	19	9	10	10	9
New Jersey	113	68	45	45	68
New Mexico	20	11	9	10	10
New York	282	163	118	129	151
North Carolina	69	13	56	66	3
North Dakota	14	10	4	5	7
Ohio	161	81	80	89	72
Oklahoma	42	9	33	36	3
Oregon	39	14	25	26	13
Pennsylvania	185	102	83	95	90
Puerto Rico	41	20	21	21	20
Rhode Island	23	17	6	6	17
South Carolina	37	6	31	37	
South Dakota	19	10	9	9	10
Tennessee	55	8	47	51	4
Texas	152	47	105	108	38
Utah	20	12	8	11	4
Vermont	12	7.5	4.5	5	7

TABLE 1.7(*Continued*)

State	Total Votes	Open Convention Vote For	Open Convention Vote Against	Presidential Nomination* Carter	Presidential Nomination* Kennedy
Virginia	64	7	57	59	5
Washington	58	24	34	36	22
West Virginia	35	16	19	21	10
Wisconsin	75	26	49	48	26
Wyoming	11	3.5	7.5	8	3
Virgin Islands	4		4	4	
Guam	4		4	4	
Latin America	4	4		4	
Abroad	4	2.5	1.5	1.5	2
Total	3,331	1,390.6	1,936.4	2,129	1,146.5

*The roll call on the presidential nomination showed a decrease of 112 votes, or 9 percent, in support for Senator Kennedy from the pledged delegates he had accumulated before the convention and before his formal withdrawal. The largest defections were District of Columbia 7; Kentucky, 7; Louisiana, 11; Michigan, 31; New York, 13; and North Carolina, 10. For details, see *Congressional Quarterly Weekly Report* 38 (9 August 1980): 2268-76. For roll calls, see *New York Times,* 12 and 14 August 1980.

tions reached a fundamental question of political theory: are elected representatives to be delegates expressing the opinions of their consitutuents, or are they to be trustees, using their best judgment on behalf of these constituents? Advocates of the binding rule argued that convention members should be delegates and that the only proper method of democratic decision was unmediated popular sovereignty. Advocates of an unrestricted decision favored allowing the convention to exercise its own collective judgment in the light of its present view of circumstances.

Yet, this debate was, in a fundamental way, off the point. The cause of the Democrats' problem in August was the new nominating process itself, particularly its effective closure in March and its year-long exclusion of the party organization. The logic of the reform process had been carried to a paradoxical conclusion disavowed by the chairs of all four party reform commissions convened in the past twelve years. Efforts to make the conventions themselves more representative and fairer had led to procedures that made the conventions irrelevant to the principal task of choosing a presidential candidate.

The ultimate result was neither popular sovereignty nor a democratically effective convention. Selection of the nominee through the apparently "open" processes of primaries and caucuses enabled the decision to be made by a minority of Democrats, to be influenced greatly by passing events and the resources of an incumbent administration, and to be closed early in the year. At the same time, the convention thus assembled was incapable of making a rational and independent judgment. An "open" Democratic convention in 1980 would have lacked experienced leaders, for few elected Democratic officials—

only 8 senators and 39 representatives — were present. The party "reforms" had made the convention members not decision makers, but recorders of decisions made in other forums.

The rules decision assured President Carter's renomination, but the drama remained to be played. After the decision, Kennedy immediately withdrew from the race; he came to the convention on its second night to speak on behalf of a minority platform plank pledging the party to a major effort to relieve unemployment. In a speech that was compared to Bryan's famous "Cross of Gold" oration, he brought the convention to its feet repeatedly, sparked a forty-minute demonstration, and compelled convention officers to accept his positions on a voice vote. Possibly envisaging a new effort in 1984, he concluded: "For all those whose cares have been our concern, the work goes on, the cause endures, the hope still lives and the dream shall never die."[40]

The remaining two days of the convention were dominated by the efforts of the Carter forces to achieve a united party. The minority planks voted on the floor were accepted "in principle" by the administration. Although the overall platform was a defense of the Carter Presidency, Senator Kennedy was paid great personal and political deference. He reciprocated by formally endorsing the President and briefly appearing with him on the podium before the convention adjourned.

In its formal action, the convention ratified the candidate choice predestined in the spring. Most Kennedy delegates continued to vote for the senator, but Jimmy Carter was renominated by a 2-1 majority, and Vice-President Mondale was named as running mate with no significant opposition. President Carter, in his acceptance speech, spoke proudly of his past achievements and drew a sharp contrast between his "realism" and the "fantasy" programs of the Republicans.[41] Nominally united, the Democrats left New York City with none of their 1976 euphoria, with some hope for a revival in the fall campaign, and with much fear for their future.

PRESIDENTIAL NOMINATIONS
AND DEMOCRACY

The presidential nominations of 1980 have significant implications for the democratic process in America. Democracy certainly means that the chosen leaders should be persons with broad popular support, ideally the choice of an appropriate majority. Nevertheless, this simple rule does not in itself define a democratic system. Which majority should make the selection? A majority of uninstructed delegates? A majority of the entire party, as represented in public opinion polls, or alternatively of those party members participating in a national primary? Or a majority of those persons who come to the caucuses in Iowa or to the polls in a few early primaries?

In one sense, the nominations of 1980 were fully democratic. Jimmy Carter was the most popular candidate in the Democratic party from the beginning to the end of the formal selection process. He won a clear, if slim, majority of the votes cast in the primaries, and led some contests in all regions. As the person most responsible for the record of the Democratic party in the past four years, it was appropriate that he personally stand on that record and receive the electorate's judgment.

Among Republicans, Reagan was also a fitting choice. He had been the favorite of party county chairmen as early as 1974; he was the early choice for 1980 of the delegates to the previous Republican convention; he had led opinion polls among Republicans since September of 1978;[42] he embodied the conservative ideology that was dominant among both party leaders and members; and he repeatedly defeated his rivals in open caucuses and primaries that attracted millions of voters.

Yet, in another sense, it is not clear that the nominations of 1980 fully contributed to a democratic selection. Each party named a candidate who reversed some of its established positions, such as a concern for unemployment rather than inflation among Democrats, or support of the Equal Rights Amendment among Republicans. Each candidate ran an individual campaign in which the power of party leaders to affect the nomination was severely restricted, and the future possibility of party coordination was consequently reduced.

Most generally, the process itself did not provide for full consideration. No possiblity existed, given the structure of rules, for either the party or the electorate to give serious thought to nominees who were not open, active, and long-standing possibilities, such as Ford among Republicans or Vice-President Mondale or Secretary of State Edmund Muskie among Democrats. There was also little opportunity for second thoughts because of the rush to decision created by the combined effects of the rules, mass media, opinion polls, and the momentum of primaries. A possible compromise choice, such as Baker, was eliminated early, as was Brown, who might have broadened his party's appeal; Kennedy's force was revealed only after the delegates were made impotent. These individuals might or might not have been better Presidents than Carter or Reagan — that is not the issue. The point is that the electorate could hardly consider them as possibilities. In the long run, a limited choice must be a poorer choice (see chapter 7).

The process of 1980 was a distorted one in which quick decisions were inflated to become definitive. The process was biased in favor of those who could make their voices heard early. It was also biased as a result regionally, for the early contests were principally in the East and South. By the end of March, the nominations were essentially decided — before a single primary had been held west of the Mississippi River. A vast proportion of the electorate was therefore effectively disenfranchised. (A system of regional primaries, a current proposal, would worsen this defect, by giving inordinate influence to the region that held the first primary.) The early end of the race meant that events such as the attempted rescue of the American hostages had no effect, that the electorate could not consider alternative programs offered to combat the highest inflation rates in American history, and that the capabilities of the candidates could hardly be glimpsed. Only by a mechanistic definition can this be considered a democratic decision.

By summer's end, the process had been completed. Reagan and Carter had the endorsement of the major parties and the legitimacy and drawing power carried by that endorsement. Yet the choices were not satisfactory to many, as evident in polls showing almost half the electorate wishing for other options.[43] The voters would need to find other outlets for this discontent.

NOTES

1. Congressional Quarterly, *Elections '80* (Washington, D.C., 1980), pp. 68-96, provides details of the state selection systems.
2. Thomas Hammond ably examines the effect of these changes in "Another Look at the Role of 'the Rules' in the 1972 Democratic Presidential Primaries," *Western Political Quarterly* 33 (March 1980): 50-72.
3. See Cornelius Cotter and John Bibby, "Institutional Development of Parties and the Thesis of Party Decline,"*Political Science Quarterly* 95 (Spring 1980): 1-27.
4. William Keech and Donald Matthews, *The Party's Choice* (Washington, D.C.: Brookings Institution, 1976), p. 13.
5. F. Christopher Arterton, "Campaign Organizations Confront the Media-Political Environment," in *Race for the Presidency*, ed. James David Barber (Englewood Cliffs, N.J.: Prentice-Hall, 1978), p. 12.
6. The definitive analysis is Thomas Patterson, *The Mass Media Election* (New York: Praeger, 1980), chaps. 3-5.
7. Thomas Marshall, *Presidential Nominations in a Reform Age* (New York: Praeger, 1981), chap. 3.
8. Keech and Matthews, *Party's Choice*, pp. 7-9; James Beniger, "Winning the

Presidential Nomination: National Polls and State Primary Elections, 1936-1972," *Public Opinion Quarterly* 40 (Spring 1976): 22-38.

9. Donald Matthews describes the process in 1976 in Barber, *Race for the Presidency,* chap. 3. For a theoretical analysis, see John Kessel, *Presidential Campaign Politics* (Homewood, Ill: Dorsey, 1980), chap. 2.

10. Adam Clymer in the *New York Times,* 4 February 1980, p. A14.

11. CBS News/*New York Times* poll, 3-6 June 1979.

12. James Fallows, "The Passionless Presidency," *Atlantic* 243 (May 1979): 46.

13. The text of the speech can be read in *Congressional Quarterly Weekly Report* 37 (21 July 1979): 1470-72.

14. *Gallup Opinion Index* 174 (January 1980): 9, 14.

15. Presidential news conference of 13 February reported in *Congressional Quarterly Weekly Report* 38 (16 February 1980): 410.

16. Norman Nie et al., *The Changing American Voter* (Cambridge, Mass.: Harvard University Press, 1976), pp. 312-18.

17. David Nexon, "Asymmetry in the Political System: Occasional Activists in the Republican and Democratic Parties, 1956-1964," *American Political Science Review* 65 (September 1971): 716-30; and Anne Costain, "Changes in the Role of Ideology in American National Nominating Conventions and Among Party Identifiers," *Western Political Quarterly* 23 (March 1980): 73-86.

18. The Republicans basically allocated delegates to the states on the basis of population. They also provided additional delegates to states that voted for Republican candidates, providing the "bonus" to states regardless of their turnout or total Republican vote. These rules particularly benefited the states of the South and Southwest.

19. The reputation index is based on CBS News/*New York Times* national polls in which respondents are asked whether they have a "favorable" or "unfavorable" view of each candidate. The proportion that has any opinion is added to the proportion with opinions whose view is favorable, the total is divided in half. The index therefore combines the total recognition a candidate receives with the positive or negative character of this recognition. A rating of 50 would be achieved, for example, by a candidate who is known to half the electorate, of which 25 percent regard him favorably and 25 percent unfavorably. The rating of 50 therefore can be considered a neutral point (although the same result can be achieved through other combinations). A candidate with limited but highly positive ratings will have his "reputation index" magnified — this result can be seen in the early ratings of Anderson and Crane — whereas a candidate who is widely

known but regarded badly will have his rating diminished, as in the case of Brown. The theoretical limits of the index are 0 to 100, allowing for simple comparisons among candidates and across time.

20. *New York Times,* 23 January 1980, p. A16.

21. Scott Keeter, my colleague at Rutgers University, coined and elaborated this term.

22. Jules Witcover, *Marathon: The Pursuit of the Presidency, 1972–1976* (New York: Viking, 1977), p. 64 f.

23. E. J. Dionne in the *New York Times,* 6 March 1980, p. D17.

24. The data are from a CBS News/*New York Times* poll of voters leaving the polling booths in New Hampshire. The total figures for alternative choices are as follows: from one conservative to another, 18 percent; from a moderate to a conservative, 14 percent; from a conservative to a moderate, 29 percent; and from one moderate to another, 39 percent.

25. *New York Times,* 2 March 1980, p. A1. The poll results are from the CBS News/*New York Times* poll, 12-15 March 1980.

26. Adam Clymer in the *New York Times,* 16 March 1980, sect. 4, p. 4.

27. Hedrick Smith in the *New York Times,* 20 March 1980, p. A1. The importance of Illinois is shown by a statistic known as "Competitive Standing," or CS, developed by John Aldrich. This statistic reaches 1.0 when a candidate is assured of victory, but tends to increase rapidly at a lower point, as candidates develop "momentum." Carter's CS jumps from .03 to .09 at the time of the Illinois primary, to .21 after the Pennsylvania contest, a critical level. Media projections of local caucus results yield still higher figures, .14 after Illinois and .30 after Pennsylvania. For the calculation, see John Aldrich, *Before the Convention* (Chicago: University of Chicago Press, 1978), pp. 94 f, 243.

28. Howard Reiter, "Party Factionalism: National Conventions in the New Era,"*American Politics Quarterly* 8 (July 1980): 303-18.

29. Table 1.3 is based on CBS News/*New York Times* polls of voters in six designated states where there were significant Republican contests. Table entries are percentages of all voters and therefore include many who did not answer a particular question. Where an entry is missing, the question was not asked in the particular state or there were insufficient answers for a meaningful entry. The question on approval of the Carter foreign policy was sometimes replaced by one asking approval on Iran specifically (and, in Florida, by a general question on the President's job performance). The first two rows summarize as multiple-choice questions the two reasons a voter chose a particular candidate. Responses of "honesty and integrity," "experience," or "judgment under pressure" are considered references to

personal qualities. Responses referring to the qualities of "consistent positions on the issues," "real liberal," "a real conservative," "not too liberal," "a strong leader," "new ideas," and "cares about people's problems" are considered references to policy positions. The choices offered were generally, but not fully, consistent in all the polls. Such responses as "lesser of two evils," "best chance to win," and "he's trying hard" were not included in either category. Race is not included because of the low number of black Republicans.

30. For immediate accounts, see Howell Raines in the *New York Times*, 18 July 1980, and Jerome Cahill in the *New York Daily News*, 18 July 1980.

31. *New York Times*, 18 July 1980, p. A8.

32. John Herbers in the *New York Times*, 10 December 1979.

33. Timothy Clark in the *New York Times*, 21 April 1980, p. A19.

34. CBS News/*New York Times* polls, 1979-80.

35. Hedrick Smith in the *New York Times*, 20 March 1980, p. A1.

36. Aldrich, *Before the Convention*, p. 135.

37. Eugene Kiely, "1980 Campaign Coverage" (manuscript, Rutgers University, 1980).

38. *Congressional Quarterly Weekly Report* 38 (5 July 1980): 1873.

39. Table 1.6 is based on CBS News/*New York Times* polls of voters in eight designated states. The questions and coding used are the same in most respects as those in table 1.3. Race is also included. The multiple-choice question on the reason for candidate choice is treated somewhat differently. The personal quality of "judgment under pressure" was not always asked of Republicans but was very relevant in Democratic contests. The quality of "experience" was less important for the Democrats and is not included in the "personal" category. Its inclusion would have further exaggerated Carter's strength.

40. *New York Times*, 13 August 1980, p. B2.

41. *New York Times*, 15 August 1980, p. B2.

42. On each of these points, see *New York Times*, 24 March 1974, p. 32; *New York Times*, 24 June 1979; p. 27; and *Congressional Quarterly Weekly Report* 37 (15 December 1979): 2825.

43. CBS News/*New York Times* poll, 18-22 June 1980.

2

Issues in the Presidential Campaign

HENRY A. PLOTKIN

In the presidential election of 1980, two major-party candidates, one near major candidate, and a myriad of minor candidates presented a wide range of alternatives to the American public. This chapter focuses on the candidates of the Democratic and Republican parties, Jimmy Carter and Ronald Reagan, and with the exception of a brief description of John Anderson's energy program, it does not attempt to assess the positions of other candidates. This is not to argue that the positions of the minor candidates did not have intellectual merit, but that none made an appreciable impact on the actual vote.

All candidates and parties were united in one general set of beliefs: our nation was facing new challenges that required new solutions. This was true even for the Democrats, who controlled both houses of Congress and the Presidency, and who stated in their platform that the 1980s presented problems that were as "monumental and fundamental as those faced during the Civil War, during the two world wars, and the Great Depression."[1]

Most campaigns tend to engage in apocalyptic rhetoric, but the 1980 campaign had more than its share. Democrat Jimmy Carter and Republican Ronald Reagan, along with independent John Anderson, seemed to be communicating different visions of a coming doom. Whether it was Carter's emphasis on the dangers of nuclear war, Reagan's prediction of economic catastrophe, or Anderson's call for sacrifice, all seemed to view the nation as standing at the edge of a precipice. Their perceptions had a certain plausibility, for the standards that had guided national policy since the end of the Second World War were no longer valid. The political, military and economic position of the United States had undergone a profound revision by the time of the 1980 election.[2]

THE CONTEXT

Political change in a democratic society seems to accumulate slowly over time until, seemingly out of nowhere, it becomes evident that something revolutionary has occurred.[3] For the United States, this is particularly the case because individual political choices, born of compromise, are largely incremental in nature. This is true of domestic politics, where a series of events spanning a variety of issues led to dramatic changes. It is also true of the international environment, where the United States in 1980 faced a world that had altered with great rapidity.

The bipolar world of the postwar era, in which the United States and the Soviet Union were the two dominant powers, slowly evolved to include an economically resurgent Europe and Japan, as well as a China that was no longer a Soviet client. In addition, the emergence of the Organization of Petroleum Exporting Countries (OPEC) meant a greater national dependence by oil-poor countries on an economically united and politically demanding confederation of Third World, mostly Arab, nations.[4]

Perhaps no other issue reflected the changed circumstances of the United States more than its dependence on foreign oil. For a nation whose industrial development was fueled by a seemingly endless supply of cheap domestic oil, the newfound dependence on foreign oil created psychological and economic shock waves. President Carter called the challenge of energy independence the "moral equivalent of war" and spent more time trying to fashion an energy policy than he spent on any other domestic program.

The growing dependence on foreign oil helped stimulate inflation, depreciated the value of the dollar abroad, shifted the balance of political power toward the oil-producing Middle Eastern nations, and helped establish a psychology of scarcity that was in sharp contrast to the American tradition of abundance. The energy issue in particular forced the candidates to offer policies that would avoid the pessimistic scenario of a national economic collapse. It became clear during the campaign that a candidate's position on energy would also have a bearing on the role of government regulation, the nature of foreign relations, and perhaps most critically, on the nation's new role in the world.

The automobile industry epitomized many problems.[5] Domestic car production was overwhelmed by high-quality, fuel-efficient Japanese and German automobile imports. Chrysler went to the brink of bankruptcy and needed federal loan guarantees in order to survive; Ford was not in much better shape and suffered huge financial losses; and at General Motors, once a symbol of American industrial success, 1980 losses were the highest in corporate history.

The decline in the U.S. automobile industry had a heavy political impact as plant layoffs placed tens of thousands of workers on the unemployment lines. There were new demands on government for protective measures against foreign imports (especially from Japan), and political leaders and United Auto Workers' representatives attempted to put pressure on foreign producers to build plants in the United States.

Clearly, the American automobile industry suffered because of painful changes caused by high energy costs, which resulted in a dramatic new public preference for small cars. Too, it became obvious that the industry was no longer a national entity but an international one. The auto industry had become so internationalized that there was no longer an American but a world car, which was assembled in and contained parts from many nations.[6]

The American automobile industry simply pointed to a much wider economic malaise. The economic autonomy of the United States was no more; the world had become more egalitarian, at least among democratic industrial states, and this egalitarianism exposed various flaws in the American economy. Underinvestment in new plants, low productivity, and a weak dollar placed the United States at a severe economic disadvantage in trading with other industrial states. A new international economic order had emerged, yet the United States seemed trapped in the assumptions of the old order, where the American economy was the wonder of the world. The economic leviathan was brought to its knees under the impact of high energy costs and a decaying industrial base.

Perhaps in no other area was the loss of autonomy seen so clearly as in the area of foreign relations. The loss of the war in Vietnam made many Americans question military policy and wonder if the United States, with its web of international alliances, had assumed too activist a role in the world. George McGovern's slogan in the 1972 campaign, "Come Home America," was in fact partially heeded by a nation reluctant to get involved in foreign adventures.

Nevertheless, the 1980 campaign raised serious questions about the level of the nation's military preparedness and the military intentions of the Soviet Union. Two events during the election year caused many Americans to rethink their foreign policy assumptions: the taking of American hostages in Iran and the Soviet invasion of Afghanistan. The fall of the Shah of Iran, who, under the Nixon doctrine, was given primary responsibility for defense of the Middle East oil supply,[7] called into question U.S. strategy in that part of the world. Concern was heightened by the capture of the U.S. Embassy in Teheran by student militants who had the implicit sanction of the revolutionary government and its religious leader, the Ayatollah Khomeini. For many, the failure to free the hostages was a symbol of American impotence.

The Soviet Union's invasion of Afghanistan caused shock and consternation in the United States. This foray into a Moslem nation was seen by the Carter administration as a radical departure from previous Soviet policy, which had limited its military activities to Eastern Europe. The fact that this invasion came when American relations with Iran had deteriorated made it all the more dangerous and a potential threat to Western oil supplies. The administration's responses — cutting American wheat sales to the Soviet Union, boycotting the 1980 Olympics in Moscow, and shelving the Strategic Arms Limitations Treaty (SALT II) — sent U.S./Soviet relations into the deep freeze of a new cold war.

What perhaps overwhelmed even these important events was the growing perception that the United States had lost its military dominance, that the Soviet Union was now at least America's equal in nuclear strategic arms and far its superior in conventional forces. This led to much soul-searching about the effects of the all-volunteer army on U.S. conventional forces and the various decisions made by the Carter administration in terms of the general defense budget. These concerns underscored one essential point: the United States had lost its military edge and was in danger of falling victim to renewed Soviet aggression.

The last set of questions that establish the context for the 1980 election have to do with management of the domestic economy. Double-digit inflation, high unemployment, and record high interest rates marked the presidential election year. The candidates devised various solutions to the nation's economic ills; nevertheless, it was clear that something was fundamentally wrong with the conventional wisdom about economics (drawn mostly from Keynesian theory) and perhaps most profoundly, with the capacity of American political institutions to develop programs comprehensive enough to grapple with today's economic problems.

In many respects one can draw an analogy between the weaknesses in the nation's economic infrastructure and the political infrastructure. Both in large measure had been allowed to atrophy, had proven unable to respond to the changed circumstances, and had lost the faith of the consumers. For political institutions, the fragmented nature of power made it difficult to develop and sustain policies that would systematically deal with the twin evils of inflation and unemployment. The complexity of these issues, along with those of energy, presented national institutions with problems that might be beyond their current capacity to resolve. Indeed, a fundamental issue of the 1980s may well be the inability of institutions developed in the eighteenth century to contend with twentieth-century problems that require more developed and authoritative political institutions.[8]

This, then, is the context that framed the issues of the 1980 election. The campaign itself raised many superficial points — whether President Carter was mean; whether his brother, Billy, was an appropriate choice to assist in the Iranian crisis; whether Ronald Reagan was a warmonger; whether John Anderson was a spoiler — but many significant and important issues also were raised and debated. Indeed, two of the platforms reached back to thè 1952 campaign of Adlai Stevenson and quoted his famous remark, "Let's talk sense to the American people."[9] The competition for votes lay beyond media hype; it involved attempting to persuade reasonable men and women about what was indeed sensible.

Although this chapter explores the relevant differences between the two major parties and their nominees on the significant issues of the campaign, it should be noted that there was broad agreement on many matters. Both candidates spoke of the need to revitalize U.S. cities through the use of tax incentives and tax-free economic zones. There was also agreement on such questions as economic revitalization of the nation's industries, making the government more efficient, expanding export markets, and combatting crime. On international affairs, both sides agreed on the need to halt terrorism, the desirability of maintaining American alliances, and the importance of avoiding war. The once crucial issue of race seemed to fade into the background.

All presidential campaigns raise a seemingly endless array of issues. As the role of government expands, so too does the range of issues on which candidates for the Presidency have to take positions. This chapter distills from the myriad issues those that seem the most critical, not necessarily from the public's perception (that question is dealt with elsewhere in this book), but from the perspective of issues that are most central and enduring to the life of the nation. Hence, a large degree of selectivity has been utilized in order to give some understanding of the broad questions facing the nation and how the two major-party candidates sought to answer them.

E N E R G Y   P O L I C Y

Energy was the single issue that every American faced. This became a touchstone issue, reflecting both the loss of energy independence and the growing realization that inflation, unemployment, and foreign policy were ultimately influenced by the degree to which the United States remained dependent on foreign oil. It also became clear that the various programs proposed to solve the energy problem would required sacrifice on the part of the public. No issue was more politically explosive for the major candidates.

The Democrats

President Carter's energy program had two essential goals: to conserve present resources through the more efficient use of energy, and to create new environmentally secure sources of energy.[10] Specifically, the Carter program entailed several major points, central among them being the slow decontrol of the price of domestic oil. Historically, the price of domestic crude has been regulated by the federal government. The primary reason for this regulation, ironic in the present context, has been to prevent the nation from being swamped with cheap Arab oil. The federal government, in order to protect domestic producers, has controlled the price of oil and kept it above world market prices.[11]

The Carter plan argued for a windfall profits tax as a way of amassing the needed capital for an elaborate program to develop alternative sources of energy. Specifically the plan called for a crash program in solar energy, synthetic fuels, and any other related energy source that would make the nation less dependent on foreign oil. In addition, the plan asked for the establishment of an Energy Mobilization Board to circumvent unnecessary red tape in the quest for new energy sources. Such "red tape" would include environmental laws or state regulations that the EMB determined were blocking the sensible "construction of needed energy facilities."[12] For many environmentalists, the EMB represented a direct threat to the ecological safeguards that the Environmental Protection Agency had promulgated over the last decade.

A second institutional proposal in President Carter's energy policy was the establishment of an Energy Security Corporation that would finance the alternative fuels program by using the windfall profits tax. The ESC represented a bold extension of federal power and resources into the area of energy development.

The Carter administration also called for standby authority to ration gasoline, a program to be implemented "in the event of a serious supply interruption." Congress quibbled about the definition of a "serious supply interruption," but it was clear that the Carter plan sought to limit consumption by the price mechanism and, failing that, was willing to use forced conservation as well.[13]

In all, the Carter program was a balanced one, and to use one of his favorite words, a "comprehensive" one. He could point with some pride to the success of the program by mid-1980: the United States was importing a million fewer barrels of oil a day from OPEC than it had imported a year ago, oil exploration was at an all-time high, and the use of solar energy had increased dramatically.

Despite the partial success of the Carter program, many people harbored grave doubts about its ultimate efficacy. Criticisms ranged from those of the environmentalists, who feared that the emphasis on synthetic fuel (especially shale oil) would destroy the ecology of certain western states, to others who feared that the President's support of the Alaska land bill, which sought to preserve vast tracts of natural wilderness from exploration, was artificially inhibiting the discovery of new energy sources.

What is perhaps most interesting about the energy question is the difficulty of striking a balance between contending political forces. No energy program can, at once, please both environmentalists and those who believe in the unlimited availability of fossil fuel. President Carter and, especially, the Department of Energy were caught between two worlds: the traditional one of cheap and abundant resources, and the new one of limited resources. It became almost a popular sport to blame the President and Secretary of Energy James Schlesinger for the energy crisis. In significant ways the test of Carter's energy program was not whether it was a sensible one but whether the public *thought* it was. Clearly, no public consensus supported the Carter energy policies.

The Republicans

The response of Ronald Reagan and the Republican party to the Carter plan was direct and blunt:

> The answer is more domestic production of oil and gas. We need greater use of nuclear power within strict safety standards. We need more research and development for energy substitutes for fossil fuel. We need capital markets that can grow . . . we need savings. Putting the market system back to work for these objectives is an essential first step for their achievement.[14]

For Reagan, the answer to the energy question lay in the marketplace. Indeed, at the heart of the issue, the position of Reagan and the conservative wing of the Republican party was that the government was the chief enemy of economic growth and that a bloated federal bureaucracy prevented the marketplace from providing for the needs of the public. Moreover, the modern welfare state was pernicious; it operated out of a logic of its own, to fulfill its own needs, not those of society. On this topic Reagan made his disagreement with Carter clear. During the debate with Carter, Reagan asserted:

> I just happen to believe that free enterprise can do a better job of producing the things the people need than government can. The Department of Energy has a multi-billion dollar budget in excess of $10 billion — it hasn't produced a quart of oil or a lump of coal or anything else in the line of energy.[15]

Hence, a solution to the energy crisis involved the rapid decontrol of oil and natural gas prices, abolition of the Department of Energy, a relaxation of environmental rules, and the freeing of federal funds for oil exploration. While Reagan made vague allusions to the need to conserve scarce resources, his fundamental assumption was that there was an abundance of energy resources and that the private sector, unfettered by government regulation, would be able to discover them.

For Reagan, belief in the efficacy of the marketplace was not merely a question of economic efficiency. It represented a moral precept, involving a conviction that the free market was essential in a political democracy, and that economic messages transmitted from consumers to producers were not simply more rational than any other system but also the only way to ensure freedom.[16] Reagan and the movement he represented questioned the economic and moral underpinnings of the welfare state, arguing that, whatever its good intentions, they had become perverted by an excessive centralization of power in Washington.

Reagan flatly rejected any program that held the price of energy at an "artificially low" level; he also rejected a windfall profits tax. The Republican platform bluntly stated: "We reject unequivocally punitive gasoline and other energy taxes designed to artificially suppress domestic consumption."[17] The Republican program even called for higher prices for oil and natural gas with the profits from these higher prices retained by the oil companies to finance resource exploration.

The distinction between Carter's and Reagan's energy programs was in how dramatically Carter stressed a cooperative relationship between the public and private sectors, while the Reagan program called for a greater reliance on the private sector. Also, implicit in this debate was how each felt about economic growth. The Carter plan, with its emphasis on conservation, seemed to be assuming an "era of limits." That is, the fuel availability is limited and, barring some technological breakthrough, people have to learn to live with less. For Reagan, the idea of limits was anathema, a further example of government's attempts to stifle the entrepreneurial inclinations of the American public. Indeed, a populist theme was inherent in Reagan's belief in economic progress: social justice and equality would best be achieved by a return to rapid economic growth. Anything less would prevent the upward mobility of citizens, which was, for Reagan, the essence of America.

A Note on the Anderson Difference
Independent candidate John Anderson distinguished himself from the two major-party candidates on the energy issue. In fact, it was his position on energy, with its seeming call for sacrifice, that helped bring him into national prominence during the Republican primaries. Anderson called an increase in

gasoline prices, through taxation, the best way to ensure conservation. The Anderson platform called for:

> Substantially increasing the federal tax on gasoline and use of the proceeds to lower the payroll taxes and increase social security benefits. A fifty-cent per gallon tax would achieve a reduction in gas consumption of as much as 700,000 barrels per day in the short run and over one million barrels per day in the longer term. It would also generate over $50 billion per year in net revenues to be returned to consumers through offsetting tax relief.[18]

This energy plan was designed to encourage conservation through pricing; unlike the Reagan plan, however, Anderson intended to return the price increase to the public through reduced social security taxes. Hence individuals would not pay higher taxes; rather, the tax burden would be reallocated to reduce energy consumption. Anderson's argument had as its premise that the supply of oil and natural gas was limited and that the United States was becoming dangerously dependent on unreliable sources of foreign oil. The key to any energy plan therefore involved fairly severe conservation measures that would include, aside from price increases, home energy audits, investment in solar and wind power, and a limited use of nuclear power. The Anderson plan was a broad and comprehensive one that added much to the quality of the public debate over this vital issue.

THE ECONOMY

Elections are won and lost for many reasons, but none is as critical as the state of the nation's economy. It is as likely as anything else that Jimmy Carter met his Waterloo on Election Day because he had failed to correct three critical aspects of the economy: inflation, unemployment, and interest rates (see chapter 3). His administration tried various policies ranging from tight money policies to wage-price guidelines to still the fire of inflation. None seemed to work. Inflation kept escalating, and so did the rates of unemployment and interest. The prime interest rate (the rate banks charge their most credit-worthy customers) stood at 15½ percent on Election Day; the rate of inflation for 1980 was in excess of 12 percent; and unemployment stood at 8 million for the year.[19] As if this weren't enough, unemployment of black teen-agers in some central cities reached astronomical proportions of over 40 percent and over 200,000 auto workers were on layoffs.

Still, of all the challenges to the Carter administration, the most perplexing was inflation. Indeed, it was inflation that rankled most Americans, especially those on fixed incomes, and probably was as responsible as anything for the public's disaffection for the President's performance. Carter lost the war against inflation. Alfred Kahn, the President's "inflation fighter," asked if the war against inflation was winnable, replied, "Well obviously. Fred Kahn couldn't do it. Can anybody do it? I don't know. Can a President do it? I don't know. All I can say is that we have to do it."[20] These words, from an economist as distinguished as Kahn, offered faint hope, but the parties did present to the nation two distinct remedies for its economic ills.

The Democrats
The Democrats were the incumbents at a time when the economy was ailing. This made it difficult to offer plausible policies that would persuade the public that the President's reelection would alter the present course. Democratic problems were compounded when Senator Edward Kennedy, representing the left wing of the party, challenged the President during the primaries. Kennedy offered a broad range of programs as alternatives to the President's. They included advocacy of wage/price controls, national health insurance, and a $12 billion jobs program and opposition to the decontrol of oil and natural gas prices.[21] The Kennedy program was self-consciously designed to continue the traditional commitment of liberals to the extended welfare state. Kennedy, who attempted to place himself in the tradition of Franklin D. Roosevelt, Harry S Truman, John F. Kennedy, Lyndon B. Johnson, and Hubert H. Humphrey, derided the Carter performance as more Republican than Democratic.

Unfortunately for President Carter, he could not engage in speculations about future abundance but was forced by his incumbency to justify what had been done and argue that there was a light at the end of the tunnel of economic decline. So the President's position was:

> This inflation took fifteen years to build up; it cannot be eliminated overnight. The Administration's anti-inflation program was designed to cope with very specific inflation factors confronting our nation. So far double digit price increases have been heavily concentrated in the areas of energy and housing. In the short term the goal of anti-inflation policy must be to "Quarantine" these increases and prevent them from spilling over into the base wage price structure of our economy.[22]

The Carter perspective on the economy assumed that problems which had evolved over many years were immune to short-term fixes; what was required was a balanced program of a tight budget, a restrained monetary policy, and private restraint on the part of management and labor. Carter assigned much of the blame for inflation to the OPEC nations and asserted that a reduction in imported oil was the most important first step in reducing inflation.

President Carter also sought ways to overcome the debilitating effects of the wage/price spiral, in which higher prices beget higher wage demands, which beget higher prices, etc., by proposing a tax-based incomes policy. This would involve using tax penalties and rewards as a mechanism to control wages and prices.[23] This policy had been discussed during Carter's administration and was seen as a creative halfway point between the jawboning of wage/price guidelines and the stringency of the wage/price controls advocated by Senator Kennedy.

Carter's economic program attempted to walk a fine line between the demands of various Democratic constituencies and his own ideas on what was fiscally prudent. The Democratic platform reiterated its commitment to the Humphrey-Hawkins Full Employment Act, stating that full employment was necessary "to the pursuit of sound justice, and to the strength and vitality of America."[24] To buttress this pledge, the platform called for a $12 billion anti-recession jobs program that would add 800,000 new jobs for those who were most in need.[25] While committing themselves to job programs and expressing a "sensitivity to those who look to the federal government for help," however, the Democrats also stated: " . . . as long as inflationary pressures remain strong, fiscal prudence is essential to avoid destroying the progress made to date in reducing the inflation rate."[26]

Although Carter and the Democrats came out flatly against a constitutional amendment requiring a balanced budget, they did support a restructured fiscal policy that would lead to a balanced budget. This position was made even more necessary because of the $59 billion deficit over the previous fiscal year, a deficit blamed by many for the nation's high rate of inflation.

In all, as far as the economy was concerned, Carter was trapped by a need to limit spending while reconciling the values of traditional welfare-state Democrats. Hence the platform would praise the Carter administration for having increased spending in such programs as Head Start (77 percent), basic skills programs (233 percent), Job Corps (157 percent), Native American education (124 percent), Medicare (54 percent), and child nutrition (43 percent);[27] and at the same time would claim fiscal restraint and the necessity of a balanced budget.

The tax-cut issue highlighted the dilemmas of the Carter economic program. The President argued against large individual tax cuts, claiming they would be highly inflationary. Instead, Carter offered a $27 billion tax cut, primarily designed to offset 1981 increases in the social security payroll tax.[28] Other tax cuts would be directed primarily at the business community with no proposal for a reduction in the personal income tax. This meant that Carter, unlike the Republicans, was not promising any immediate improvement to the individual taxpayer. His emphasis during the campaign was on belt tightening and, at least temporarily, on austerity. And while he did not renew his pledge to balance the budget, it was clear that Carter economics offered the public no easy path to an economic utopia.

The Republicans

If Ronald Reagan and the Republicans did not exactly promise a utopia, they did tell the American public "that we can and will resurrect our dreams."[29] The dream of economic abundance rejects flatly any call for an "age of limits" or any sprightly sayings that "less is more." Instead, it suggests that there is no limit to what free men and women can accomplish. Further, it holds that the chief enemy of economic progress is the national government. Again, as with their energy policy, the Republicans stressed the importance of unfettered economic markets as the best mechanism to achieve renewed prosperity.

The Republicans called inflation "the greatest domestic threat facing our nation today."[30] They charged the Carter administration with responsibility for the rate of inflation's moving to a high of 18 percent in 1980 from the 4.8 percent rate that existed in 1976 when Gerald Ford was President. In many ways the Republican platform reads not only as an indictment of President Carter specifically but also of the entire idea that governmental policies can assure economic growth. For the Republicans, the solution to the nation's economic ills was straightforward: "The Republican party believes inflation can be controlled only by fiscal and monetary restraint, combined with sharp reductions in the regulatory disincentives for savings, investments and productivity."[31]

The Republicans rejected wage/price controls as a possible solution and instead argued for "lower taxes, less spending and a balanced budget." Specifically, they called for the enactment of the Kemp-Roth tax bill that would reduce personal income taxes by 30 percent over a three-year period. The theory behind this bill is that a reduction in personal income tax leads to more savings, which increases the capital markets so that industries can expand their operations. Reagan also argued that, when coupled with a reduced federal budget, an increase in spending would not cause higher rates of inflation. During the debate with Carter he asserted that "we don't have inflation because the people are living too well. We have inflation because the government is living too well."[32]

The Republican economic program was based on the conviction that the best way to prosperity was to shift resources away from the public sector and on to the private sector. This idea, commonly referred to as supply-side economics, assumes that government tax and regulatory policies cause economic stagnation. Supply-side economics has at its core assumption the belief that a substantial tax cut will produce more revenues from increased economic activity than it loses. Hence, one can have it both ways: reduce taxes and generate more revenue for the government.[33] As the Republicans saw it, the new theory would replace the Democratic orthodoxy of more taxes and more government spending to solve problems. The Republicans and their candidate saw government programs as failures and believed that only the marketplace could get the nation out of its current bind.

In significant ways the Republican program was a repudiation of the welfare state. They argued that government spending, with its huge budget deficits, had placed the nation on the brink of financial ruin. A theme that ran through many of their statements was the deplorable increase in private-sector dependence on governmental largesse. This represented a threat to political freedom, as well as a threat to the work incentive. That the government now spent 21 percent of the gross national product, that federal credit (various loan programs) had soared to nearly $600 billion, and that regulatory policies had increased in both scope and complexity were evidence of this dangerous trend.[34]

In one sense the Republicans were attempting to restore autonomy to the private sector. They rejected the ideal implicit in the welfare state that a redistribution of income is necessary for a healthy and just society. Rather, they argued that only an expanding economy could produce abundance for all. As Reagan stated: "When government takes more of one person's income the larger it is, and gives it to someone else for having a smaller income, each person suddenly has more to lose by earning more. The government has effectively raised the tax on the efforts of both."[35]

Hence, the overall goal of Reagan's economic program was to "offer broad new incentives to labor and capital . . . to stimulate a great outpouring of private goods and services and to create an abundance of jobs."[36] There was a messianic urgency in Reagan's economic message. He was calling for a "new beginning" and for a return to those older economic verities of hard work, self-reliance, and limited government that had ostensibly made the American economy the wonder of the world. His call was for a return to a time when the scale of governmental activity was more contained. Indeed, Reagan described himself as leading a crusade. The purpose of that crusade would be to "take the government off the backs of the great people of this country and turn you loose again to do those things that I know you can do so well, because you did them and made this country great."[37]

Issues involving energy and the economy were of major importance, but for many people the overwhelming issues of the 1980 campaign were social. These included questions about abortion, the Equal Rights Amendment (ERA), prayer in the schools, crime, pornography, and the general state of the nation's morality. The rapid changes in American society made it difficult for citizens to adopt secure and certain standards and beliefs with which to judge a changed world. Life styles changed, as did opinions on morality, making it more difficult for people to know what should be tolerated and what should not.[38]

For many, the responsibility for the moral climate of the nation lay at the feet of a government that had been too indulgent, too tolerant of what many saw as moral excesses. In fact, the 1980 campaign was to witness the rise of evangelical religious groups, many of whom used television as their pulpit and involved themselves directly in the political process as a way of stopping what they took to be the nation's drift into moral decay.

The social issues discussed during the campaign raised complex legal as well as moral questions. The conflict between individual rights and community interests has always been a perplexing problem for the United States with its racial, ethnic, and religious pluralism. In America, toleration is important not only for reasons of fairness but for prudent reasons as well. Nevertheless, for many Americans, public tolerance of certain forms of behavior had gone too far. Still, for others, the government was seen as their only hope for achieving equality and justice.

The Democrats
The Democratic party has long prided itself on its commitment to the liberal principles of justice and equality. In the 1980 campaign it stressed its support for the floundering ERA. Indeed, on the question of the ERA, the Democrats went even further than simply calling for its ratification. Their platform stated: "The Democratic party shall withhold financial support and technical campaign assistance from candidates who do not support ERA. The Democratic party further urges all national organizations to support the boycott of the unratified states by not holding their national conventions in those states."[39]

This statement represented a bold departure from normal party policy on binding candidates to specific issue positions. On no other issue was there the threat of withholding party support nor the recommendation for using economic boycotts against recalcitrant states. This victory by feminists and their sympathizers was, however, illustrative of the strong positions the Democrats took on a host of civil liberties questions.

They made clear their advocacy of equality for minorities and the handicapped, of affirmative action, and of basic civil rights. On the issue of abortion the party declared that "reproductive freedom is a fundamental human right. We therefore oppose government interference in the reproductive decisions of Americans, especially . . . poor Americans."[40] This latter point meant that the Democrats were supporting federally funded abortions for the poor, a position that Jimmy Carter had not previously endorsed. Yet what all these strong positions reflected was the power within the Democratic party of the forces of modern liberalism. The overall attitude of these forces was to use basic constitutional precedents to change what they took to be inequities in the private order. A major tenet of modern liberalism is the extension of individual choice and equality throughout society.

What is interesting about the 1980 Democratic platform is that support for many controversial issues is maintained, while certain buzzwords are eliminated. Thus, instead of "abortion," the Democrats speak of "reproductive rights"; instead of "busing," they refer to their opposition to "efforts to undermine the Supreme Court's historic mandate of school desegregation."[41] This indicates two things: (1) within the Democratic party, the influence of minorities and women is not to be denied; and (2) Democrats realize that many issues, among them abortion, the ERA, integrated housing, raise significant public opposition.

In some ways, the problems the Democrats faced on social issues reflects a problem inherent in liberal ideals. That is, classical liberalism as a political form assumes that the private order is cohesive, that religion, political community, and moral teaching all exist and have authority. Liberal thought does not see government as a redemptive force. Redemption must occur privately, and all that a liberal government can do is to ensure respect for basic rights under the law.[42] Yet, it becomes increasingly clear that the private order is *not* cohesive; divorce rates soar, church membership declines, a common morality becomes fragmented — all of which makes the sources of social understanding and unity more problematic (see chapter 7).

The question that current liberalism has yet to answer is how it can help rebuild the social order. Jimmy Carter in the 1976 campaign said that his major goal as President was to help rebuild the American family. While such statements have the ring of campaign puffery, it is true that the family as the basic unit of society has undergone profound changes and that, in some sense, the state is being asked to play a larger role in what used to be an exclusively private concern. Hence, day-care centers, the care of the aged, prenatal advising, and a host of other traditionally private concerns have, over the last two decades, become public ones.

The redefinition of private issues as public issues had caused great consternation in many quarters, for the more activist role of government in these formerly private areas has been seen as contributing to the decline of the social order. The ERA, perhaps more than any other question, became the focal point for discontent about the state's attempts to impose egalitarian standards onto traditional relationships between the sexes. Hence, the commitment of the liberal wing of the Democratic party to reform in the private sector led to a counter mobilization among those who wanted to maintain the values and traditions of the private order. Indeed, it was the opposition to activist liberal principles and the defense of earlier liberalism that induced many to seek an alternative to the Democratic nominee.

The Republicans

At sharp variance with the Democratic position, Reagan and the Republicans represented a revolt against secularism. In significant ways the Republican party was captured by those who wanted to return to traditional values and who additionally blamed the intrusion of the federal government for the decline in morality. Hence, the party argued with some vehemence for the reestablishment of prayer in the schools, for the right to bear arms, for the centrality of the family in American life, and most importantly, for the federal government to cease and desist from intruding on the autonomy of the private order.

The grievances of the Republican right-wing against the national government are of long standing. The nomination of their candidate, Ronald Reagan, gave them the chance to proclaim publicly their discontent with secular liberalism's vision of equality and justice.[43] For this wing of the party, as distinct from the moderate wing of George Bush, Howard Baker, and Gerald Ford, the Republican convention provided an opportunity to make questions involving morality important again. This entailed revising the Republican ERA position, which had been supportive, and arguing instead that the amendment should not be ratified. The platform stated: "We support equal rights and equal opportunity for women, without taking away traditional rights of women such as exemption from the draft. . . . We oppose any move which would give the federal government more power over families."[44] The platform supported equal pay for equal work, urged the elimination of all discrimination against women, but also argued that traditional distinctions between the sexes be maintained. And most importantly, it advocated that the federal government refrain from interfering with the privacy of married people.

On the abortion issue, the Republicans and their candidate were also clearly distinguishable from the Democrats. Said the Republicans: "We affirm our support of a constitutional amendment to restore protection of the right to life of unborn children. We also support the congressional efforts to restrict the use of taxpayers dollars for abortion."[45] Two distinct views of what was socially tolerable emerged. This split demonstrated a sharp cleavage within the nation between those who believed in individual choice enforced by the national government, as the basis of morality, and those who believed that traditional religious and community values ought to dominate.

The ostensible goal of the Republicans was to restore parental authority to the schools to replace the authority of the state. They found "amoral indoctrination" existing in the schools. This is an interesting concept, which can be contrasted to Reagan's suggestion, at one point in the campaign, that evolutionary theory should not be taught in the schools because it contradicted the vision of Genesis found in the Old Testament. And while this idea evoked memories of the famous Scopes monkey trial of the 1920s, it signaled the Republicans' belief that secular education not rooted in theology was responsible for the marked increase in immoral behavior. The Republicans wanted to return control of the schools to localities and advocated the abolition of the newly created Department of Education, which they saw as a symbol of the usurpation of local rights by the federal government.[46]

What underlay most of the Republicans' positions on the social issues, like most of their positions on energy and economics, was a belief that a return of autonomy to the private sector would correct all the abuses of the last several decades. There was a strong element of nostalgic wistfulness in this position, which saw all virtue in the people and all vice in government. Implicit was a belief in the natural goodness of men and women, who became corrupted when government intervened in their lives.

There was, in addition, a rejection of the values of eastern intellectuals, of those who hold secular as opposed to traditional values. For secularists were the state planners who sought, it was argued, to impose their values on the people. Hence, what was needed was a redistribution of power away from Washington and back to the states and localities. Indeed, the Republican party was seeking to reverse the trend of nationalizing political issues by returning them to the states where, it was felt, traditional values still flourished.[47]

The Republicans made one further pledge to the nation and that involved the selection of judges. They asserted: "We will work for the appointment of judges on all levels of the judiciary who respect traditional American values and the sanctity of innocent human life."[48] This pledge was consistent with the views of conservatives that the court system, especially the U.S. Supreme Court under Earl Warren, was largely responsible for the threats to moral values. Hence, the Republican platform promised a litmus test for all prospective judges, their opposition to abortion. More generally, the Republicans wanted judges who would not be "activist" in the progressive sense but would act to restore the traditional "rights of law abiding citizens."[49] This translates into less emphasis on procedural due process for criminals and a greater respect for the rights of victims.

The Republicans' position on the social issues had an element of inconsistency. On the one hand, they argued that government should not attempt to instruct individuals on moral questions; on the other hand, they sought to use the power of the state to ban abortion or to eliminate pornography. In some cases, such as wiretapping, they invoked national security as a justification for the abrogation of private rights. This seeming confusion about the appropriate role for the state in the social order reflects two distinct concerns of conservatives — to preserve the traditional order and to favor that "government which governs least." On many issues these positions were not always compatible.

William Safire argues that American conservatism has two strands: traditionalism and libertarianism.[50] The former group holds that government ought to "uphold society's values," including those of the family, common morality, and religion; the libertarian wing is "fierce in its belief that government is wrong to legislate morality."[51] This, Safire argues, is the dimension of the coming debate among conservatives. How this debate will be resolved in a highly pluralistic society remains to be seen but what should not be underestimated is the seriousness of purpose of both the traditionalist and the libertarian. Each seeks to dramatically reverse what is felt to be the use of big government to achieve secular ends.[52]

FOREIGN POLICY AND DEFENSE

Fears about America's loss of autonomy were voiced most directly on the issue of foreign policy and defense. The 1980 election provided an opportunity to reassess America's international posture at a time when the trauma of Vietnam

had significantly abated. The behavior of the Soviet Union, the hostages in
Iran, and the ability of the military to protect the nation were all debated during
the 1980 campaign.

The Democrats

The Carter administration served during a time of rapid change in the international arena. As President, Carter could point with pride to some of his accomplishments: the Panama Canal treaty, the Camp David accords between
Egypt and Israel, avoidance of a race war in Zimbabwe, the emphasis on human rights, and a normalization of relations with China. Nevertheless, there
were the nagging problems of Soviet aggression in Afghanistan, the fall of the
Shah of Iran, and the holding of 52 American hostages in Iran. The Iranian
crisis, perhaps more than any other, came to symbolize for many Americans
their nation's impotence in the modern world.

Carter faced the same problem as many statesmen. As Henry Kissinger
pointed out, leaders rarely receive credit for crises avoided, but they have to accept blame for those that are not.[53] Carter also had to reckon with the problem
of making foreign policy in a democratic nation, which in some respects means
that foreign policy is an extension of domestic policy. Hence, Carter paid an
enormous price among Jews, for example, for the seeming inconsistency of the
U.S. position on Israel in the UN.

Carter's position on foreign policy and military issues was primarily a
defense of what he had accomplished. In this context he cited his foreign policy
accomplishments and went on to emphasize his commitment to arms control,
specifically to the signing of the SALT II treaty with the Soviet Union. Carter
argued that the United States must learn both to compete and cooperate with
the Soviet Union. He presented himself as a peacemaker and an experienced
statesman and attempted to brand his opponent as trigger-happy: "I think
habitually Governor Reagan has advocated injection of military forces into
troubled areas when I and my predecessors . . . have advocated resolving those
troubles . . . peacefully, diplomatically, and through negotiation."[54]

On a more substantive level, Carter argued that his basic foreign policy
had been successful and that the United States had made inroads in Third
World countries, strengthened the Western alliance, and was working toward a
new world economic order. In addition, Carter justified his human rights policy
as consistent with fundamental American beliefs. While he did not spend as
much time on human rights as he had in the 1976 election, he did assert that
U.S. efforts in that difficult area had been useful in Latin America, the Philip-
pines, and South Korea.[55]

On the question of defense, the Democratic platform paid traditional obeisance to America's strength and claimed that "America's military strength is and must be unsurpassed."[56] The platform further claimed that the present administration had clearly reversed the "threatened decline in America's world position" brought about by the Nixon and Ford administration.[57] This was a somewhat paradoxical comment, given Carter's 1976 pledge to cut the defense budget.

The Carter defense program had several major themes. First, it emphasized the modernization of strategic weapons such as the MX, Trident, and Cruise missile systems, while finding the current U.S. nuclear deterrent adequate. Second, it stressed the need to beef up conventional forces, specifically with the addition of a rapid deployment force and peacetime draft registration (including the registration of women). Third, it argued the need to continue to bargain for a strategic arms limitation agreement with the Soviet Union.[58]

The Carter defense program sought to walk a delicate line between hawks and doves, arguing as it did for both an increase in military spending and a SALT II agreement. The Jimmy Carter of 1980 clearly was not the Jimmy Carter of 1976. He had become much more hawkish on foreign policy and more deeply suspicious of Soviet intentions. Indeed, in his 1980 State of the Union Address, the President stated: "Let our position be absolutely clear; any attempt by any outside force to gain control of the Persian Gulf region will be regarded as an assault on the vital interests of the United States and such an assault will be repelled by any means necessary, including military force."[59]

This was a direct warning to the Soviet Union that the United States would be willing to go to war to protect the West's supply of oil. But it also showed how much Jimmy Carter had been forced to change his basic foreign policy and defense posture.

The 1980 campaign found President Carter and his party unable to persuade the public about the cohesiveness of their policies. Liberals attacked them for spending too much for defense, while conservatives talked about the weakness of the Carter foreign policy. In some respects, Carter did not articulate the foreign policy and defense issues well, but it is also true that the press showed a morbid fascination with conflicts between the head of the National Security Council, Zbigniew Brzezinski, and Secretary of State Cyrus Vance, instead of discussing more meaningful questions.[60]

In many ways the foreign policy and defense issues that Jimmy Carter presented to the American public lacked an overall sense of purpose becaus‒ the President, in an age when American autonomy is severely reduced, ca‒ easily present a unified and certain position. While Carter was not alwa‒

sistent, the complexities of the world often make consistency not the most desirable of virtues.

The Republicans

Reagan and the Republicans had a field day attacking the Carter administration's record on foreign policy. They presented a vision of an incompetent, cowardly President with an uncertain foreign policy vainly attempting to hold back the inexorable march of the Soviet Union: "Overseas, conditions already perilous, deteriorate. The Soviet Union for the first time is acquiring the means to obliterate or cripple our land-based missile system and blackmail us into submission. Monstrous tyrannies spread more rapidly through the third world and Latin America. Our alliances are frayed in Europe and elsewhere."[61] If we continued to drift aimlessly, the Republicans argued, "the American experiment, so marvelously successful for 200 years, would come strangely, needlessly, tragically to a dismal end early in our third century."[62] Such visions of the apocalypse were fairly common during the campaign, for the Republicans clearly felt that the President's foreign policy had failed.

The Republicans paid the most attention to what they termed the "confusion" in Carter's foreign policy. Reagan sent several broadsides against his Democratic opponent. He charged that human rights was a policy used against American allies but not against the most flagrant violators of human rights: the Soviet Union, Vietnam, and Cuba. Reagan's argument about human rights was reminiscent of Henry Kissinger's in its reliance on quiet diplomacy as a way of persuading American allies to be more respectful of their citizens' rights. Indeed, a consistent argument the Republicans made was that President Carter's use of human rights policy helped to undermine the Shah of Iran, by encouraging his enemies to think that the United States was supportive of the position of the Shah's opponents.

In terms of American/Soviet relations, Reagan seemed less optimistic than Carter about the potential for cooperation. Reagan and the Republican right-wing had historically invested the Soviet Union with demonic qualities. And while some of the harsher rhetoric of Reagan's past was moderated during the campaign, he did present a foreign policy not unlike the cold-war perspective of the 1950s. One had the impression of the United States locked in never-ending struggle with the Soviet anti-Christ.

The basis of Reagan's attack on Carter's policies was that he had allowed a massive Soviet buildup of arms. Reagan assserted: "When one side [the United States] reduces while the other [the USSR] carries out the greatest military buildup in the history of mankind . . . the cause of peace has not been advanced."[63]

For Reagan, the goal of the United States must be to strengthen its military capability. During his debate with Carter he stated that "America has never gotten into a war because it was too strong." What Reagan proposed was a substantial increase in the defense budget to assure American security and, from that position, to negotiate an arms control treaty. There was some quibbling during the debate about whether Reagan wanted superiority or simply a stronger negotiating position. What he did claim was that "Carter had canceled the B-1 bomber, delayed the MX, delayed the Trident submarine, delayed the Cruise missile, shut down the Minuteman production line. . . ." These policies, Reagan charged, weakened the American negotiating position because they told the Soviets that "we had gone forward with unilateral concessions without any reciprocity from them whatsoever."[64]

The Republican candidate also attacked President Carter for allowing U.S. conventional forces to decline, and although Reagan opposed draft registration,[65] he did argue for higher pay for the military in order to halt the alarming rate of attrition in the armed services. In all, Reagan regarded the nation's defense budget as in need of a massive infusion of capital to establish the "margin of safety" the nation had lost during the Carter years.

Reagan's position on other foreign policy issues is somewhat difficult to assess. At one time he violently opposed the Panama Canal treaty, but barely alluded to it during the campaign. Reagan's position on China was somewhat ambiguous. At first he argued for the restoration of "official" relations with Taiwan, but after the Chinese explained to the vice-presidential candidate, George Bush, that such restoration was unacceptable, Reagan backed off and seemed to accept the current formula worked out by Carter. That formula makes U.S./Taiwan relations informal, thus conceding to Peking their assertion that there is only one China.

Reagan sounded most hawkish on the Middle East, calling the Palestine Liberation Organization a terrorist group and chiding Carter for allowing UN Ambassador Andrew Young to meet with them. It is not at all clear, however, what Reagan would do beyond the Camp David accords, which he pledged himself to support. During the campaign Reagan offered no new proposals to deal with the thorny problems in the Middle East except to say that he supported Israel's right to exist, and to call the Israelis good allies.

On U.S. policy toward its NATO allies, Reagan called for closer consultation and claimed that the Europeans had lost confidence in Carter. Nevertheless, most of his criticisms seemed leveled at Carter's image, not at concrete policy differences. One of the interesting facts about the European allies' relationship with America is that in some measure the Europeans are always dissatisfied with American leadership. If an administration attempts détente with the Soviets, the Europeans feel threatened by being excluded. And if attempts are made to take a harder line with the Soviet Union, the Europeans worry about a war.[66] Carter bore criticisms no matter what he did. When the SALT II treaty was near ratification, the Europeans, especially the Germans, worried about their defenses. And when Carter took a hard line over Afghanistan, the Europeans were less than enthusiastically supportive.

Serious differences between the candidates were noted in their views on the Third World. Reagan was skeptical both about human rights policy and about attempted North/South dialogue on the distribution of the world's resources. Reagan has an abiding suspicion of such grandiose attempts to redistribute economic goods and seemed to feel that less developed countries would progress more rapidly economically if they were more informed by American capitalism than by socialism or communism.

Generally, the Reagan vision of international affairs is of a world grown hostile to American interests. His solution to this challenge was to have a more powerful military establishment, one able to protect American interests against any contingency. Reagan's rhetoric during the campaign was reminiscent of the cold-war era of the 1950s. It remains to be seen whether President Reagan will behave as Candidate Reagan seemed to suggest (see chapter 6).

The 1980 campaign was one in which many issues were debated and dozens of position papers distributed, all in an attempt to persuade the public to choose its national leaders on the basis of their positions on the issues. Ronald Reagan's victory, especially its margin, came as a surprise to many. Whether it represents a real turn away from the assumptions of the New Deal welfare state is not yet clear, nor are the ways in which foreign policy will change at all certain.

Reagan and the Republican right-wing have criticized big government for the past twenty years, arguing that the nation is better served by giving free rein to the private sector. Indeed, this was the fundamental issue on which Reagan ran. Whether he can truly persuade a nation that has gotten used to the entitlements of federal support to give them up remains an open and fascinating question. So too is the question whether, in the modern world, nations can effectively function when ruled by the logic of markets rather than the political leadership of men.

During the campaign, Ronald Reagan was fond of referring to America as a "city upon a hill," which was originally stated by John Winthrop in his *Model of Christian Charity*. A more complete quotation reads:

For we must consider
that we shall be as
A city upon a Hill
The eyes of all people
Are upon us.[67]

Over three centuries have passed since the Puritans came to this land, and although the nation has accomplished much, it is still far from clear that we have satisfied "the eyes of all people." President Reagan's promise to the American public was to begin to prod the nation in the noble direction John Winthrop spoke of many years ago. As Reagan begins his Presidency, he might want to remember what Winthrop wanted America to provide for its posterity:

> . . . to follow the Counsell of Micah, to do justly, to love mercy, to walk humbly with our God, for this end, wee must be knitt together as one man, wee must entertaine each other with brotherly attention, wee must be willing to abridge ourselves of our superfluities. . . . [68]

Whether President Reagan can fulfill this promise of American life is his challenge and the nation's hope.

NOTES

1. The 1980 Democratic Platform, *Congressional Quarterly Weekly Report* 38 (5 August 1980): 2390.
2. For an interesting argument about the dimensions of this change, see Theodore Lowi, *The End of Liberalism* (2nd ed.; New York: Norton, 1974), particularly his discussion of "the second American republic." See also Lester Thurow, *The Zero-Sum Society* (New York: Basic, 1980) for his analysis of the limits of economic choice.
3. See E. E. Schattschneider, *The Semi-Sovereign People* (New York: Holt, Rinehart and Winston, 1975); and Charles E. Lindblom, "The Science of 'Muddling Through,' " *Public Administration Review* 19 (Spring 1959).
4. For an informed discussion of American oil policy and its implications, see Robert Engler, *The Brotherhood of Oil* (Chicago: University of Chicago Press, 1977). For a useful analysis of current energy problems, see Robert Stobaugh and Daniel Yergin, eds., *Energy Future* (New York: Random House, 1979).
5. Much has been written about this topic. Among the most prescient of analyses is Emma Rothchild, *Paradise Lost: The Decline of the Auto In-*

dustrial Age (New York: Random House, 1973). See also Charles G. Burch, "The Comeback Decade of the American Car," *Fortune* 10 (2 June 1980), for a somewhat more optimistic assessment of the automobile industry's future.

6. Edwin McDowell, "Made in U.S.A. – With Foreign Parts," *New York Times,* 9 November 1980.

7. See Richard M. Nixon, *R.N.: The Memoirs of Richard Nixon* (New York: Grosset and Dunlap, 1978); and Henry Kissinger, *White House Years* (Boston: Little Brown, 1979).

8. See Grant McConnell, *Private Power and American Democracy* (New York: Knopf, 1967), for an explanation of why American political institutions remain fragmented.

9. 1980 Democratic Platform, p. 2390; and Anderson/Lucey National Unity Campaign Platform, p. 2.

10. *The Candidates 1980* (Washington, D.C.: American Enterprise Institute, 1980). This is a useful little book in which each of the candidates was asked an identical set of questions.

11. Engler, *Brotherhood of Oil.*

12. *The Candidates 1980,* p. 27.

13. 1980 Democratic Platform, p. 2390.

14. *The Candidates 1980,* p. 67.

15. "Transcript of the Carter-Reagan Debate," *New York Times,* 29 October 1980, p. A28.

16. For the philosophical basis of this belief, see Milton Friedman, *Capitalism and Freedom* (Chicago: University of Chicago Press, 1963).

17. The 1980 Republican Platform, *Congressional Quarterly Weekly Report* 38 (18 July 1980): 2045.

18. Anderson/Lucy Platform, p. 7.

19. *New York Times,* 9 November 1980, p. 3.

20. Ibid.

21. These positions were argued in Kennedy's Georgetown speech of 28 January 1980 (see *New York Times,* 29 January 1980) and in his support of the minority plank at the Democratic convention, *Congressional Quarterly Weekly Report* 38 (15 August 1980).

22. *The Candidates 1980,* p. 28.

23. *New York Times,* 2 November 1980, p. 15.

24. 1980 Democratic Platform, p. 2391.

25. This plank in the Democratic platform represented Carter's compromise Kennedy. Kennedy agreed not to push for wage and price controls as his part of the bargain.

26. Ibid., p. 2391.

27. Ibid., p. 2392.

28. Ibid.

29. 1980 Republican Platform, p. 2031.

30. Ibid., p. 2047.

31. Ibid.

32. "Transcript of the Carter-Reagan Debate," p. A26.

33. This idea has been expressed by many in recent times. See, for example, Jude Wanniski, *The Way the World Works* (New York: Basic, 1977).

34. 1980 Republican Platform, p. 2047.

35. *The Candidates 1980*, p. 68.

36. 1980 Republican Platform, p. 2030.

37. "Transcript of the Carter-Reagan Debate," p. A27.

38. For a fascinating discussion of this question, see Daniel Bell, *The Cultural Contradictions of Capitalism* (New York: Basic, 1978), particularly his discussion of the "untrammeled self" on pp. 144-45.

39. 1980 Democratic Platform, p. 2404.

40. Ibid., p. 2405.

41. Ibid.

42. See John Locke, *The Second Treatise on Government* and *A Letter Concerning Human Understanding*, ed. J. W. Gough (New York: Barnes and Noble, 1966), for the classic statement on liberalism. For an interesting criticism, see George Santayana, *The Birth of Reason and Other Essays* (New York: Columbia University Press, 1968), especially for his understanding of the social basis of liberalism.

43. For an informed discussion of American conservatism, see Irving Louis Horowitz, *Ideology and Utopia in the United States 1956–1976* (New York: Oxford University Press, 1977), esp. pp. 133-61.

44. 1980 Republican Platform, p. 2033.

45. Ibid., p. 2034.

46. Another of the issues the Republicans cited as an example of federal usurpation of power was the 55 mile-per-hour speed limit.

47. For an informative collection of essays about conservative theory in America, see William F. Buckley, Jr., ed., *American Conservative Thought in the Twentieth Century* (Indianapolis: Bobbs-Merrill, 1970).

48. 1980 Republican Platform, p. 2046.

49. Ibid.

50. William Safire, "The Good Right Fight," *New York Times*, 17 November 1980, p. A23.

51. Ibid.

52. It might be noted, parenthetically, that the distinction between these two conservative wings is probably as wide as the one they both have with liberalism.

53. Kissinger, *White House Years.*

54. "Transcript of the Carter-Reagan Debate," p. A26.

55. *New York Times,* 14 October 1980, p. 42.

56. 1980 Democratic Platform, p. 2413.

57. Ibid.

58. "Transcript of the Carter-Reagan Debate," p. A27.

59. Quoted in the 1980 Democratic Platform, p. 2413.

60. Even after the election, the conflict between Vance and Brzezinski still commanded newspaper headlines. See *New York Times,* 3 December 1980, p. A1.

61. 1980 Republican Platform, p. 2031.

62. Ibid., p. 2030.

63. "Transcript of the Carter-Reagan Debate," p. A26.

64. Ibid.

65. Ronald Reagan's opposition to the draft was symptomatic of one consistent strand in the campaign. The Republicans asked no sacrifices of the American people. They opposed not only the draft but also the wheat embargo, as the latter position appealed to agricultural interests. Their tax policy promised more disposable income as well as a balanced budget, reduced unemployment, and a lowering of the inflation rate.

66. Kissinger, *White House Years.*

67. John Winthrop, "A Model of Christian Charity," in *Puritan Political Ideas,* ed. Edmund S. Morgan (Indianapolis: Bobbs-Merrill, 1965), p. 93.

68. Ibid., p. 92.

3

The Presidential Election

GERALD M. POMPER

You have sat too long here for any good you have been doing.
Depart, I say, and let us have done with you.
In the name of God, go!

—Oliver Cromwell, to the
Long Parliament, 1653

The results were clear: Ronald Reagan was decisively elected President on November 4, 1980. Jimmy Carter was trounced in his attempt to win reelection. John Anderson and other independent candidates had little effect on the outcome of the election.

The meaning of the results was less obvious. Did Reagan's success constitute a personal mandate for the former California governor or a repudiation of the incumbent Democratic President? Did the election portend an enduring shift in American voting patterns or a more simple intention to "throw the rascals out"? Would the Republican party now be able to construct a new majority coalition, or would the trend toward party deterioration, evident in the presidential nominations, continue? In this chapter we argue that the presidential election outcome was predominantly a negative reaction to the leadership of Jimmy Carter, which yet provides an opportunity for building a Republican majority.

THE RESULTS

Geography
The Reagan victory was undoubted. He won 44 of the 50 states (he lost the District of Columbia), amassing 489 electoral votes of the national total of 538.

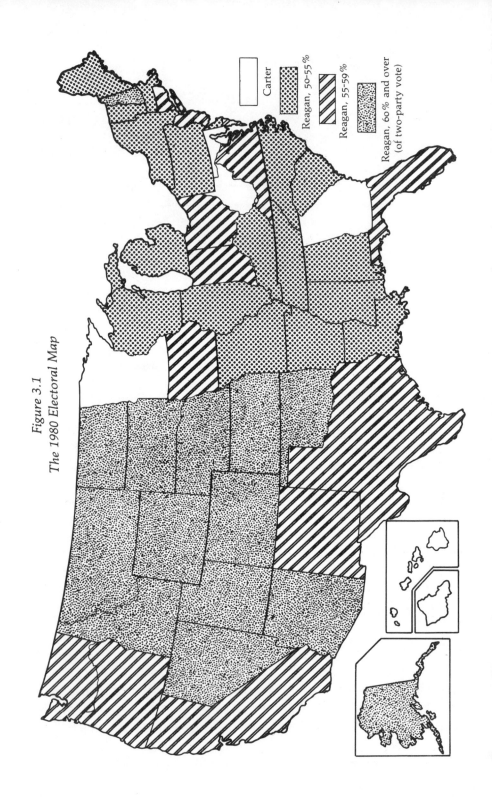

Figure 3.1
The 1980 Electoral Map

Carter

Reagan, 50-55%

Reagan, 55-59%

Reagan, 60% and over
(of two-party vote)

He led in every area of the country including liberal Massachusetts, economically depressed Michigan, booming Texas, traditionalist Utah, and contemporary California. Of the 86 million Americans who cast their ballots, the Republican candidate won a clear majority, and he gained an even larger share of the vote for the two major parties, 55.3 percent.[1]

Still more impressive were the dimensions of Jimmy Carter's defeat. Only twice in the twentieth century had an elected incumbent President been denied a second term—William Howard Taft when his party split in 1912 and Herbert Hoover during the Great Depression in 1932. Carter rewrote this record. He received the lowest percentage of the popular vote of any incumbent Democratic President in American history and gained fewer electoral votes than any sitting chief executive except Taft, who lost most of his party to Theodore Roosevelt. Only four years earlier, Carter had won a slight majority, 51 percent of the national two-party vote, and had carried 23 states. After one term in office, his net loss was 10 percent of the national vote—almost one of very five previous supporters, and all but six states and the District of Columbia.

These defections are striking, especially when portrayed on a map (see figure 3.1). Yet Carter was vulnerable to any level of defection. In 1976 he had won only the narrowest of victories. In that year a small, 2 percent shift of the vote to the Republicans would have meant an electoral disaster for Carter, only 185 electoral votes of the 270 needed for his election. That shift—and more— occurred in 1980. Overall, there was over a 6 percent change between the two elections in the Democratic proportion of the two-party vote, and change was evident in most of the individual states as well.

A striking feature of the electoral map of 1980 is the relative consistency of results across the country. Not only did Ronald Reagan win, but he won with fairly similar margins almost everywhere. A majority of states fell to the Californian by percentages that were within five points of his national average. The exceptions were essentially those states salvaged by Carter (white on the map) and those that gave three-fifths or more of their vote to Reagan (shaded on the map). The similarity of results is an indication that the contest was determined by forces moving all of the nation in a Republican direction, not by influences that had contrary effects among different regions or voting groups.*

In many ways, the 1980 electoral map is like that of the past presidential election. The areas of relative Democratic and Republican strength are similar —but with the crucial difference that the absolute Republican strength was much higher, the Democrats lower. Thus, in 1980, the Democrats ran best in

---

*The standard deviation of the vote measures the similarity of results among the states. In 1980, it was 7.9 percentage points, historically a relatively low figure, although higher than the 6.3 recorded in 1976.

TABLE 3.1
THE 1980 PRESIDENTIAL VOTE

State	Electoral Vote		Popular Vote		Percentage of Three-Candidate Vote			Percentage of Two-Party Vote	
	Carter	Reagan	Carter	Reagan	Carter	Reagan	Anderson	Carter	Reagan
Alabama		9	636,730	654,192	48.7	50.0	1.3	49.3	50.7
Alaska*		3	41,842	86,112	26.5	54.7	18.8	32.7	67.3
Arizona		6	246,843	529,688	28.9	62.1	9.0	31.8	68.2
Arkansas		6	398,041	403,164	48.3	49.0	2.7	49.7	50.3
California		45	3,083,652	4,524,835	36.9	54.2	8.9	40.5	59.5
Colorado		7	368,009	652,264	32.0	56.7	11.3	36.1	63.9
Connecticut		8	541,732	677,210	38.9	48.7	12.4	44.4	55.6
Delaware		3	105,754	111,252	45.3	47.7	7.0	48.7	51.3
District of Columbia	3		130,231	23,313	76.8	13.7	9.5	84.8	15.2
Florida		17	1,419,475	2,046,951	38.9	55.9	5.2	41.0	59.0
Georgia	12		890,955	654,168	56.4	41.4	2.2	57.6	42.4
Hawaii	4		135,879	130,112	45.6	43.6	10.8	51.1	48.9
Idaho		4	110,192	290,699	25.8	67.9	6.3	27.5	72.5
Illinois		26	1,981,413	2,358,094	42.2	50.4	7.4	45.6	54.4
Indiana		13	844,197	1,255,656	38.1	56.8	5.1	40.2	59.8
Iowa		8	508,672	676,026	39.1	52.0	8.9	42.9	57.1
Kansas		7	326,150	566,812	34.0	58.9	7.1	36.6	63.4
Kentucky		9	617,417	635,274	48.1	49.5	2.4	49.3	50.7
Louisiana		10	708,453	792,853	46.4	51.9	1.7	47.2	52.8
Maine		4	220,974	238,522	43.1	46.5	10.4	48.1	51.9
Maryland	10		726,161	680,606	47.5	44.6	7.9	51.6	48.4
Massachusetts	14		1,053,800	1,056,223	42.2	42.4	15.4	49.9	50.1
Michigan		21	1,661,532	1,915,225	43.2	49.7	7.1	46.4	53.6
Minnesota	10		954,173	873,268	47.6	43.7	8.7	52.2	47.8
Mississippi		7	429,281	441,089	48.6	50.0	1.4	49.3	50.7
Missouri		12	931,182	1,074,181	44.7	51.6	3.7	46.4	53.6
Montana		4	118,032	206,814	33.3	58.4	8.3	36.3	63.7

Nebraska	5		166,424	419,214	26.4	66.5	7.1	28.4	71.6
Nevada	3		66,666	155,017	27.9	64.8	7.3	30.1	69.9
New Hampshire	4		108,864	221,705	28.7	58.3	13.0	33.0	67.0
New Jersey	17		1,147,364	1,546,557	39.2	52.8	8.0	42.6	57.4
New Mexico	4		167,826	250,779	37.4	56.0	6.6	40.1	59.9
New York	41		2,728,372	2,893,831	44.8	47.6	7.6	48.5	51.5
North Carolina	13		875,635	915,018	47.5	49.6	2.9	48.9	51.1
North Dakota	3		79,189	193,695	26.8	65.3	7.9	29.1	70.9
Ohio	25		1,752,414	2,206,545	41.6	52.4	6.0	44.3	55.7
Oklahoma	8		402,026	695,570	35.4	61.2	3.4	36.6	63.4
Oregon	6		456,890	571,044	40.1	50.1	9.8	44.5	55.5
Pennsylvania	27		1,937,540	2,261,872	43.1	50.4	6.5	46.1	53.9
Rhode Island		4	198,342	154,793	48.0	37.5	14.5	56.2	43.8
South Carolina	8		430,385	441,841	48.6	49.8	1.6	49.4	50.6
South Dakota	4		103,855	198,343	32.1	61.3	6.6	34.4	65.6
Tennessee	10		783,051	787,761	48.8	49.0	2.2	49.8	50.2
Texas	26		1,881,147	2,510,705	41.7	55.8	2.5	42.8	57.2
Utah	4		124,266	439,687	20.9	74.0	5.1	22.0	78.0
Vermont	3		81,952	94,628	39.3	45.4	15.3	46.4	53.6
Virginia	12		752,174	989,609	40.9	53.9	5.2	43.2	56.8
Washington	9		650,193	865,244	38.2	50.9	10.9	42.9	57.1
West Virginia		6	367,462	334,206	50.1	45.6	4.3	52.4	47.6
Wisconsin	11		981,584	1,088,845	44.0	48.8	7.2	47.4	52.6
Wyoming	3		49,427	110,700	28.7	64.3	7.0	30.9	69.1
National Total	489	49	35,483,820	43,901,812	41.7	51.6	6.7	44.7	55.3

*Alaska third-party vote includes 18,479 votes for Ed Clark, Libertarian party, as well as 11,156 votes for Anderson.

Georgia and received their lowest percentage in Utah, while Oregon stood in
the exact middle of the ranking of the states by Democratic vote. In 1976,
Georgia also had led the party to victory, Utah had provided the least support,
and Oregon had stood 27th in the ranking of 51 areas (including the District of
Columbia).*

Geographical vote patterns of this kind usually reflect a national response
to current events, bringing victory to the incumbent party in a "maintaining"
election (when voters are satisfied) or that party's defeat in a "deviating" election
(when voters are discontented).[2] More basic changes in voter loyalties occur in
"realigning" contests, when party loyalties shift to new dimensions. On a
geographical basis, the overall 1980 results do not evidence fundamental shifts.
The results show more variation than in 1976, however, possibly indicating
some realignment.** While almost every state increased its Republican vote
over the four years, this trend was particularly strong in the Mountain and
Plains states. These areas, Republican in earlier elections, brought in astonish-
ing margins for Reagan and may now have become virtually one-party states in
presidential elections.

Demography

Divisions of the vote among groups of voters provide additional clues, summarized in table 3.2. Since the 1930s, the Democrats had comprised a majority
coalition based largely on social class rather than geography. The most significant elements were minority groups including blacks, Catholics, and Jews;
those of lower income and in working-class occupations; residents of the larger
cities; members of labor unions; and southerners, particularly those of lower
status and in rural areas. The loyalties of these voters had been forged before
and during the Great Depression and had been solidified by the social welfare
programs of the New Deal. Even decades after these events, their political
effects could still be seen in the common characterization of the Democrats as
"the party of the people" and in the Democratic loyalty of 40 percent of the electorate. By comparison, only 23 percent of the voters were Republicans, and 37
percent were self-declared Independents.[3]

For some time, it has been evident that the position of the Democrats has
been weakening. Personal memories of the New Deal are retained only by persons of retirement age so that loyalty to the Democrats is much weaker among

---

*The rank-order correlation of states (Spearman's rho) in 1976 and 1980 is an impressively
high .88. The linear correlation is also high historically, at .84, for the two-party vote.

**In 1980, 24 states differed considerably (by more than five points) from the national
Republican percentage. This is a noticeable increase from 1976, when only 18 states showed such
variation.

TABLE 3.2

SOCIAL GROUPS AND THE PRESIDENTIAL VOTE, 1980 AND 1976

	1980			1976	
	Carter	Reagan	Anderson	Carter	Ford
Party*					
Democrats (43%)	66	26	6	77	22
Independents (23%)	30	54	12	43	54
Republicans (28%)	11	84	4	9	90
Ideology					
Liberal (18%)	57	27	11	70	26
Moderates (51%)	42	48	8	51	48
Conservatives (31%)	23	71	4	29	70
Race					
Blacks (10%)	82	14	3	82	16
Hispanics (2%)	54	36	7	75	24
Whites (88%)	36	55	8	47	52
Sex					
Female (48%)	45	46	7	50	48
Male (52%)	37	54	7	50	48
Religion					
Protestant (46%)	37	56	6	44	55
White Protestant (41%)	31	62	6	43	57
Catholic (25%)	40	51	7	54	44
Jewish (5%)	45	39	14	64	34
Family Income					
Less than $10,000 (13%)	50	41	6	58	40
$10,000-$14,999 (15%)	47	42	8	55	43
$15,000-$24,999 (29%)	38	53	7	48	50
$25,000-$50,000 (24%)	32	58	8	36	62
Over $50,000 (5%)	25	65	8	—	—
Occupation					
Professional or manager (39%)	33	56	9	41	57
Clerical, sales, white					
collar (11%)	42	48	8	46	53
Blue-collar (17%)	46	47	5	57	41
Agriculture (3%)	29	66	3	—	—
Unemployed (3%)	55	35	7	65	34
Education					
Less than high school (11%)	50	45	3	58	41
High school graduate (28%)	43	51	4	54	46
Some college (28%)	35	55	8	51	49
College graduate (27%)	35	51	11	45	55

TABLE 3.2 (Continued)

| | 1980 | | | 1976 | |
	Carter	Reagan	Anderson	Carter	Ford
Union Membership					
Labor union household (28%)	47	44	7	59	39
No member of household					
in union (62%)	35	55	8	43	55
Age					
18-21 years old (6%)	44	43	11	48	50
22-29 years old (17%)	43	43	11	51	46
30-44 years old (31%)	37	54	7	49	49
45-59 years old (23%)	39	55	6	47	52
60 years or older (18%)	40	54	4	47	52
Region					
East (25%)	42	47	9	51	47
South (27%)	44	51	3	54	45
White South (22%)	35	60	3	46	52
Midwest (27%)	40	51	7	48	50
Far West (19%)	35	53	9	46	51
Community Size					
Cities over 250,000 (18%)	54	35	8	60	40
Suburbs-small cities (53%)	37	53	8	53	47
Rural and towns (29%)	39	54	5	47	53

*The figures in parentheses are the percentges of the 1980 voters belonging to each group. The table entries are percentages, which total approximately 100 percent in each row for 1980 or 1976. Missing data account for those categories that do not total 100 percent.

SOURCE: CBS News/New York Times interviews with 12,782 voters as they left the polls, as reported in the New York Times, 9 November 1980, p. 28, and in further analysis. The 1976 data are from CBS News interviews. For that year, the large-city vote is for communities over 500,000 population.

younger generations. Some groups in the Democratic coalition have become smaller in number over the years as the population has moved from older cities into new suburbs, as some once-poor ethnic groups have risen into the middle class, and as membership has declined in industrial unions, once most supportive of the party. The South has been transformed by industrial development and the consequent movement of rural populations into metropolitan areas and the immigration of northerners and Republicans. These trends have produced an evident weakening of party loyalty on the presidential level. From the end of the Second World War, the Democrats have won only one convincing national election, in 1964; in eight other contests, the party has achieved three additional but narrow majorities and has lost five times.

As the party lost loyalists in some groups, it replaced them with others, but these new recruits only partially compensated for the defections. Young voters were more likely to be Democrats, but were largely independent of both major groups. Blacks and Hispanics increased both in numbers and voting turnout, stimulated by voting rights laws and registration campaigns, and became the most loyal Democratic partisans. These groups were not fully mobilized, however, and their voting rates lagged behind those of whites. The women's movement brought feminists into an active role in the party, but its liberal demands also aroused countervailing, more conservative attitudes among both sexes.

By 1980 voters were ready to abandon party loyalty in the voting booth. From their days in school to their nights before television sets, Americans were urged to "vote for the man or woman, not the party." Mass media presented elections as contests between individuals, not partisan teams. Candidates argued their own merits and largely ignored those who shared with them a line on the ballot or a philosophy of the party. Consequently, voters gave little thought to parties. Even those who did admit to being Democrats or Republicans were increasingly inclined to describe themselves as "weak" in loyalty. In assessing the reasons for their vote, relatively few voters mentioned the parties; in contrast to the past, a majority held negative evaluations of both major parties.[4]

The election of 1980 brought the culmination of these trends. Party loyalty failed Jimmy Carter. Having been first elected as an "outsider" successfully challenging the "establishment" within the Democratic party, having maintained his independence of the traditional coalition, and having argued against the orthodox party positions of Edward Kennedy in the nominating contest, he could not call upon traditional loyalties in his hour of need. A third of the self-identified Democrats rejected him, as did an even larger proportion of the self-identified liberals who comprised the ideological core of the party. Unable to hold this base, Carter was far less successful in gaining support from other segments in the political spectrum — Independents and Republicans, moderates and conservatives.

As Carter lost support, Reagan made gains that, significantly, were most evident in many demographic groups included in the traditional Democratic coalition. White Catholics gave Carter about the same proportion of the vote as the rest of the nation, instead of producing their past Democratic pluralities; Jews defected both to Reagan and to John Anderson; white southerners joined the majority groups in the population — Protestants, suburbanites, and non-union members — in strong support of Reagan.

The established Democratic coalition could be glimpsed only fleetingly among a few groups. Blacks provided strong support for Carter, as much support as in 1976, and they were joined by a majority within the small but growing ranks of Hispanics. Women showed more electoral support for Carter than did men, possibly reflecting feminist concerns, and younger voters were slightly more favorable to the incumbent. Union members and their families provided a bare plurality in favor of Carter, but gave him a lower vote than all other recent Democratic candidates except George McGovern. Even in these islands of relatively high ground for the Democrats, the waves of voter discontent caused considerable erosion.

With few exceptions, the most apparent feature of the vote was the wide degree of support won by Reagan. His majority was not fashioned from the coalescence of some groups in the population in opposition to others. Rather, that support was broadly distributed, at least among whites, throughout the electorate. This feature of the polling results indicates that there is not yet a distinctive coalition ready to endorse a new Republican direction in public policy. At the same time, the breadth of the voting support provides many opportunities for fashioning such a coalition.

THE CAMPAIGN

Strategies

Discontent was the principal characteristic of the 1980 campaign. The voters did not see their options as happily selecting one of two (or more) acceptable candidates to be President. Instead, it was to be a forced choice of the "lesser of two (or more) evils," leading one wag to bewail "the evil of two lessers."

Humor itself was one indication of voter unhappiness. An air of gallows gaiety pervaded the contest. Referring to Reagan's statement that plants were a major source of air pollution, students put signs on a tree imploring, "Chop me down before I kill again!" Reagan advocates responded that the only thing worse than "the fear of the unknown" (Reagan) was the "fear of the known" (Carter), and the Republican candidate answered his opponent's charges with a quip, "I'll confess to being irresponsible if he'll admit to being responsible" for the nation's problems. A Republican county chairman complained that it was difficult to get voters to back Reagan when they believed "he wants to take the fluoride out of the water and poison the Chinese with it." Nor could Carter be happy about supporters who chose him because "we know what he's *not* capable of."[5] Even John Anderson was not spared. One comedian quoted an apocryphal remark of the independent candidate: "Some people falsely claim I am self-righteous. May God forgive them!" Johnny Carson seemed to capture the nation's reluctance when his audience mildly cheered the suggestion that Anderson quit the race and then wildly acclaimed the thought that both Reagan and Carter withdraw.

Voter dissatisfaction was also shown by more precise indicators. Only a bare majority of the electorate was highly favorable to either candidate — the least enthusiasm displayed in three decades.[6] These critical attitudes were reflected by voter behavior. The proportion of undecided voters remained high throughout the fall. Almost a fourth of the nation did not reach a decision until the last week, and the actual voting turnout fell for the fifth straight election and came close to an historic ebb.

Voter hesitancy was shown in the pattern of opinion polls. As seen in figure 3.2, the lead in the Gallup surveys changed five times in the course of the election year. A persistent Carter advantage became a decisive Reagan margin during the summer, only to be eliminated by the end of the Democratic convention and then partially restored during the month of October. A week before Election Day, on the eve of the only debate between the two major candidates, Carter seemed to have gained an edge, then lost it immediately after the televised confrontation. Until the end, no candidate was able to build a secure position, as if the voters were alternately repelled by whichever man seemed likely to be President.

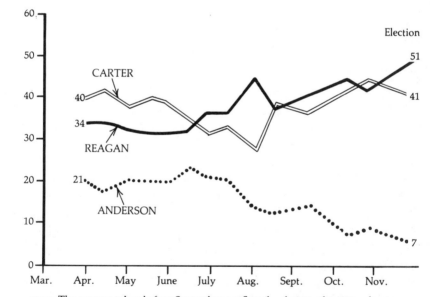

NOTE: The surveys taken before September 1 reflect the choices of registered voters. The surveys taken after September 1 reflect the choices of likely voters. Late October results based on partial survey taken before the October 28 debate.

Figure 3.2
The Presidential Race in 1980 Gallup Polls

In retrospect, these campaign trends evidence some logic. The basic political premise of the 1980 election was that Jimmy Carter was widely unpopular. On the basis of this unpopularity, a political scientist would have predicted that he would receive only 46 percent of the vote—nearly the exact proportion of the two-party vote he did achieve.[7] The question to be answered in the campaign was whether Ronald Reagan would be viewed as a satisfactory alternative to an unpopular President. Ultimately, the voters clearly answered yes (see chapter 4).

As President, Carter was the inevitable target of accumulated national discontents. The United States had seen itself as a strong, self-reliant, and prosperous country. Events of recent years had severely shaken confidence in this national image. Rather than achieve its will in international affairs, America was unable to gain the release of its hostages in Iran either through diplomatic or military means, and was forced to endure a year-long humiliation. Rather than control its own affairs, America saw its life style, its economy, and its foreign policy subject to the unilateral decisions of Arab oil producers. Rather than improve its standard of living, America saw record levels of interest rates and inflation combined with rising unemployment and industrial decay. By 1980, the real income of the average American family, once wages were discounted by inflation and taxes, had fallen 5 percent below the level at the beginning of the Carter term. The electorate was prepared to shout, in imitation of the battle cry of the film *Network*, "I'm mad as hell and I'm not going to take this anymore!"

Jimmy Carter, of course, did not bear sole personal responsibility for these accumulated problems. The decline in national power abroad, the rise of OPEC, and the stagnant economy had been evident for some time, certainly before the Georgian's inauguration. Nevertheless, the public still found Carter wanting. The most persistent criticism of him related to his inability to seize control and point to solutions to national problems. Voters seek, above all, competence in the Presidency, and "the most appropriate job-related information upon which to base a projection of future performance is the current performance of an incumbent."[8] Voters know whether they are satisfied or dissatisfied with an office-holder; they can only guess whether his opponent could have done better. This inevitable public emphasis on Carter's performance in office underlined his electoral vulnerability.

Inescapably running on his record, President Carter had three strategic options: to praise his accomplishments and promise future improvements (the most common technique, used by Lyndon Johnson in 1964 and Gerald Ford in 1976); to blame others for failures (as Harry Truman did in 1948); or to attempt to change the public's focus to the defects of the opposition. The Carter campaign, while mixing in the other options, relied primarily on the last strategy.

At the outset, the Carter emphasis had been on the President's positive accomplishments and his standing as a Democratic spokesman. As his campaign developed, however, a shift occurred toward an attack on Reagan, as well as John Anderson. The Carter campaign chairman, Robert Strauss, described the principal effort "to portray Reagan as 'simplistic' and 'not equipped to be President.' " A contrast would be drawn with Carter, who would be pictured as hard-working, aware of complexity, and knowledgeable about foreign affairs.[9] Little attention was given to Carter's future plans, and the President did not deliver a single major policy speech. Instead, dominant attention was given to Reagan's philosophy and personal qualities. The Carter forces no longer asked, as in 1976, "Why not the Best?" Instead, they argued, "It could be worse."

Aside from its unorthodoxy, this strategy had its dangers. It implied a considerable change from the 1976 characterization of Carter as a competent manager of government. The strategy was also open to counterattack. If Reagan could present himself and his programs decently, he could ride to victory on public discontent with the undefended Carter record. Still, despite its problems, the Carter strategy appeared to be succeeding — until Election Day.

The Reagan strategy was more conventional. In keeping with the expected stance of the challenger, Reagan emphasized the alleged failings of the Carter administration. The thrust of the Republican campaign was summarized in two slogans — the party national convention's theme, "Together, A New Beginning," and its televised advertising phrase, "For a Change." These slogans were empty of any substantive comment; they only promised something different. Reagan himself articulated the challenge at the conclusions of the televised debate and his preelection address. He asked the voters:

> Are you better off than you were four years ago? Is it easier for you to go and buy things in the stores than it was four years ago? Is there more or less unemployment in the country than there was four years ago? Is America as respected throughout the world as it was? Do you feel that our security is as safe, that we're as strong as we were four years ago?[10]

The attack on the Carter record was specified in much detail, such as charges of high taxes, prices, and unemployment; inadequate defense spending and foreign policy failures; excessive government regulation; and general national demoralization (see chapter 2). While Republicans also suggested solutions to the problems they found, and the party platform was the longest in its history, the emphasis in the campaign itself was on Carter deficiencies. Reagan offered a general conservative philosophy and a vague vision of better times, while emphasizing that "this country doesn't have to be in the shape that it is in."

Reagan also defended himself against Carter attacks. The most frequent Republican television advertisement presented details of Reagan's record as governor of California, to emphasize his governmental experience and competence. An exhausting campaign itinerary served to refute any suspicions about his health. Days were spent in preparation for each of two televised debates so that Reagan would be seen as knowledgeable and reasonable. The premise of these efforts, according to Republican National Chairman Bill Brock, was that "the undecided voters really weren't undecided about President Carter. They were undecided about Governor Reagan because they didn't know him."[11] Through the campaign, they came to know him and, if not to love him, to accept him.

The courtship of the electorate involved considerable alteration and explanation of policy positions. Reagan had come to political prominence, and had won the Republican nomination, because of his championing of conservative causes. The philosophy he espoused had been written into the party platform, but it received little emphasis in the campaign. Instead, Reagan sought to assure various groups that his election would not represent a threat to their vital interests.

Reversing positions he had held at one time or another, Reagan endorsed the farm-parity system, federal aid to New York City and automobile manufacturers, occupational health and safety regulations, prevailing wage laws, and union exemption from antitrust acts. His opposition to the Equal Rights Amendment was replaced by endorsement of statutory enactment of the same principle, and his endorsement of a constitutional amendment to ban abortion was replaced by silence. Downplaying his past antipathy toward communist regimes, he supported recognition of the People's Republic of China and nuclear arms negotiations with the Soviet Union. Reagan presented himself as a moderate, rather than as an ideological conservative. Barry Goldwater, in 1964 the last conservative Republican candidate, would "rather be right than President." Reagan preferred to be elected — and so he was.

Events

From the end of the Democratic convention in mid-August, the campaign went through four overlapping phases, each leading to an apparent change in the race. The first of these periods was one of Reagan's decline. Though he emerged from his own party convention with a large lead in the polls and a united Republican organization, the Californian was soon lagging. The exciting contest and ultimate reconciliation at the Democratic conclave brought many of that party's voters back into the fold. At the same time, Reagan appeared to be confirming many of the worst fears about himself. In the early weeks of the campaign he rekindled old antagonisms about the Vietnam war by calling American intervention there "a noble cause"; he appeared to oppose the theory of evolution; he inaccurately and ineptly criticized Carter for attending a rally at "the birthplace of the Ku Klux Klan," while he himself visited a Mississippi county fair favored by segregationists; and he suggested renegotiating the agreement that had led to diplomatic relations with China. These actions led to embarrassing explanations, apologies, and even a transoceanic argument between Reagan and his running mate, George Bush. The errors were easily used by the Democrats to argue that Reagan was both unknowledgeable and reactionary.

For their part, the Carter forces used the powers of presidential incumbency, as they had during the nominating contest. Reagan's assertions on foreign policy were refuted by the ambassador to China and by Secretary of State Edmund Muskie. Vindicating the administration's military record, Secretary of Defense Brown confirmed a leak that the United States was developing a bomber that would be virtually invulnerable to Soviet radar — while downplaying the fact that the airplane would be unavailable for many years. Refurbishing his image as Middle East peacemaker, Carter announced that Israeli Prime Minister Menachem Begin and Egyptian President Anwar Sadat would join him in a postelection summit conference.

Throughout the fall, the administration employed its executive authority to court crucial votes. Vice-President Walter Mondale announced that large naval repairs would be done in Philadelphia, providing jobs in the closely contested states of Pennsylvania and New Jersey rather than in Virginia, which was considered lost to Reagan. Seeking the vital electoral bloc of a New York burdened by welfare costs, Carter endorsed a federal takeover of Medicaid payments, although he had previously opposed the action. In the Midwest, he suggested restrictions on imported steel and automobiles as possible means to relieve the region's unemployment. Wherever possible, federal grants were announced during campaign trips, with $50 million provided for Michigan alone during one week and $20 million to the Cleveland area in a single day.[12]

The second phase of the campaign, extending roughly through the latter part of September and the first week of October, saw a Reagan revival. His campaign speeches were reviewed more carefully, new advisers accompanied him on the campaign plane, and he eliminated most news conferences or appearances before right-wing groups. These steps were taken, as his former campaign chairman foresaw, to avoid Reagan's need for "explaining every day why you're not an idiot."[13] Most importantly, Reagan gained a national television audience of 50 million voters by appearing in a debate with John Anderson.

The debate was the first of four planned by the League of Women Voters. As a private organization, the League could invite whichever candidates it chose. Unlike the television networks, it was not required to include minor aspirants. Once the League decision was made, the networks were free to cover the debate as a news event, unrestricted by legal guarantees of "equal time" to other candidates.

The League's own tradition was one of open access to all serious candidates. Moreover, John Anderson had great personal support among members of the organization, who responded to his intellectual ability and his strong feminist position. In issuing its invitation, the League created a new standard — it would include any candidate who, because of a 15 percent rating in public opinion polls (and official placement on state ballots), had a significant chance of winning the Presidency. When Anderson barely met this standard early in September, he was invited to a debate on September 21, along with Carter and Reagan. The Carter campaign refused. Seeing Anderson as a direct competitor for the liberal votes they sought, they hoped that Carter's absence would deprive Anderson of attention and would make the debate unimportant.

The Carter strategy did succeed in reducing the television audience — aided by ABC's counterprogramming of a motion picture. Reagan still used the occasion for his own benefit. While he did not change any of his positions drastically, he presented his arguments moderately and thereby served to dispel some doubts about his candidacy while undercutting Anderson's appeal to Republicans. Although few viewers said their preferences had been changed by the debate itself, the opinion polls showed that Reagan converted a 4 percent deficit into a 5 percent lead over Carter and that most voters were now convinced — contrary to their earlier views — that Reagan "understood the complicated problems a President has to deal with."[14]

The Democrats were now fully engaged in attacking Reagan as dangerous, as untrustworthy with control of nuclear weapons, and as a threat to the social welfare benefits of the aged, poor, and minorities. Carter himself pressed these points, depicting the election as a "choice between peace and war," hinting that Reagan promoted racism, and suggesting, "if I lose this election, Americans might be separate, black from white, Jew from Gentile, North from South, rural from urban."[15]

Reagan's response to these attacks was largely cool, such as his depiction of the President as subject to "fits of childish pique," but occasionally sharp, as in his characterization of Carter as "the greatest deceiver ever to occupy the White

House."[16] The press found Carter's rhetoric "mean" and "vindictive" and one liberal columnist complained that "all along the President has acted as if a successful 1980 campaign could consist of nothing more than horror stories about Ronald Reagan."[17] The public, too, reacted; a near-majority now believed that Carter "says too many things carelessly, without considering the consequences."[18]

No candidate could benefit from these characterizations, but they were especially serious as criticisms of Carter. He had been attempting to focus the campaign on Reagan's personal deficiencies, but now found he was the target. Moreover, Carter's greatest personal assets were threatened—his past reputation as a moral and decent individual, and the esteem of the presidential office he held. His vitriolic attacks on Reagan diminished his standing and demeaned his office. Carter, realizing the error of his ways, offered a semiapology in a television interview, initiating the third phase of the campaign.

In this period, President Carter rallied the traditional Democratic coalition. Buoyed by the endorsements of most major unions, he emphasized the social welfare programs of the Democratic party. Carter conducted a series of televised "town meetings" around the nation, in which he responded to easy questions from citizen audiences and demonstrated his command of the government and his personal involvement in particular problems. Through visits to black churches, union halls, and senior citizen centers, he sought to spur these groups to revived party loyalty. Hopeful signs of economic recovery began to appear and were emphasized by the administration.

There also were signs that foreign policy questions were beginning to have an impact. The public's greatest concern about Reagan continued to be his ability and moderation as a possible commander-in-chief. This shift in attention was accelerated by events abroad. Iran, still holding the American hostages, was invaded by the neighboring country of Iraq, and it soon became evident that Iran could not repel the invasion but would need outside assistance. Thus, the Iran-Iraq war might lead to a release of the hostages in exchange for the release of Iranian assets impounded in the United States. It was widely believed that, if this deal were made, Carter would be seen as a national hero and would be triumphantly reelected. Fearing this result, the Reagan camp attempted to discount its impact in advance, warning that Carter planned this "October surprise" and complaining about the "cynical manipulation" of the public by the administration.

As the campaigners neared the finish line, the race became extremely close, with Carter apparently moving toward a narrow victory. The Reagan camp, which had hoped simply to hold its early lead, now saw the need for more dramatic action and revived discussion of a second televised debate. Previously, the Republican campaigners had acted cautiously, fearing a spontaneous error by their candidate. They had insisted that Anderson be included in any confrontation, knowing that Carter would not agree to this condition. With news about Iran blanketing the press, however, they feared that their own messages would be lost, and began to call anew for a debate.

President Carter had left the door open by saying that he would engage Reagan alone. The League of Women Voters, noting Anderson's decline in the polls, reversed its past policy that the congressman would be included in all debates. Instead, it accepted Carter's condition, and Reagan promptly agreed to a two-man event. While Carter advisers, by this point, had "all pretty well reached the conclusion that a debate could only hurt us,"[19] Carter himself eagerly accepted the challenge. The ninety-minute confrontation was scheduled for one week before the election.

The debate itself probably contributed considerably to public awareness and decision. Over 100 million persons watched as each candidate argued his basic campaign themes. Carter stressed the benefits of his programs to specific constituencies, placed himself in "the mainstream of the Democratic party" and emphasized his experience in office (mentioning the President's "Oval Office" ten times). He attacked Reagan's statements on such policies as Medicare, and even — at his own initiative — cited his teen-age daughter as a source for his concern over the spread of nuclear weapons. Reagan had prepared for three days for the debate. He offered detailed and moderate answers, cited his record as governor of California several times, and was ready to respond to all criticisms, leavening his factual rebuttals with deprecating humor. The difference in the candidates' tones can be seen in this exchange regarding the strategic arms limitation treaty:

> Carter: This [Reagan's] attitude is extremely dangerous and belligerent in its tone, although it's said with a quiet voice.

> Reagan: I know the President's supposed to be replying to me, but sometimes I have a hard time in connecting what he's saying with what I have said or what my positions are.[20]

Many newspaper comments and public opinion polls were devoted to the question of who "won" the debate. As is common with such events,[21] relatively few voters actually changed their preference as a direct result, although these few did favor Reagan. The more important effect of the debate was to reinforce previous commitments and again center the election on the basic question: Was Reagan an acceptable alternative to Carter? Because Reagan showed himself as competent, because he made no errors, and because he appeared pleasant and reasonable, he was able to settle any doubts raised during the campaign. By not losing, he won; the polls now showed him in the lead.

This lead was transformed into a Reagan sweep on Election Day. Events in Iran contributed to the shift (as discussed in chapter 4). The Iranian government seemed ready to release the American hostages, but then established four prior conditions for the freedom of the captives. President Carter flew back to Washington to direct preparation of an American response, but he could take no quick, dramatic action to resolve the situation. Instead, the nation would suffer another disappointment on the very anniversary of the takeover of the Teheran embassy. There was no "October surprise," feared by the Republicans, but only a "November frustration" for Carter and the nation.

While these events did not cause the late changes in and of themselves, they served as "metaphor" and "catalyst" for the expression of long-standing antipathies toward the Carter administration.[22] Again, the United States was shown dependent on the whims of another nation's leaders. Again, presidential desires had been frustrated by legislative delay — and this time not by an American Congress but by a body with strange customs and unknown members. Again, President Carter had seemed to promise a happy result, only to act indecisively and unsuccessfully. Discontent had been the keynote of the election year; on November 4, the keynote swelled to a chorused disapproval.

RESULTS AND IMPLICATIONS

The Anderson Difference
Throughout this book, we have focused discussion on Carter and Reagan. In the race itself, much attention was devoted to a third candidate, John Anderson. The congressman received considerable acclaim from the press and from some groups in the electorate for his intelligence, persistence, and willingness to take specific and unpopular policy positions. He faced difficult odds, beginning his independent candidacy late, supported by no formal party organization, and bereft of secure financing. In these circumstances, he did relatively well. A bipartisan national ticket was established, with former Wisconsin Governor Patrick Lucey the running mate in Anderson's "National Unity Coalition." The ticket secured a place on the ballot of all fifty states, despite formidable legal and political hurdles. The campaign raised almost $12 million, largely through direct-mail contributions, even though federal law limited individual contributions to a $1,000 maximum, and Anderson actually received money from more individuals than did the national Democratic party. By securing 7 percent of the national vote, Anderson laid the groundwork for a more ambitious future effort.

The Anderson campaign failed in its ostensible objective: presidential victory. Organizational difficulties, advertising and money shortages, the diversion of time and money into the struggle to win legal access to the ballot, and the remaining strength of the two major parties explained part of this failure. Furthermore, Anderson himself never won widespread popular enthusiasm. At no point did he gain a plurality of favorable comments from the electorate, and his "reputation index" (see chapter 1) actually declined over the course of the campaign, while that of the two major candidates rose slightly.[23]

The independent candidate never developed a strong electoral base. His appeal remained largely restricted to the "young, liberal, well-educated, white and affluent" voters and extended little into the broader ranks of the middle and working classes. Moreover, Anderson's support was inherently soft, concentrated among younger persons, who vote infrequently, and among persons who were least certain of their own preferences. Most importantly, there was no distinctive ideological character to this vote. Anderson ran as a middle-of-the-road candidate in a race in which his opponents also claimed the same place on the political highway. Unlike most protest candidates, his dissent lacked a strong emotional issue, such as Vietnam for McGovern or civil rights for George Wallace.[24] Indeed, at times, the greatest Anderson appeal seemed to be not his own positive qualities but the voters' negative reaction to all the candidates. As one of his advocates said, "There's something soothing to one's soul to say, 'I didn't help any of them get in.' "[25]

In the final results, Anderson's efforts were not decisive. Even if all the Anderson voters had chosen Carter instead, Carter still might have been defeated, although the race would have been considerably closer. The Democrats devoted much of their effort to achieving such a switch, arguing that "a vote for Anderson is a vote for Reagan." On the last weekend of the race, Carter extended the appeal, showing the similarity of some of his positions to those of the Illinois congressman and pleading for support by Anderson's voters.

The Democratic effort was based on an incorrect premise. Those who liked Anderson did so precisely because they did not like Carter, as well as not liking Reagan. As one prominent liberal Democrat put it, "I cannot see that on his record President Carter has earned 20 more seconds — not to speak of four more years — in the White House."[26] Urging these dissidents to support Carter was asking them to abandon the strong emotional antipathy they held toward the President. Even if Anderson had been removed from the race, moreover, it is doubtful that Carter would have benefited. Anderson won most of his votes from Independents, rather than committed partisans, and of the remaining support he received almost as much from Republicans as Democrats (see table 3.2). Those who remained with Anderson to the end actually preferred Reagan to

Carter, and his elimination from the ballot actually might have further swollen the Reagan majority.[27]

While not affecting the final results, Anderson certainly affected the campaign, particularly the Democratic effort. Concern about Anderson dominated and warped many of Carter's strategic decisions. His forces spent much time and money in a futile effort to deny Anderson access to the ballot — in the process arousing Anderson's ire and determination to remain in contention, even if Reagan were elected. Because Anderson won the important endorsement of the Liberal party in New York, a traditional backer of Democrats, the Carter campaign devoted exceptional efforts to that state. With funds running low, the opportunity to campaign elsewhere was lost.[28] Carter's evasion of the first debate, and his attacks on the Anderson candidacy, contributed to the deterioration of his own reputation. Furthermore, by delaying the debate with Reagan in order to exclude Anderson, that single confrontation gained exceptional importance. With no time for a second meeting with Reagan, President Carter was proven vulnerable. By contrast, Reagan, also accepting the premise that Anderson would take votes from Carter, was free to appear magnanimous toward the independent candidate.

The ultimate decline of the Anderson effort is a testament to the institutional strength of the two-party system in the United States. As a new and independent candidate, Anderson had to devote weeks and thousands of dollars to earning a place on state ballots. The major candidates had automatic access and were free to devote themselves to addressing the voters. While Republicans and Democrats each had $29.4 million in federal funds for their campaigns (and their parties could raise an additional $4.6 million), Anderson had to raise all his money privately. By winning over 5 percent of the national vote, he did receive, retroactively, partial federal financing, but he could not secure advance bank loans on this uncertain collateral — and the Carter administration pressured banks to deny him such loans

The Anderson decline was basically due to the realities of two-party power in the nation, the ultimate fact that the elected President would be either a Democrat or a Republican. While he received over 20 percent of polled preferences during the summer, Anderson finally held only a third of his potential support. Even if unhappy with the choice, most voters still wanted to make a President, not merely to make a protest. With the race perceived as close, the value of each vote increased, and the luxury of an Anderson ballot became too costly.

The Election Mandate

The extensive Reagan victory immediately raises basic questions of its ideological meaning and its impact on the relative future strength of the two major parties. Can the Republican triumph be seen as a victory for the conservative ideology? Can the victory then be understood as a realignment of American politics around a "new Republican majority," comparable to the critical elections of 1928–36, which created the Democratic New Deal majority?[29]

Certainly, voter discontent is apparent in the congressional as well as presidential results. In the Senate, Democratic liberals were almost entirely the targets of this discontent, while House races brought the defeat of major leaders of the congressional party and its left-wing (see chapter 5). These results have a decided partisan character, with the voters choosing not only a Republican President but a Republican and conservative-to-moderate government. Party, however, is more important than ideology in explaining these outcomes. Particularly in the presidential race, the weight of the evidence is that the 1980 election was a negative landslide based on dissatisfaction with Carter and his record rather than a direct endorsement of conservative philosophy.

Elections that involve upheavals in the party coalitions have certain hallmarks, such as popular enthusiasm and diverse voting shifts. These indicators are largely lacking in 1980. Turnout actually falls, instead of showing the increase that would be expected in the enthusiasm of a rising cause. The victorious candidate, Reagan, lacks the personal popularity we would expect of the leader of a mass crusade. Neither geographical nor demographic data, as reviewed above, show the countervailing two-way shifts we would expect in a realigning election; instead, they evidence the consistent and one-way movements common to elections based on short-term influences.

TABLE 3.3
PARTISANSHIP AND IDEOLOGY IN THE
1976 AND 1980 ELECTIONS
(In percentages voting Democratic)

| | | Partisanship | | |
		Democrats	Independents	Republicans
Ideology	Liberals	$86/70$	$64/50$	$17/25$
	Moderates	$77/66$	$45/31$	$13/11$
	Conservatives	$64/53$	$26/22$	$6/6$

Analysis of the effect of ideology and partisanship on the vote provides further evidence. There is a striking similarity in the voting patterns of 1976 and 1980. If the Reagan victory marked a major partisan change based on conservative philosophy, we would expect to find that the Republican vote had become distinctly more conservative, while the Democrats were reduced to a predominantly liberal party. Table 3.3 does not show such a shift; instead, there is a continuity between these two years.

The table entries show the vote for Carter in these two elections for various combinations of partisanship and self-declared ideology. The first number in each cell is the percentage Carter received in 1976; under it is his share in 1980. Thus, among liberal Democrats — the entry in the upper-left-hand corner — Carter won 86 percent in 1976 and fell to 70 percent in 1980. Two points are clear from this table: (1) the vote was affected more by party loyalty than by ideology in both contests; and (2) particularly relevant to this discussion, Carter lost support among all groups in 1980, and lost more among liberals and Democrats. The President's change in fortunes was not the result of conservatives rallying around the Republican cause; his defeat was the effect of a widespread desertion from his own ranks.[30]

Another way of looking at the results is to determine the ideological character of the candidates' coalitions (i.e., to see whether their constituencies lean toward the liberal or conservative direction). Table 3.4 presents these figures for 1976 and 1980. A striking feature of the table is the lack of any change in the parties' ideological constituencies over the two elections. Carter in 1976 won the bulk of his vote from moderates, while tilting in a liberal direction. His 1980 coalition was essentially identical, but he received fewer votes from every group across the philosophical spectrum. The two Republican candidates were virtually carbon copies of each other. Both Reagan and Ford got their votes principally from moderates, with a considerable proportion of conservatives and a noticeable sprinkling of liberals. In summary, Reagan's victory came from getting more voters, from every group, not from the arousal of a conservative mandate.*

The cause of the shift to Reagan was primarily economic. His greatest strength was among those who believed their economic position had worsened in the past year, and among those who considered inflation the primary prob-

TABLE 3.4
IDEOLOGICAL COMPOSITION OF CANDIDATE COALITIONS

	Carter 1976	Carter 1980	Ford 1976	Reagan 1980
Liberals	28%	27%	10%	10%
Moderates	54	55	47	48
Conservatives	18	18	43	42
Total	100%	100%	100%	100%

*Another way to consider the vote is to compare the 1980 ballots to those cast in 1976 by the same individuals. Carter held only 62 percent of those who supported him in the earlier race — 28 percent going to Reagan, 6 percent to Anderson. Reagan kept 84 percent of those who had voted for Ford, losing 10 percent to Carter and 5 percent to Anderson. Of new voters and previous nonvoters, Carter and Reagan each received 44 percent, Anderson 9 percent. The method is used by V. O. Key in *The Responsible Electorate* (Cambridge, Mass.: Harvard University Press, 1966).

lem facing the nation. Over three-fifths of these groups voted for the Republican. Those who felt their financial condition to be improving, and even those who worried most about unemployment, remained with Carter. This Republican support from persons concerned with inflation is not new, but the pervasiveness of the concern meant that the party's candidate would win millions of votes previously in the Democratic column. Those who saw their financial condition worsening completely reversed their 1976 ballots: three-fourths of them had endorsed Carter in 1976; now, three-fourths voted against him.

Economic grievances were at the heart of the Reagan vote. A steel union official complained, "Carter ignored the steel workers for three and a half years, and now he comes around asking for our votes. Well, he's not getting them." Understanding these attitudes, Douglas Fraser, president of the automobile union, had earlier worried, "We've always told our people to vote their pocketbooks, and this year they may do it."[31]

TABLE 3.5
THE CARTER VOTE AND ECONOMIC SATISFACTION*

	Improved Economic Position	Worsened Economic Position
Democrats	77	47
Independents	45	21
Republicans	18	6
Liberals	65	44
Moderates	59	26
Conservatives	33	16
Protestants	51	24
Catholics	53	28
Jews	52	30
Union households	65	34
Nonunion households	48	22
Total	53	25

*Each entry in the table is the percentage of the designated group voting for Carter, e.g., Carter received 77 percent of the votes of Democrats who believed their family finances had improved in the past year.

Economic dissatisfaction is the most direct influence on the 1980 vote, and it has a greater impact that any other issue. As seen in table 3.5, it substantially diminishes the association between party or ideology and the vote. Despite their philosophy, those liberals who felt worse off financially opposed Carter. Despite their partisanship, those Democrats suffering economically defected to Reagan and Anderson. Traditional supporters of the party, such as Catholics and unionists, remained loyal—but only when their pocketbooks remained full. More widespread economic satisfaction would have brought the President reelection, by a two-party margin over Reagan of at least 53–47.[32] Jimmy Carter was not defeated in the marketplace of ideas; he was trounced in the marketplace of food and gasoline and mortgages.

The Republican Opportunity

If the election provides no mandate for conservatism, it does provide the opportunity for Republicans to develop an electoral majority that will consistently support a conservative direction in public policy. The Reagan administration has a chance similar to that of Franklin Roosevelt in 1932. That President, too, was elected in a time of economic distress, when the voters dismissed an incumbent chief executive (who also happened to be an engineer). Those who turned to the Democrats that year were not advocates of a New Deal program that had not yet been created, but they and their children became its loyal supporters when that program improved their lives. A Reagan Presidency—supported by a Republican majority in the Senate and a conservative, if Democratic, House —may have similar effects (see chapters 6 and 7).

A major change in American politics did not occur in 1980—but it may be coming. "Every American election," wrote Theodore White, "summons the individual voter to weigh the past against the future."[33] In 1980, neither Carter nor Reagan facilitated this process. Rather, as James Reston complained early in the fall, the contest was "a phony campaign of pretense, with Carter and Reagan savaging each other and blowing off about the past in order to avoid the hard questions of the future."[34]

The failure to address these questions was particularly marked for the Democrats, who prided themselves on being the party of innovation. President Carter had rejected some elements of traditional Democratic liberalism in his nominating campaign against Senator Kennedy, but he presented no alternative ideology. Ultimately he returned to the older ideas. Unconvincing in this late philosophical rebirth, he lost substantial support from liberals without making compensating gains among other groups. Essentially, on the presidential level, no modernized liberal ideology was presented. Its appeal, therefore, was not rejected; it was simply untested.

Carter persistently discussed past errors, or present difficulties, not future possibilities. This had been his focus in 1976 when he stressed the deficiencies of Gerald Ford. In 1980 he turned toward the past again—the old statements of Reagan, not his own intentions and directions. The lack of attention to the future, an opposing strategist argued, was Carter's major philosophical problem. "He had to . . . come before the people and say, look, I didn't know as much as I told you I did. I'm sorry and here is what I'm going to do in the next four-year term. He didn't do that." As a Democratic campaigner agreed, "We gave them all the reasons to be against the other person. We gave them no sense of the vision. No sense of why they should really want to participate in the 1980 election."[35]

Reagan, for his part, also provided little specific direction for the future. His program was criticized for offering nothing more than a nostalgic and impossible return to the 1950s or, as Garry Trudeau satirized it in his *Doonesbury* cartoons, for replacing clear forward-looking vision with rose-colored hindsight. The Reagan campaign, too, came to stress the past — both its reputedly glorious years before Carter and its failings under the incumbent administration.

Nevertheless, the Reagan candidacy did present a more hopeful stance toward the future, despite the lack of novelty in its policy proposals. His vision was vague, but it was still more inspiring than Carter's condemnation of American "malaise." By calls to patriotism, the recitation of established homilies, and the re-creation of the national past, Reagan was able to invoke the concept of American exceptionalism, of the United States as "a city on a hill," providing world leadership.

The Iranian revolution had shown the power of appeals to traditional morality and nationalistic purpose. Combining these romantic images with pocketbook complaints of economic distress, Reagan received public recognition as "a strong leader" who "offers a vision of where he wants to lead the country."[36] As Thomas Cronin had forecast earlier in the year, "the 1980s will be shaped by people and Presidents who have confidence in themselves and can radiate confidence in the nation. . . . Today, the bully pulpit — amplified as it is by the remarkable electronic opportunities of the age — beckons once again."[37]

There is an opportunity for Reagan, building on the public's desire for leadership, to develop a dominant coalition. Such opportunities are not always taken, and they can be lost through circumstances. Lyndon Johnson after 1964 was unable to develop his Great Society because of Vietnam, and earlier Republican prospects were subverted after 1972 by Nixon's Watergate corruption. Reagan and the Republicans now have a second chance. The election of 1980 was not an endorsement of their programs, but successful programs can lead to future and persistent electoral endorsement.

In the effort to develop a new majority among the electorate, Reagan will have the benefit of two political assets. Population changes and movements, the first asset, are tending in directions that largely favor the Republicans. The 1980 election was conducted on the basis of the outdated population figures of 1970; future contests will be based on the just-completed census of 1980. This census will necessitate a decided shift of congressional representation and presidential electoral votes away from the Northeast and Midwest — areas of relative Democratic strength — and toward the Far West and the sunbelt states such as Florida and Texas — areas of relatively high Republican strength. States that gave Reagan above-average support will gain sixteen electoral votes.

Changes among population groups, as well as among states, will also benefit Republicans. Large cities, the core of the Democratic majority, have lost enormous numbers of residents — nearly a million persons in the case of New York City alone. The population is aging, and there will be fewer young voters as the impact of the low birthrates of the 1960s begins to have political effects. In the past decade, senior citizens have grown in number by a fourth, and the median age has increased two years, to thirty.[38] These pro-Republican trends are reinforced by the growth of suburban and nonmetropolitan areas. They will be offset by the countervailing growth of nonwhites in the population, as the large numbers of black and Hispanic youth reach political maturity. If the Republicans can reduce the antagonism of these groups, the general population trends can work in their favor.

Reagan's most important political asset is the Republican party. Although the GOP is still a distinct minority in the electorate, it has become an ideologically coherent and organizationally efficient party. The most significant aspect of the Republicans' victory in 1980, in the long run, may be precisely that it was a Republican victory rather than the triumph of particular individuals. While Reagan won his nomination as an individual factional leader, he did represent the core of the party. While Reagan won the election as an individual challenger to a particular incumbent, he did campaign as a Republican spokesman, unlike Eisenhower and Nixon. For first time in fifty years, a President has been elected who admits that he is a Republican.

The Reagan campaign was a party effort, closely coordinated with a year-long national effort to rally support for Republican candidates for the Senate and House. The coordination of these campaigns was dramatized by a joint appearance of Reagan and most Republican congressional candidates on the steps of the Capitol during the fall. Announcing a "solemn covenant with the American people," the party leaders subscribed to a series of pledges to cut taxes, reduce the federal budget, increase military weaponry, and promote business investment.[39] This program approximated the ideal of party government, in which parties "bring forth programs to which they commit themselves" and "possess sufficient cohesion to carry out these programs."[40]

Promoting this unity is the remarkable organizational revival of the national party. Unlike the Democrats, who have attempted reform through broadened mass participation, the Republicans have devoted their efforts to increased electoral efficiency. Fund raising has been extended through direct-mail programs and administratively centralized in the national committee. Under the leadership of Chairman Bill Brock, the party has sought to revitalize its basic leadership by active recruiting of candidates for public office from the state legislatures to Congress. The national party provided low-budget surveys of public opinion, conducting 250 local polls. It dispatched organizational experts to congressional constituencies, conducted 100 training sessions on the use of the mass media and other electioneering techniques, and ran a regular series of workshops for campaign managers, culminating in the graduation of 160 persons from a "campaign management college." Computerized data analysis and policy research were coordinated, a permanent headquarters was established, and a party journal of opinion, *Commonsense*, was published regularly. Finances were integrated so that the contributions from state parties were pooled with national resources. Furthermore, the central party provided $3 million for state legislative candidates (in contrast to the national Democrats' total neglect of these races).

The most hopeful sign for the party is that their candidate won a presidential election on economic issues. For five decades, these issues have been the major advantage of the Democrats. Having won popular support on these basic questions, the Republicans have successfully attacked their opponents at their strongest point. If they can deal with the problems of inflation, endemic unemployment, energy, and industrial decay, the Republican party will be well along in the construction of a new and persistent majority coalition. If the economic problems of the United States are too deep-rooted for political solution, the Republican victory will prove shallow and short-lived.

The Democratic Opposition
The Republican triumph also provides opportunities for the Democratic party. Defeat also has its uses, even if they are less enjoyable than the possibilities created by victory. The Democrats can exploit weaknesses evident in the Reagan electoral coalition, while they use the time out of power to regroup.

The most disturbing aspect of the Reagan victory is the exclusion from the winning majority of almost all blacks and the majority of Hispanics. Republican programs will not succeed if they lack concern for these groups. Politically as well, the Republican coalition will be vulnerable if it ignores the claims of groups that represent an increasing proportion of the population. Morally, a purely white majority would violate basic human and American values of equality and opportunity. The Democrats can still prosper as the party demanding empathy for minority groups.

There also are prospects for the Democrats among the near-majority of the population that did not vote in 1980. Turnout has always been greater among persons of high social status, particularly those with the most education. Until 1980, this difference did not affect the electoral outcome greatly.[42] In the last contest, however, there was a marked contrast between voters and nonvoters. Reagan's forces were more likely to register and actually to come to the polls. While four out of five Reagan backers registered, the proportions fell to three of four Carter supporters and to two of three Anderson enthusiasts. If all adults had voted, Reagan still would have won the election, but his lead would have been cut in half, to only a 5 percent margin over Carter. The large number of unregistered and nonparticipating citizens offers the Democrats a possibility for political mobilization.[43]

To exploit the possibility, Democratic rebuilding is necessary. The party emerges from the election of 1980 still predominant in the loyalties of the voters, and still in control of most of the state legislatures and governorships and of the U.S. House of Representatives. Inevitably it will return to national power. Restoring its long-term dominance, however, will require more than awaiting the swing of the electoral pendulum. The organization is weak and, despite four years in the White House, the national party is still heavily in debt. The core of its leadership has been eliminated through deaths and electoral defeats. Party reform has preoccupied the Democrats for a dozen years, but has not contributed substantially to the basic goal of any political party — winning office. Democratic resurgence will require much attention, beginning with such mundane activities as compiling lists of contributors and preparing attractive television spots.

Technical expertise will not renew the party. The fundamental need of the Democrats is for ideas that are meaningful and convincing. There is some effort in the Republican party to develop new ideas, a Democratic strategist admits, while in 1980 "the Democrats tended to run on the basis of being Democrats."[44] Party loyalty and old ideas are no longer sufficient. The 1980 election, for the Democrats, was "the end of an idea whose time has passed. Liberalism has come unstuck. Now, compassion has to be separated from dependence on government programs."[45] New thinking is the basic requirement for the future revival of the Democrats (see chapter 7).

The Party Future
For both Republicans and Democrats, the future of the two-party system remains questionable. John Anderson was ultimately eliminated as a factor in the presidential race, but nearly 7 million voters indicated their discontent with the major parties by casting ballots for him, Ed Clark, and Barry Commoner. Ideological and single-interest groups continue to challenge the parties for the loyalties of the electorate. Philosophically, conservative groups are particularly active. Unrestricted by federal election laws, they spent some $8 million in the 1980 election, while all political action committees, predominantly representing business, spent $60 million. These interests not only challenge liberal

"targets" but have already indicated their distrust of George Bush and their wariness even of Ronald Reagan. Both parties will be electorally ineffective if they are captured by narrow groups, such as anti-abortionists applying loyalty tests to Republicans or feminists applying loyalty tests to Democrats. Both parties are challenged by the rise of independents, the prevalence of split-ticket voting, and the virtually unprecedented division of control of the two chambers of Congress. Both parties should be concerned about the substitution of mass media campaigning for personal contact with the voters and about the decline of local party activity.

The parties, and the nation, continue to need the stability, continuity, and democratic responsibility that exist in a strong two-party system. Reagan and the Republicans now hold the power of government, nominally, and Democrats will surely recapture it at some time in the future. More basic innovations in politics are needed, however, than the changing of the guard. Without them, American politics will remain vulnerable to deadlock, inconsistency, frustration, and citizen withdrawal. Even as we near the two-hundredth anniversary of the Constitution, the renewal of political institutions remains the critical American issue.

NOTES

1. The voting results are from *Congressional Quarterly Weekly Report* 39 (17 January 1981): 138. Of minor party candidates, Ed Clark of the Libertarian party received 921,188 votes and Barry Commoner of the Citizens party received 234,279.

2. See Walter Dean Burnham, *Critical Elections and the Mainsprings of American Politics* (New York: Norton, 1970).

3. These data, from the studies of the University of Michigan's Center for Political Studies, are presented in John Kessel, *Presidential Campaign Politics* (Homewood, Ill.: Dorsey, 1980), p. 224.

4. Norman Nie et al., *The Changing American Voter* (Cambridge, Mass.: Harvard University Press, 1976), p. 59.

5. Adam Clymer, in the *New York Times*, 26 October 1980, sect. 4: E1.

6. E. J. Dionne, in the *New York Times*, 2 November 1980, p. 37. By contrast, in 1956, 92 percent of the voters were highly favorable to Eisenhower and/or Stevenson.

7. The percentage would be received by a President with only a 30 percent popularity rating in the Gallup poll — Carter's standing before the election. See Lee Sigelman, "Presidential Popularity and Presidential Elections," *Public Opinion Quarterly* 43 (Winter 1979): 534.

8. Jeffrey A. Smith, *American Presidential Elections: Trust and the Rational Voter* (New York: Praeger, 1980), p. 151.

9. *Time* 116 (15 September 1980): 11. The shifts in television advertising are reported in the *New York Times*, 17 September 1980, p. 33; 26 September, p. A18; and 1 October 1980, p. B7.

10. *Congressional Quarterly Weekly Report* 38 (1 November 1980): 3289.

11. *New York Times*, 9 November 1980, sect. 4: E1.

12. *New York Times*, 2 October 1980, p. 1; and 26 October, p. 41. For a general discussion of such tactics, see Edward Tufte, *Political Control of the Economy* (Princeton: Princeton University Press, 1978), chaps. 1 and 2.

13. John Sears, quoted in the *New York Times*, 27 August 1980, p. A17.

14. CBS News/*New York Times* poll, 19-25 September 1980.

15. *New York Times*, 26 September 1980, p. A18; and 7 October, p. D21. The "war and peace theme was cited so often that the President's plane was nicknamed 'Tolstoy' "—*Newsweek* 96 (3 November 1980): 34.

16. Howell Raines in the *New York Times*, 12 October 1980, p. 32.

17. Anthony Lewis, "Carter Against Himself," *New York Times*, 16 October 1980, p. A31.

18. CBS News/*New York Times* poll, 16-20 October 1980.

19. *New York Times*, 9 November 1980, p. 1.

20. The text of the debate can be found in *Congressional Quarterly Weekly Report* 38 (1 November 1980): 3279-89, the quotation on 3285.

21. See Sidney Kraus, ed., *The Great Debates* (Bloomington: Indiana University Press, 1962, 1979).

22. George Will, "Rebuke to a Party," *Manchester Guardian Weekly* 123 (16 November 1980): 17.

23. From June to August and then to late October, Anderson's score on this index changed from 47 to 52 to 46. For Reagan, the ratings were 65, 68, 68; for Carter, 64, 63, 67.

24. These weaknesses were seen early in the *Los Angeles Times* poll, 15 July 1980.

25. Steven Roberts, in the *New York Times*, 13 June 1980, p. A14.

26. Arthur Schlesinger, Jr., in the *Wall Street Journal*, 31 October 1980.

27. The final CBS News/*New York Times* poll before the election showed 38 percent of the Anderson supporters preferred Carter as a second choice, 42 percent preferred Reagan, and 13 percent would not vote in a two-man race. The survey of voters on Election Day found that of those actually casting Anderson ballots, 33 percent preferred Carter to Reagan, 29 percent were more favorable to Reagan than Carter, and 33 percent would have abstained in a two-man race.

28. See *New York Times*, 15 August 1980, p. A1; and 15 October, p. A26.
29. On the Democratic coalition, see Kristi Andersen, *The Creation of a Democratic Majority* (Chicago: University of Chicago Press, 1979); and Everett C. Ladd and Charles D. Hadley, *Transformations of the American Party System* (New York: Norton, 1975). On recent prospects, see Kevin Phillips, *The Emerging Republican Majority* (New Rochelle: Arlington House, 1969); Richard Scammon and Ben Wattenberg, *The Real Majority* (New York: Coward-McCann, 1970); and James Sundquist, *Dynamics of the Party System* (Washington, D.C.: Brookings Institution, 1973). The original concept is found in V. O. Key, "A Theory of Critical Elections," *Journal of Politics* 17 (February 1955): 3-18.
30. The data are from the Election Day CBS News/*New York Times* exit poll. The pro-Carter change of liberal Republicans is an intriguing exception but involves only a tiny, 2 percent share of the total electorate.
31. *Time* (17 November 1980): 24; and *Newsweek* (17 November 1980): 32.
32. This would have been the result if the election were confined to those voters who felt their financial situation had improved (16 percent of the nation) or had stayed the same (40 percent) in the past year.
33. *The Making of the President, 1960* (New York: Atheneum, 1961), p. 254.
34. "The Political Traps," *New York Times*, 3 September 1980, p. A19.
35. John Sears and Peter Hart in the *New York Times*, 9 November 1980, sect. 4: E3.
36. In the CBS News/*New York Times* poll of 16-20 October 1980, 62 percent and 67 percent, respectively, agreed with each of these characterizations of Reagan.
37. "Looking for Leadership," *Public Opinion* 3 (February/March 1980): 19-20.
38. John Herbers, in the *New York Times*, 2 November 1980, sect. 4: E3.
39. *New York Times*, 16 September 1980, p. B4.
40. "Toward a More Responsible Two-Party System," *American Political Science Review* 44 (September 1950): 1,supplement.
41. See the essays by John Bibby and Charles Longley in Gerald Pomper, ed., *Party Renewal in America* (New York: Praeger, 1980); and Francis Clines, in the *New York Times*, 23 July 1980, p. A14.
42. Raymond Wolfinger and Steven Rosenstone, *Who Votes?* (New Haven: Yale University Press, 1980), esp. chap. 6.
43. See E. J. Dionne, in the *New York Times*, 5 November 1980, p. A23; and Adam Clymer's analysis of the CBS News/*New York Times* exit poll in the *New York Times*, 16 November 1980, p. 1.
44. Patrick Caddell, in the *New York Times*, 9 November 1980, sect. 4: E3.
45. Jeff Greenfield, in his election night analysis on CBS.

4

Public Opinion Trends

KATHLEEN A. FRANKOVIC

Perhaps Jimmy Carter's major obstacle to renomination and reelection in 1980 can be best illustrated by the following fictitious account of a corporation that manufactured dog food: Sales of the dog food were lagging, and so the company hired an advertising agency, at great expense, to design a campaign about the virtues of the product. Despite the expense, and the publicity, sales did not improve. Then a graphic arts firm, equipped with the latest academic research on labeling's effect on marketing, redesigned the dog food's package. Still no improvement in sales. Finally, the company hired yet another expert, who after only two days of study, returned to the company president with the solution to the poor sales. "It's simple," he said, "the dogs simply can't stand the food."

The final 1980 vote count also demonstrated convincingly that "the dogs" simply couldn't stand the product.

The year 1980 was often characterized as one of great "volatility" in public opinion, and there was evidence of large voter shifts, but there were also impressive continuities in popular attitudes. The most significant was the consistently negative portrait painted of Jimmy Carter in the minds of the public. The dark portrait was lightened only by a brief improvement following the taking of American hostages by Iranian militants in November 1979.

Jimmy Carter spent most of 1980 with a national plurality disapproving of his job performance, and with a plurality also viewing him unfavorably in personal terms. Disapproval and dislike of the incumbent outweighed any other single explanation for supporting Ronald Reagan on Election Day. Even the final changes in vote intention came most frequently from those citizens who regarded Jimmy Carter negatively. Voter discontent extended as well to Ronald Reagan, whose sizable margin camouflages relatively widespread concern

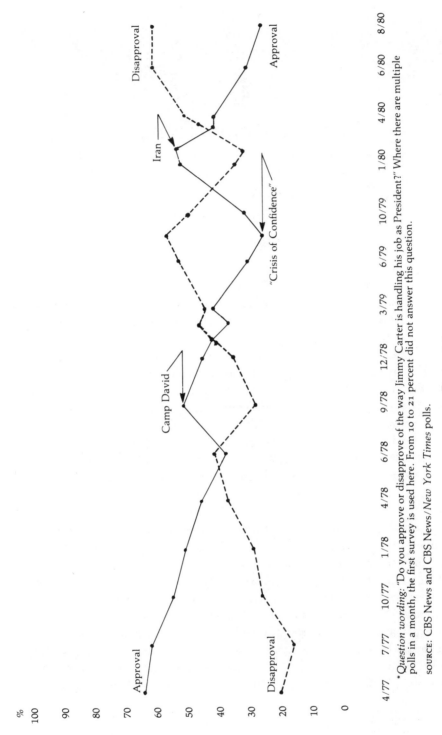

Figure 4.1

*The Public's Rating of President Carter**

Approval

Disapproval

Camp David

Iran

"Crisis of Confidence"

Approval

Disapproval

%
100
90
80
70
60
50
40
30
20
10
0

4/77 7/77 10/77 1/78 4/78 6/78 9/78 12/78 3/79 6/79 10/79 1/80 4/80 6/80 8/80

*Question wording: "Do you approve or disapprove of the way Jimmy Carter is handling his job as President?" Where there are multiple polls in a month, the first survey is used here. From 10 to 21 percent did not answer this question.

SOURCE: CBS News and CBS News/*New York Times* polls.

about his likely performance in the Presidency. But the doubts about Reagan did little to overcome the dissatisfaction with Carter.

In this chapter we explore some of the measures of Carter negativism, particularly the public's evaluation of his handling of the Presidency and of Carter the individual. We also survey the assessment of the two major candidates on a variety of qualities and the impact of these attitudes on Election Day. We then evaluate the impact of the campaign on public opinion, the effect of issues on candidate choice, and the changes that occurred in the final week. Finally, we examine the meaning of the election for the Reagan Presidency and the character of his electoral mandate.

CARTER APPROVAL AND EVALUATION

Until the hostage crisis, exactly a year before the election, the voters held Jimmy Carter in such low esteem that it seemed impossible that he could win the Democratic *nomination.* Senator Edward Kennedy was the overwhelming choice of Democrats. Previously hesitant about running, he finally was convinced to declare his candidacy.[1]

Things had not always been so bad. Carter held the approval of two-thirds of the population in April 1977, after his first hundred days in office. But the President slowly dropped in public support, and reached a low point of 26 percent in July 1979 (see figure 4.1). Immediately prior to the taking of the hostages, less than a third of the public approved of the way he handled his job. After that event, his popularity nearly doubled. Once this second peak was reached in February 1980, public support slid down once again, and continued its decline throughout the primary season. The President was back at his 1979 low by August 1980, the time of the Democratic national convention. Yet this decline and fall of public approval was almost irrelevant, as Carter held more than enough delegates to secure the nomination.

A major international crisis usually has a positive effect on a President's rating, as the public "rallies round the flag" to support a leader under siege.[2] But the brief upsurge in approval of Carter that followed the Iran crisis, besides being temporary, was limited in scope. It failed to alleviate public dismay about a concern that was closer to home: the economy. In early 1980 most people approved of Carter's overall performance and his handling of foreign policy and Iran, but they did not endorse his fiscal management (see table 4.1). Carter's general and foreign policy ratings waxed and waned; attitudes toward his economic performance remained unfavorable, and these ratings fell below 20

TABLE 4.1
CARTER APPROVAL RATINGS ON THREE ISSUES*

			Percentage Approving				
	Nov. '79	Jan. '80	Feb.'80	Mar. '80	April '80	June '80	Aug. '80
Foreign policy	28	45	48	34	31	20	18
Economy	21	27	26	23	21	18	19
Iran		55	63	49	39	29	31

*Questions: (1) Do you approve or disapprove of the way Jimmy Carter is handling foreign policy? (2) Do you approve or disapprove of the way Jimmy Carter is handling the economy? (3) Do you approve or disapprove of the way Jimmy Carter is handling the crisis in Iran? Each percentage is the proportion approving Carter's actions on the stated issue.

SOURCE: CBS News/New York Times polls.

percent several times. Public hostility was especially evident in the summer of 1980, as the race for the nomination neared its conclusion.

Shifting evaluations of Carter's overall performance as President paralleled the public's evaluation of Carter the individual. At the beginning of 1980, potential voters tended toward a favorable personal impression of the man, just as they were inclined to approve of his job performance. But these positive ratings were almost equalled by negative evaluations, as can be seen in table 4.2. The President did much better among Democrats, the critical group for his nomination, and his positive balance was most evident in January and February, the critical time for wooing delegates.

This improvement in Carter's standing within his own party fortuitously came when opinions of his major Democratic opponent were falling. Senator Kennedy, the overwhelming favorite for the nomination in 1979, was perceived negatively by most voters in January 1980, and even by Democrats in later months. It is unclear whether this change was the result of the Iranian situation or the early and unexpected Carter successes in primaries in Iowa and Maine, or whether it reflected a more focused public reaction to the major Kennedy problem of Chappaquiddick. In February, better than one of every ten Democrats gave his behavior at Chappaquiddick as the primary reason they disliked the senator, and a similar proportion objected to his campaign tactics. The Carter campaign ads, which continually boasted about Carter's judgment under pressure and criticized Kennedy's judgment, may have stimulated this public dislike. A Carter ad of "on the street" interviews in Pennsylvania included comments such as, "I don't think [Kennedy] can deal with a crisis" and "I trust Carter more than Kennedy."[3]

In later months, neither Carter nor Kennedy fared well in public perceptions. In June and August, even as the President neared official renomination, his fellow Democrats regarded him ambivalently. As many in his party viewed him unfavorably as favorably, and by the June 3 primaries, many Democrats

TABLE 4.2
PUBLIC EVALUATIONS OF PRESIDENTIAL CANDIDATES*

	January 1980 Total	Dem.	February 1980 Total	Dem.	March 1980 Total	Dem.	April 1980 Total	Dem.	June 1980 Total	Dem.	August 1980 Total	Dem.
Opinion of Carter												
favorable	45%	56%	58%	62%	48%	49%	43%	52%	33%	43%	33%	46%
unfavorable	33	24	32	24	43	37	50	39	58	49	56	44
no opinion	22	20	10	14	9	14	7	9	9	9	11	10
Opinion of Kennedy												
favorable	38%	51%	25%	31%	25%	36%	27%	36%	29%	40%	28%	38%
unfavorable	50	38	56	48	63	52	62	54	59	46	49	41
no opinion	12	11	19	21	12	12	11	10	12	14	23	21

	January 1980 Total	Rep.	February 1980 Total	Rep.	March 1980 Total	Rep.	April 1980 Total	Rep.	June 1980 Total	Rep.	August 1980 Total	Rep.
Opinion of Reagan												
favorable	42%	59%	38%	51%	34%	53%	41%	61%	42%	70%	46%	75%
unfavorable	38	25	46	32	35	24	32	21	30	12	27	9
no opinion	20	16	16	17	31	23	27	18	28	18	27	16

*Question: Do you have a favorable or not favorable opinion about . . . . . , or don't you know enough about him to have an opinion?

SOURCE: CBS News/New York Times polls.

defined their votes more negatively than positively. In New Jersey, a quarter of the Democrats said they voted for the "lesser of the evils"; in California, this proportion rose to 40 percent. Nevertheless the increasing negativism among Democratic voters and their decreasing approval of the Carter Presidency never significantly turned to Kennedy's advantage in the primaries or polls. Only in mid-August was Kennedy even tied with Carter as the choice of rank-and-file Democrats for the nomination.

The Democratic convention met at a particularly bad time for Carter. The President was at a low point in public approval, and he was being drawn into the problems created by his brother's financial association with the government of Libya. Allegations of wrongdoing within the administration detracted from Carter's widespread reputation for honesty. He had been elected as someone who would never lie to the American people, but deceit was now suspected of his associates.

Carter may have salvaged his position during a midweek press conference. Prior to it, Democrats were evenly divided between Carter and Kennedy as their presidential choice; afterward, Carter had a clear lead once again.[4] At the same time, Democratic convention delegates were considering a rules change that would release them from voting for their original candidate (see chapter 1). After the press conference it became clear, from polls of delegates, that such a move would fail.[5]

President Carter was able to win the Democratic nomination despite a lack of public enthusiasm. Still, his limited support would plague him throughout the fall. His opponent was free of this problem. While Carter was losing approval both overall and within his own party, Ronald Reagan maintained a fairly even balance in perceptions among the electorate as a whole, and dramatically improved his already strong position within his own party. Prior to the Republican convention, Reagan was perceived favorably by a four-to-three margin overall and by an impressive six-to-one margin among Republicans. As table 4.2 shows, Republicans were lining up behind their party's candidate in time for his nomination. Democrats were, if anything, moving away from their nominee. Carter had not shaken the public's problems with his Presidency; these difficulties were to reassert themselves as the campaign advanced.

REAGAN VERSUS CARTER

In April of 1980, half the public claimed dissatisfaction with the possibility of a Carter-Reagan confrontation.[6] This dissatisfaction continued throughout the fall. Opinion data provide a number of indicators of this public discontent.

First, the most frequently cited reason for supporting either candidate in the fall was one that reflected negatively on his opponent. As early as mid-September, over a quarter of those who claimed they supported Reagan gave anti-Carter reasons for their choice. Just over 10 percent of Carter supporters cited anti-Reagan justifications. The smaller proportion of negative reasons given by Carter supporters, however, is misleading. Their positive reasons were only *mildly* so — Carter was doing as well as he could; Carter was trying hard; Carter was a Democrat. Or respondents fell back to what had been the greatest Carter asset of 1976 — his image as an honest person. As the election drew nearer, the proportion giving negative reasons for their vote continued to remain high, and after the election, two of every five Reagan voters explained their choice as a dislike of Carter. When asked directly, 40 percent of all voters said they voted mainly *against* another candidate.[7]

Second, the absence of positive feeling by the electorate is evident in the absence of issue content in voter's comments. Seventeen percent of Reagan supporters cited the economy as the basis for their vote; otherwise, no specific issue was named by more than 2 percent of either major candidate's supporters. Since Carter's worst approval ratings concerned the economy, there is reason to think that these Reagan voters also were motivated mainly by anti-Carter feelings.

Third, neither Carter nor Reagan was free of specific negative perceptions. Nearly all voters had some concern about each candidate's probable performance as President. In September, only a quarter had no worry about another term of a Carter Presidency, while only about a third had no worry about Reagan. The electorate spontaneously cited the incumbent's perceived inability to make decisions, a notion that he was generally doing a poor job, and the country's economic problems. Reagan was viewed as a warmonger and as too old to handle the Presidency effectively.

Fourth, voter discontent is evident in responses to specific questions about each candidate. Majorities believed Carter was a weak leader, but they also complained that Reagan said too many things carelessly, without considering the consequences. People were uncertain of Carter's or Reagan's clarity on the issues, while only bare majorities thought each candidate had good judgment under pressure. As many as two in five voters feared Reagan would get the country into a war, while more respondents thought the economy would get worse, rather than better, in another Carter administration.

The large Reagan victory can be attributed to general dissatisfaction and to specific dissatisfaction with Carter. On Election Day, nearly two-fifths of actual Reagan voters claimed their primary motivation was simply that "it was time for a change," as opposed to any positive quality or ideological stance of their candidate. The issues cited by most Reagan voters were domestic economic ones (particularly inflation), which were seen as Carter's greatest failings by both voters and the political experts.[8] Kennedy, too, had scored extremely well in the Democratic primaries among voters who had seen their financial situation worsen.

The Reagan campaign sought to make the most of these failures, and the candidate's ads pointed directly to them. In one, Reagan said: "Everywhere I travel in America I hear this phrase over and over again. 'Everything is going up. Where is it going to end?' Record inflation has robbed the purchasing power of your dollar. And for three and a half years the administration has been unable to control it."[9] In his televised debate with Carter, the former California governor hammered at the same point in his concluding argument. That appeal was successful, as Reagan defeated Carter by better than two to one among those voters who claimed their family's financial situation had worsened in the last year.

CAMPAIGN EFFECTS ON PUBLIC OPINION

Campaigns are supposed to educate the public about both the candidates' personal qualities and the major issues. In fact, without effective campaigns any level of issue voting would be impossible, since voters would be unaware of the differences between candidates on the issues.[10]

The campaign of 1980, while it did not fundamentally alter public opinion on the issues, served to make it related to vote choice. Additionally, the presidential campaign (particularly the two presidential debates) had two effects. First, it improved Reagan's image, at least temporarily. Second, it permanently dashed the hopes of John Anderson, who never recovered from the losses he suffered at the time of his debate with Ronald Reagan.

Carter and Reagan

Ronald Reagan and Jimmy Carter came into the fall campaign with relatively well formed public images. Carter, as noted, was seen as honest and experienced but also as lacking leadership and not fully competent. Public opinion of Carter hardly changed during the campaign. From the outset, the electorate characterized Reagan as a conservative and as a strong leader, knew his advanced age,[11] and expressed concern about his potentially aggressive character. Most of the perceptions of the former California governor remained constant during the campaign. There was change, however, in regard to three important characteristics.

The first of these traits was Reagan's competence. Early in the campaign, Reagan was plagued by a series of verbal errors. These gaffes — for example, his doubts about the theory of evolution or his accusation that President Carter opened his campaign in the birthplace of the Ku Klux Klan — received relatively heavy play in the press. The voting public seemed to be clearly aware of these mistakes, as two-thirds (and half of the Reagan supporters) consistently agreed that he "said too many things carelessly, without considering the consequences." These mistakes also contributed to the notion that Reagan was an intellectual lightweight, lacking adequate knowledge of the problems of the Presidency. The Carter advertising campaign attempted to exploit this perception, citing Carter as a man who did understand, and who had the experience to handle the job. One ad showed an empty Oval Office, with the following voice-over: "When you come right down to it, what kind of person should occupy the Oval Office? Should it be a person who, like Ronald Reagan, has a fractured view of America? Who speaks disdainfully about millions of us as he attacks the minimum wage and calls unemployment insurance a 'prepaid vacation'? *Or should another kind of man sit here, an experienced man* who knows how to be responsive to all Americans, all 240 million of us? Figure it out for yourself."[12]

TABLE 4.3

PRESIDENTIAL COMPETENCE OF CARTER AND REAGAN*

	Carter		Reagan	
	Yes	No	Yes	No
Mid-September	68%	27%	48%	44%
Late-September	68	29	62	32
Mid-October	70	26	51	42

*Question: Do you think that [Jimmy Carter/Ronald Reagan] understands the complicated problems a President has to deal with? Each percentage is the proportion agreeing (Yes) or disagreeing (No).

SOURCE: CBS News/*New York Times* polls.

Early in the fall, the public was much less likely to think of Reagan as a man who understood the problems of the Presidency than they were to envision Carter that way, as shown in table 4.3. After the first presidential debate between Reagan and Anderson, however, Reagan gained in public estimation. At that point, nearly as many thought Reagan understood the problems a President had to confront as thought Carter did. This gain for Reagan was short-lived, and by mid-October, again only half the electorate judged Reagan capable in this regard.

A similar short-term gain, although not as striking, appeared on the public's estimation of Reagan's clarity on the issues. (In late 1979, over half the public said they would be more likely to vote for someone with clear issue positions, even if they didn't agree with him.)[13] The proportion agreeing that Reagan had clear positions rose from 50 percent before the Reagan-Anderson debate to 57 percent afterward, then dropped back to 49 percent in mid-October. It is possible that perceptions of Reagan on these characteristics, understanding and issue clarity, showed similar changes after his late October debate with President Carter. What should be noted is that these known gains for Reagan after his debate with Anderson were temporary, effectively lasting only a week or two. Such gains, *if* they occurred after the second debate, carried Reagan through the general election.

There are indications that the Carter-Reagan debate did have such an effect on a third, and particularly important, negative trait of Reagan, his alleged aggressiveness. Throughout most of the fall, well over a third of the potential electorate feared the possibility of war under a Reagan administration. That proportion dropped somewhat after the Carter-Reagan debate, in the last week of the campaign. But, after the election, the proportion who worried about a war rose again to pre-debate levels. This suggests that Reagan's presentation during that debate (as in the appearance with Anderson) alleviated, if only temporarily, serious concerns about him held by the electorate.

While the 1980 presidential debates had some effect on qualitative assessments of Reagan, they appeared to have little effect in transmitting knowledge about his issue positions. If anything, they clouded the public's perceptions of his stands. Still, Reagan went into his first debate with many of his issue positions already well known by the electorate. Just about half the voters, both before and after the first debate, identified the Republican as wanting to decrease spending on domestic programs. Before the debate, two-thirds identified Reagan as wanting U.S. military superiority over the Soviet Union, while a sizable plurality knew he favored a large cut in income taxes. Half were aware that he opposed the Equal Rights Amendment.

Reagan's views at that time were even better known by the voters than those of Jimmy Carter. While a large majority of the voters knew Carter favored the Equal Rights Amendment, fewer knew his positions on other issues. Pluralities did agree that Jimmy Carter favored keeping domestic spending at about the same level it was, and that he supported a tax cut smaller than Reagan's. There was no such clear agreement on Carter's policy concerning U.S. military strength.

Reagan's debate with Anderson actually mitigated the characterization of Reagan as a conservative. The proportions believing the Republican supported U.S. military superiority and a large tax cut actually *decreased* after the debate (see table 4.4). On the other two issues, there was no change. These modified perceptions probably benefited Reagan, since fewer people now characterized him as a strict ideologue on all issues.

TABLE 4.4
ISSUE PERCEPTIONS AND THE REAGAN-ANDERSON DEBATE*

	Perception of Reagan		Perception of Anderson	
	Pre-Debate	Post-Debate	Pre-Debate	Post-Debate
Domestic Spending				
favors increase	13%	14%	10%	14%
favors decrease	49	49	17	20
favors keeping the same	12	15	18	23
don't know	25	22	56	43
U.S. vs. USSR				
should be stronger	67%	59%	21%	21%
should be equal	14	17	18	26
should be less strong	2	3	7	7
don't know	17	21	54	46
Tax Cut				
favors large cut	44%	36%	11%	10%
favors smaller cut	25	28	19	24
favors no cut	9	13	12	22
don't know	22	23	58	44
Equal Rights Amendment				
supports	28%	30%	43%	47%
opposes	48	46	9	9
don't know	22	24	48	44

*Questions: (1) Does [Ronald Reagan/John Anderson] favor increasing government spending for domestic programs, reducing government spending, or keeping it about the same? (2) Does [Ronald Reagan/John Anderson] think the military strength of the United States should be superior to the Soviet Union, should be about equal in strength, or that the United States doesn't need to be exactly as strong as the Soviet Union? (3) Does [Ronald Reagan/John Anderson] favor a large income tax cut, a smaller tax cut, or no tax cut? (4) Does [Ronald Reagan/John Anderson] favor or oppose the Equal Rights Amendment?

SOURCE: CBS News/*New York Times* polls, 19-21, 23-25 September 1980.

John Anderson

While Reagan and Carter had well-formed public images at the beginning of the campaign, the third major challenger, John Anderson, was unknown to a large share of the public. For him, the television exposure of a presidential debate should have been critical. The evidence is that the Reagan-Anderson debate and the publicity surrounding it was just that, but in a surprisingly negative way. Instead of serving merely as an alternative to two unsatisfactory major contenders, Anderson became an option in his own right — with all the warts of a potential President.

In the early autumn, Anderson's support hovered around 15 percent of potential voters, approximately half of whom supported him for *negative* reasons, such as a general dislike of both Carter and Reagan. The congressman's support at the beginning of the campaign came almost equally from respondents who would have supported Carter and those who would have supported Reagan in a two-way election. Just two weeks later, Anderson was the choice of only 9 percent of the electorate, and for the first time, his supporters were predominantly independents, Democrats, and liberals. Also at this time, slightly more of his support came from those who would have supported Carter rather than Reagan in a two-man race. Anderson's appearance on the televised debate with Reagan did not improve his level of support; he continued to be the choice of fewer than 10 percent of the electorate for the remainder of the fall. Eventually, he drew his 7 percent share of the vote equally from Carter and Reagan.

Apparently, Anderson lost support from those respondents who were farthest apart from him on the issues. Most of the drop in his support came from Republicans and conservatives. These voters presumably lost interest in the Anderson difference once they learned what it was. This learning process occurred *before* the debate, apparently in the week before, when Anderson, in qualifying for the League of Women Voters sponsored debate, was prominently featured in the campaign news.

Anderson made little headway among the electorate from the debate itself. While he only narrowly trailed Reagan among the proportion of the electorate who thought he had "won" the debate, public perceptions of his leadership, judgment, and other personal qualities changed not at all after the confrontation. On specific issues, the public claimed greater awareness of Anderson's positions after the television event, but there was no general movement toward more *accurate* knowledge. The only exception was on Anderson's position on cutting income taxes. As seen in table 4.4, voters were more likely to think, correctly, that Anderson favored a small tax cut or no cut at all after the debate than they did before it.

ISSUES AND CANDIDATE CHOICE

The debates, and perhaps the entire campaign, had only a limited effect on knowledge of the issues among the voters. The public's own issue positions also remained relatively constant. The opportunity for change was limited by the way candidates posed policy questions. Carter and Reagan dealt mostly in generalities, such as the economy and defense, and did not fully articulate specific proposals to solve those problems, such as reducing the prime interest rate or building a new missile.

Despite these limitations, the campaign did change the way issues affected voters. Early in the season, there was relatively little relation of issues to vote, but by Election Day, a respondent's issue position was often directly related to his or her presidential choice (although it is unclear whether the voters were aware of this change). In general, two patterns of change affected presidential choice, as illustrated by table 4.5. Some issues emerged as dividing candidate supporters as early as mid-September; others did not surface until later in the fall.

Early alignment of issue and candidate preferences can be seen on the issue of tax cuts combined with a balanced federal budget. Reagan, early and often, argued that both objectives could be accomplished. The Democrats, picking up a note from George Bush, Reagan's running mate and chief opponent during the Republican primaries, called the idea "voodoo economics." And John Anderson

TABLE 4.5
ISSUE POSITIONS AND CANDIDATE PREFERENCES, 1980*

| | Cut Taxes and Balance Budget | | Equal Rights Amendment | | U.S. vs. USSR | |
	Possible	Not Possible	Favor	Oppose	Should Be Stronger	Should Be Equal
August 1980						
Carter	26%	28%	30%	24%	28%	25%
Reagan	53	44	38	59	50	46
Anderson	13	15	20	8	10	16
September 10-14, 1980						
Carter	27%	45%	45%	30%	39%	34%
Reagan	46	27	25	48	38	35
Anderson	15	16	19	10	11	19
October 1980						
Carter	34%	49%	49%	34%	41%	45%
Reagan	50	34	33	55	46	38
Anderson	9	12	12	7	7	12
November 1980 (voters)						
Carter	N/A	N/A	51%	27%	39%	43%
Reagan	N/A	N/A	38	66	53	47
Anderson	N/A	N/A	8	5	5	8

*Questions: (1) Do you think it's possible to balance the federal budget and cut income taxes at the same time? (2) Do you favor or oppose the Equal Rights Amendment — also known as ERA — the Constitutional Amendment concerning women? (3) Do you think the military strength of the United States should be superior to the Soviet Union, should be about equal in strength, or doesn't the United States need to be exactly as strong as the Soviet Union? Each percentage is the proportion of persons with a particular issue position who favor the designated candidate. For each time period, the percentages add vertically to 100 percent, except for those with no candidate preference.

SOURCE: CBS News/*New York Times* polls.

reminded voters that the only way to accomplish both goals was by mirrors. In August, there was almost no relationship between attitudes on this question and candidate preferences. By September, and for the rest of the campaign, the issue clearly divided Carter and Reagan supporters.

Another traditional economic issue has been the relative importance of inflation and unemployment. Separating Democrats from Republicans in the past, it again separated Carter from Reagan supporters in 1980. The division was clear by mid-September. That pattern changed little during the rest of the campaign, and continued to Election Day.

One other domestic item became closely related to presidential choice in September. That was the Equal Rights Amendment, on which both major candidates and both political parties clearly differed. In August, both supporters and opponents of the ERA favored Reagan, though by varying margins. By September, polarization had occurred. The Equal Rights Amendment continued to divide the voters throughout the fall, and the difference was clearly visible at the ballot box.

Foreign policy issues caught on more slowly than did domestic and economic concerns in the public's mind. This lag may have been reflected in the lesser salience of those issues earlier in the campaign. Their effect may also have been reduced by the public's personal concern about Reagan's "warmongering." In any case, foreign policy issues at first were not related to candidate choice. In August, Reagan held similarly wide leads both among those who supported U.S. military superiority and those who did not. Likewise, in mid-September, even though Carter had closed the gap between himself and Reagan, the military issue was not related to voter preferences between them. A month later, there were moderate preference differences among supporters and opponents of American military superiority. While this issue did not polarize voters as much as economic items did, Reagan convincingly captured those who favored heavier armaments and split with Carter those who supported U.S.-USSR military equality.

It is somewhat surprising that the armaments question, which many voters considered very important, took so long to have an effect. It may be a matter of more rapid assimilation on the part of the 1980 electorate of the candidates' domestic rather than foreign issue stands. In late September, 40 percent of the electorate knew *both* Carter's and Reagan's positions on the Equal Rights Amendment; about a third correctly gave both positions on a large-scale tax cut. Yet only a quarter of potential voters were aware of both candidates' positions on U.S. military superiority. Polarization on the military issue did occur among those particular voters who knew the difference between Carter and

Reagan. As the campaign wore on, more voters may have learned of Carter's and Reagan's positions, facilitating the impact of the issue on the vote.

It is conceivable that domestic questions become more highly related to candidate preference at an earlier stage than foreign items in *all* campaigns, not just that of 1980. However, the campaign of 1980, with two well-known contenders, each with exploitable negative qualities, may have served to underplay the early importance of the issue of military superiority. Carter chose to distinguish himself from Reagan on foreign policy, and many of Carter's campaign ads focused on his image as a "man of peace" by picturing him with Begin and Sadat at the Camp David summit. Other Carter ads attacked Reagan. In one, Carter said of the arms race: "We are not dealing with just another shootout at the O.K. Corral. We are dealing with the most important issue facing human beings on this planet."[14] Another ad concluded with an on-the-street comment: "I think it's a big risk to have Reagan as President. Reagan scares me. He really scares me."[15]

At least for a time in the fall, Carter was able to keep the differences between himself and Reagan on the issue of U.S. military *strength* as distinguished from nuclear weapons control from affecting votes. (After the election, peace was cited as the major success of the Carter years.) Differences on U.S. strength finally may have become salient, however, after Reagan's effective and calm performance in the final campaign debate, and after the failure of last-minute attempts to free the U.S. hostages in Iran.

THE LAST DAYS OF THE CAMPAIGN

In 1980, the voters disliked both major candidates. These feelings may have spurred an unusually large last-minute switch in candidate preference. In a situation like that of 1980, preferences may be both transient and limited, no matter what people tell the pollsters.

The data show considerable fluidity and uncertainty in the voters' minds, and last-minute gains for Reagan. Thus, one-tenth of the prospective Carter voters ultimately decided just to stay home, while only 5 percent of the early Reagan supporters abstained. Fully one-seventh of those who did vote changed their minds or made up their minds in the last two days of the campaign; and again, Reagan, not Carter or Anderson, benefited. As can be seen in table 4.6, a majority of those who decided in the last few days voted for Reagan. By contrast, prior to the election, Carter led Reagan 2 to 1 among these potential voters.

TABLE 4.6

VOTING CHOICES OF LATE DECIDERS

	Preelection Preference	Reported Vote
Carter	32%	29%
Reagan	16	51
Anderson	22	13
Not sure/Other	26	7

SOURCE: CBS News/*New York Times* pre- and postelection polls, 30 October–1 November, 7-12 November 1980. The table includes voters who either changed their minds or reached a final decision only in the last two days.

Voters who made late decisions sometimes expressed a sense of futility and/or dismay with the alternatives. These sentiments were more evident among the switchers than among the stay-at-homes. While one in five pro-Carter abstainers expressed dissatisfaction, most cited illness, work, and other claims on their time. By contrast, half of the switchers from Carter gave reasons that suggest a reevaluation of their choice and a negative evaluation of Carter. In fact, these voters became increasingly negative in their overall evaluation of the President in the week of the election.

Did the October events in Iran affect the vote? There is little evidence of a direct influence. Only 3 percent of all switchers volunteered the hostage situation as the principal reason for changing their minds; and when asked a direct question, only 16 percent agreed that Iran affected their vote.[16] Furthermore, vote switchers were no more likely than other voters to cite the hostages as Carter's most conspicuous failure. Instead of a direct impact, it is more likely that the events of the last few days before the election served as a catalyst that reminded voters of, and reinforced, generally negative images held about Jimmy Carter most of the year.

On other issues, particularly those that separate liberals from conservatives, voters who changed their minds in the final preelection days resembled voters who did not change. The two groups were alike in their opinions about government abortion financing, regulation of business, military superiority, tax cuts, spending on domestic programs, and the ERA. Like those who held firm to their preelection preference, the switchers saw the economy as far and away the most important of the country's problems, and viewed inflation as more important than unemployment.

What did set the switchers apart was their skeptical attitude about the importance of the election itself. Half of all the people who voted said there were major differences between the Republican and Democratic parties, but only a third of those who changed their minds agreed. While two out of ten voters agreed that it really didn't matter who was elected President, more switchers — three out of ten — concurred. To many switchers, the act of changing their minds was not agonizing, and could be motivated by minor events, both public and private. Changes of this sort probably occur immediately before every election. In 1980, however, instead of random change that benefits and hurts both candidates equally, there was a pattern of change that greatly contributed to the Reagan landslide.

The last-minute switchers in 1980 also were concentrated in particular social groups. They were less educated than the nonswitchers, more likely to live in the East, more likely to be liberal, more likely to be female, and much more likely to live in rural areas. One might expect, from the public opinion literature, that women and less educated adults might be less likely to hold firm opinions in any election year.[17] Yet the changes in the East and among liberals (two of Carter's strongest preelection groups) support the argument of a special anti-Carter bias among the last-minute deciders in 1980. The mood of those voters, in a year of negatives, is best illustrated by the close of a sermon given by a Massachusetts minister on the eve of the election, "Oh, thank God only one of them can be elected!" This year, the negatives spoke mostly against the reelection of Jimmy Carter.

A MANDATE FOR REAGAN?

Our explanation of the 1980 election as a referendum on the Carter Presidency is supported by the electorate's mixed feelings about the winner, Ronald Reagan. Moreover, there is no evidence that indicates a turn to the right by the nation. Reagan was not elected because of increasing conservatism of the country.

The public has a peculiar assessment of Reagan as an individual. While praising some of his attributes, such as leadership, a majority thinks he speaks carelessly, without regard to consequences. Many voters doubt he understands the complexity of the problems Presidents face. Many citizens fear he will get the United States into a war. One Reaganite typifies this ambivalence. Favoring Carter until a few days before the election, this voter chose Reagan, while fearing his election might result in war. Why switch? The answer: "War is inevitable. I would rather have someone in the White House who is a leader."[18] Unlike Carter, Reagan does have the advantage of being viewed as a strong leader, but he has other weaknesses. These deficiencies in public perceptions were evident even in polls taken after Reagan's election triumph.

The electorate also lacks enthusiasm for right-wing ideology. In 1980, voters were no more likely to call themselves consevatives than they were in 1976. Additionally, substantial segments of the electorate, including many

TABLE 4.7

IDEOLOGICAL AND ISSUE PREFERENCES, 1976 TO 1980*

Ideology	November 1976	November 1980
Liberal	20%	18%
Moderate	48	51
Conservative	32	31

Domestic Spending	November 1976	November 1980
Increase	23%	12%
Decrease	45	49
Keep the same	26	33

Welfare Payments	July 1977	November 1980
Not needed	54%	51%
Necessary	31	39

Payments For Abortions	January 1978	November 1980
Favor	42%	38%
Oppose	50	55

Business Regulation	January 1978	November 1980
Too much regulation	58%	65%
Right amount	31	27

Regulate Pornography Sales To Adults	January 1978	November 1980
Yes	42%	32%
No	53	63

Effect of '60s Programs	January 1978	November 1980
Made things better	31%	30%
Made things worse	14	20
Had no effect	46	42

*Questions: (1) Are you in favor of increasing government spending on domestic programs, reducing it, or keeping it about the same? (2) In your opinion, do you think that most people who receive money from welfare could get along without it if they tried, or do you think they really need this help? (3) The government should help a poor woman with her medical bills if she wants an abortion. Do you agree or disagree? (4) The government has gone too far in regulating business and interfering with the free enterprise system. Do you agree or disagree? (5) Should government, at some level, restrict the sale of pornography to adults, or should adults be permitted to buy and read whatever they wish? (6) There were many government programs created in the 1960s to try and improve the condition of poor people in this country. Do you think these programs generally made things better, made things worse, or do you think they didn't have much impact one way or the other?

SOURCE: CBS News/*New York Times* postelection polls, 1976 and 1980; CBS News/*New York Times* polls, July 1977 and January 1978; CBS News/*New York Times* 1980 Election Day poll; CBS News 1976 Election Day poll. The first two items were asked of actual voters in 1976 and 1980, the others of national samples of the public.

Reagan voters, were opposed to many of his issue positions. In 1976, just about a third of actual voters called themselves conservatives. About half said they were moderates, and the remaining fifth labeled themselves liberals. In 1980, the proportions in each group differed from those in 1976 by no more than three percentage points. This is not a significant change; more importantly, any shift was into the moderate category (see table 4.7).

The voters supported Reagan on two issues and disagreed with him on two others. They agreed that the United States should be more forceful in its dealings with the Soviet Union, even at the risk of war, and agreed, as Republicans traditionally have argued, that inflation was more important than unemployment. But, unlike Reagan, the electorate supported the Equal Rights Amendment, and disagreed with him about the Reagan-Kemp-Roth 30 percent tax cut.

Furthermore, there is no indication that the electorate in 1980 was significantly more conservative on *specific* issues than it had been four years before. In 1976, just under half the voters thought domestic spending should be decreased. In 1980, that proportion had increased, but the increase was barely significant. Fewer voters now favored an increase in domestic spending, but more felt that domestic spending should be maintained at the same level.

The public was as likely as it was three years before to think that welfare recipients could get along without welfare payments, just about as likely to oppose government payments for abortions, and just about as likely as before to think the government programs of the 1960s had little or no impact in solving the country's problems. On two different measures of liberalism and conservatism, there was contrary movement. The public was more likely than three years before to oppose government restrictions on the sale of pornography to adults, a question of social liberalism. On the other hand, they were also more likely to agree that the government is overregulating business and industry, a question of economic conservatism.

Overall, there is no reason to accept the election outcome in 1980 as indicating a conservative tide in this country, even though the elected candidate was clearly known and perceived by a majority of the electorate as a conservative. Movements on specific issues were minor, and while some of the issues were related to candidate preference in 1980, these issues have historically separated Democratic and Republican voters.

This lack of definitive trends toward conservatism among the electorate in general is reinforced when one examines particular social groups, especially those that have been considered part of the Democratic coalition since the critical elections of the 1930s: blacks, the religious minorities of Catholics and Jews, blue-collar workers, union members, and white southerners. As seen in table 3.2 and discussed in chapter 3, Carter suffered dramatic losses between

1976 and 1980—in most cases over ten percentage points—among all these groups, with the sole exception of blacks. The Carter losses were not necessarily equalled by Reagan gains. For example, while Jewish support for the President dropped from 64 to 45 percent, the group's vote for the Republican nominee rose only five points, to 39 percent. Much of the Carter loss among Democratic groups can be attributed to John Anderson, who appeared to siphon off at least half of the Carter losses among traditional partisans (white southerners being an exception). Since Anderson was uniformly perceived to be to the left of Reagan on most issues, his capture of some potential Carter votes cannot be attributed to a conservative tide. Reagan's vote, moreover, is not distinctively ideological. Among all groups, self-identified liberals, moderates, and conservatives, the Reagan percentage of the presidential vote matched that of Gerald Ford, within sampling error (see table 3.4).

Along with no change in the overall distribution of ideology in the electorate, there also were no major differences in the 1976 and 1980 ideological composition of the groups identified as being part of the Democratic coalition. Although there seems to be a slight drop in the proportions of Democrats, Catholics, and blacks calling themselves liberal, there is no corresponding increase in the proportions identifying themselves as conservatives. The increase appears to be among self-identified moderates. Most surprising, there is a statistically significant *decrease* in Jewish and southern white conservative identification. Again, in both cases, it is movement into the moderate area.

There is no clear ideological mandate for the Reagan administration. Dissatisfaction with the Carter administration's performance on the economy, concern over Carter's handling of Iran, and the consistent general dislike of the incumbent all contributed to the Reagan victory. Ronald Reagan, in contrast to

TABLE 4.8

POLITICAL PHILOSOPHY OF VOTING GROUPS, 1976-80

	1976			1980		
	Liberal	Moderate	Conservative	Liberal	Moderate	Conservative
Democrats	27%	51%	22%	24%	57%	20%
Independents	20	50	30	19	52	29
Catholics	22	50	28	18	55	27
Jews	42	39	19	41	47	12
Blue-Collar Households	19	52	29	19	51	30
Union Households	22	51	27	20	52	28
Blacks	32	45	23	28	47	24
White Southerners	13	46	41	13	50	37

SOURCE: CBS News/*New York Times* 1980 Election Day poll; CBS News 1976 Election Day poll.

a President who talked about the difficulties and complexities of the job, presented a hopeful vision of the future, a vision grasped by most of the public. Whether his specific solutions to the problems he sees will be enacted and will be accepted by the public is a matter for the future. The new President does not have a mandate for conservative policies; instead, he has a mandate to be different from Jimmy Carter.

NOTES

1. Unless otherwise noted, data are taken from the CBS News/*New York Times* national polls, and the CBS News/*New York Times* primary and general Election Day polls of voters. Footnotes are used only if the dates of interviewing and/or the question wording are crucial to the analysis.
2. John E. Mueller, *War, Presidents and Public Opinion* (New York: Wiley, 1973); and idem, "Presidential Popularity from Truman to Johnson," *American Political Science Review* 64 (March 1970): 18-34.
3. Bernard Weinraub, in the *New York Times*, 28 May 1980.
4. CBS News /*New York Times* poll, 2-7 August 1980. The Carter press conference took place on 4 August, in the middle of the interviewing period. Respondents interviewed before and during the conference, and those interviewed afterward, were treated as distinct samples and weighted separately, so the resulting distribution of respondents from both groups are the same for age, education, race, sex, region, and political party.

	Democratic Preference	
	Before Conference	After Conference
Carter	43%	57%
Kennedy	43	32

5. CBS News interviews with delegates to the Democratic convention.
6. CBS News/*New York Times* poll, 10-14 April 1980. The question asked was: "Suppose Jimmy Carter and Ronald Reagan *were* the two parties' candidates in November. Would you be satisfied choosing between them, or would you want other choices?" 48 percent said they would be satisfied, 47 percent said they would want other choices. The question was repeated in June with almost exactly the same results. In June and September, respondents were also asked if they were satisfied with the *three* choices facing them. 45 percent of the registered voters interviewed in mid-September said they wanted more than those three choices.

7. Voters reinterviewed after the election were asked two separate questions about the reasons for their vote. The first was: "What would you say was the single most important reason you had for voting for − − −?" The second was: "Did you decide on your candidate mainly because you liked him, or because you didn't like the others?"

8. CBS News/New York Times 1980 Election Day poll. Respondents were asked to choose two out of ten listed reasons for supporting their candidate and to select two of eight issues as the issues that most affected the way they voted. "It's time for a change" was checked by 38 percent of the Reagan voters. The next most frequently cited reasons were "He's my party's candidate" and "He has good judgment," each named by 12 percent of Reagan's voters.

9. Bernard Weinraub, in the New York Times, 19 October 1980.

10. On the role of issues in elections, see Richard Niemi and Herbert Weisberg, Controversies in American Voting Behavior (San Francisco: Freeman, 1976), chaps. 2, 3; Benjamin Page, Choices and Echoes in Presidential Elections (Chicago: University of Chicago Press, 1979); and Gerald Pomper, Voter's Choice (New York: Harper & Row, 1975).

11. As early as January 1980, two-thirds of the public knew Reagan was at least in his sixties. While relatively few persons claimed his age would determine their vote, public awareness of this characteristic was extremely high for a presidential challenger, particularly at this early point in the campaign.

12. Robert G. Kaiser, in the Washington Post, 20 September 1980. Emphasis added.

13. CBS News/New York Times poll, 29 October-3 November 1979. The question was: "Would you be more likely or less likely to vote for someone who had clear positions on the issues, even if you disagreed with many of them, or won't that make much of a difference to you?" 53 percent said they would be more likely to vote for such a candidate.

14. Bernard Weinraub, in the New York Times, 19 October 1980.

15. Adam Clymer, in the New York Times, 1 October 1980.

16. Respondents who reported a vote different from their stated intention in the preelection interview were asked one open-end question: "What was it that caused you to change your mind?" and a specific question about the relationship of Iran to the change: "Did the news the weekend before the election about the hostages in Iran enter into your voting decision?"

17. See Donald Rapoport, "What They Don't Know Can Hurt You," American Journal of Political Science 23 (November 1979): 805-15.

18. Interview schedule, CBS News/New York Times postelection poll.

5

The Congressional Elections

CHARLES E. JACOB

The drama of national elections is heightened by the element of surprise. Occasionally surprise becomes astonishment, as in the unexpected triumph of Harry S Truman in 1948. More often, surprises are of a milder sort in this age of frenetic poll-taking and media forecasting prior to the vote. Either the presidential race is "too close to call," and the electorate is not really surprised at the victory of *either* contender, or one candidate is so far ahead in the polls that the event of his triumph is met with fatalistic acceptance. Most of our surprises have come to be of a more modest proportion: perhaps the size of the winning margin, a loss in this state or a narrow win in that, the defeat of a party stalwart, or the emergence of a new legislative personality.

One place Americans have learned *not* to look for electoral surprise is in the legislative arena. Congress is always Democratic — more or less. In 1980, anyone whose past votes had contributed to Republican congressional majorities had to be a half-century old or more. And so it seemed on election eve. The most dedicated partisan opponent could not have been surprised at the Reagan victory, although the landslide quality *did* surprise nearly everyone. Yet real surprise, indeed astonishment, came in the most unfamiliar area. When the 97th Congress assembled in January 1981, Republicans controlled the Senate for the first time in twenty-eight years and the Democratic majority in the House was as thin as it had been at any time during that period. The numbers were as follows:

House: 243 Democrats, 192 Republicans
Senate: 53 Republicans, 47 Democrats

The first observation to come out of these electoral counts is that the American people resoundingly reversed the verdict of 1976. In that year, in addition to electing a Democrat as President, the voters registered partisan sentiments by reinstating the extraordinary (over two-thirds in the House) Democratic majorities in Congress. Four years later, in a determination for political change, not only was an administration turned out of office but its cohorts in Congress were punished. In retrospect, perhaps the most significant quality of the 1980 elections at the national level will be the judgment of a party victory.

ELECTIONS AND THE NEW CONGRESS

It is a truism that American political parties are coalitions of ideologically diverse groupings in the polity. Yet these coalitions have left-liberal (Democratic) and right-conservative (Republican) centers of gravity, and the numerical weight of one over another tends to accentuate that center. Moreover, to a President, the force of the symbolic party tie of his political brethren is a natural and promising target of persuasion. Thus Presidents appreciate Congresses controlled by their partisan associates. During the past half century, the usual lack of legislative party control has bedeviled Republican Presidents. For, while party fortunes have experienced their ups and downs, only rarely have majorities of Republicans been returned to office with Republican Presidents. Indeed, President Eisenhower was the last Republican to enjoy partisan congressional kinship for even a brief time (1953-55). To survey how Congresses have varied more recently, consider table 5.1

A number of observations can be made. First, the largest Democratic majorities in recent years coincided with the Johnson landslide election of 1964. The first Nixon election of 1968 brought with it only slight increases in the size of the Republican congressional contingent, still a minority in the 91st Congress. The Nixon reelection landslide of 1972 coincided with a Republican House minority increase of only eleven members, and Republican Senate strength actually *decreased* by two. The close Carter victory in 1976 coincided with only the slightest increase in congressional majorities. On the other hand, attention to midterm election results (even-numbered Congresses) discloses a consistent decline in the representation of the President's partisans, validating the conventional wisdom that the President's party can expect to lose seats at midterm. Nonetheless, an interesting variation in the size of these losses will be taken up when we consider the future of the Republicans in Congress later in this chapter.

TABLE 5.1

CONGRESSIONAL PARTY CONTROL, 1965–83*

Congress	Years	Party Alignment			President
97th	1981-83	House:	243D,	192R	Reagan (R)
		Senate:	53R,	47D	
96th	1979-81	House:	276D,	159R	Carter (D)
		Senate:	59D,	41R	
95th	1977-79	House:	292D,	143R	Carter (D)
		Senate:	62D,	38R	
94th	1975-77	House:	291D,	144R	Ford (R)
		Senate:	61D,	39R	
93rd	1973-75	House:	248D,	187R	Ford, Nixon (R)
		Senate:	57D,	43R	
92nd	1971-73	House:	255D,	177R	Nixon (R)
		Senate:	55D,	45R	
91st	1969-71	House:	243D,	192R	Nixon (R)
		Senate:	58D,	42R	
90th	1967-69	House:	248D,	187R	Johnson (D)
		Senate:	64D,	36R	
89th	1965-67	House:	295D,	140R	Johnson (D)
		Senate:	67D,	33R	

*At election.

SOURCES: *Congressional Quarterly Weekly Report* 38 (8 November 1980): 3300; *Congressional Quarterly Weekly Report* 36 (11 November 1978); *Congressional Quarterly Weekly Report* 34 (6 November 1976): 3123; *Congressional Quarterly Weekly Report* 32 (9 November 1974): 3060; *Congressional Quarterly Weekly Report* 30 (11 November 1972): 2952, 2958; and U. S. Government, *Statistical Abstract of the United States* 93 (1972): 366.

The House

If the main point of the electoral outcome in the House is the surprising gain of 33 seats by the Republicans, resulting in the largest GOP contingent since 1956,[1] the contrapuntal theme is the survival and vitality of incumbent advantage. The potency of incumbency, usually taken to result from constituent service performed by legislators, has received much attention in recent years by students of American politics.[2] For, while 31 incumbents were defeated, this is a number only marginally larger than the average mortality rate in recent elections. Consider the overall results.

The 435 seats of the 96th Congress were up for election. Forty-three incumbents retired, including a handful who were defeated in primaries. This left

392 incumbents who contended. Of these, 361 were reelected (92 percent). There were 74 freshmen, of whom 52 were Republicans and 22 were Democrats. The remarkable thing in partisan terms is that only 3 of the defeated incumbents were Republicans. The number of freshmen has been nearly the same for the past three elections, and the high survival rate among those freshmen resulted in a 97th Congress in which just short of a majority of the membership has served for two terms or less.

Although the loss of 33 seats, as such, is less than devastating for the Democrats, the real toll of 1980 was the defeat of an unusually large number of House leaders. At least 8 Democrats who held leadership positions were ousted. The most important included John Brademas of Indiana, the Chief Whip (and thus in direct line for the Speakership); Al Ullman, chairman of the key Committee on Ways and Means; three other committee chairmen; and the head of the Democratic Congressional Campaign Committee, James Corman.[3] The portentous lesson that should be drawn is that in 1980 the Republicans rediscovered the joys of party. That is, a concerted, centrally directed and funded national party campaign was conducted to persuade the electorate to "Vote Republican. For a Change." A multimillion-dollar national television campaign for a Republican Congress emphasized the main themes of "getting government off the people's back" and repairing a damaged defense establishment.[4] With the additional aid of independent political action committees (most notably, the National Conservative Political Action Committee), key congressional leaders were targeted for defeat. The strategy worked to a great extent, producing a large conservative Republican minority and the promise of a conservative congressional majority for the 97th Congress.

The Senate

While Republicans as a party made great strides in the House elections, the Senate takeover was a victory beyond expectations. As in the recent past, incumbent advantage did not serve the senators well. Of 25 incumbents who stood for reelection, only 16 survived, or slightly less than two-thirds (compared to the 92 percent House survival rate). Of the 34 Senate seats up, 9 senators retired or, in the case of 4, suffered primary defeats. Every one of the 9 incumbents who lost was a Democrat; the Republicans experienced a net gain of 12 seats, the largest for either party since 1958. The Republican majority of 53 is the largest since the days of Herbert Hoover (1929-31).[5] Finally, of the 18 new freshmen senators, 16 are Republicans (with a six-year lease on political life). Consider the body of defeated Democratic incumbents, as shown in table 5.2.

The table reveals that 156 years of senatorial seniority were washed out in November, but that is surely secondary to the more meaningful retirement of a

TABLE 5.2
DEFEATED SENATE INCUMBENTS, 1980

Member	Party	State	Terms Served
Talmadge	Democrat	Georgia	4
Church	Democrat	Idaho	4
Bayh	Democrat	Indiana	3
Culver	Democrat	Iowa	1
Durkin	Democrat	New Hampshire	1
Morgan	Democrat	North Carolina	1
McGovern	Democrat	South Dakota	3
Magnuson	Democrat	Washington	6
Nelson	Democrat	Wisconsin	3

SOURCES: *Congressional Quarterly Weekly Report* 38 (8 November 1980): 3302; and *Congressional Directory* (1979), 96th Congress, 1st sess. passim.

generation of Senate leaders. Repeating the lesson of the House with greater impact, conservative Republican party leadership mounted a supremely effective campaign against not only Democrats, but liberal Senate leadership. Fifteen months before the elections, the National Conservative Political Action Committee mounted a $700,000 campaign to defeat those whom it characterized as the "most distasteful" members of the Senate.[6] The initial political "hit list" consisted of Church, McGovern, Culver, Bayh, and Cranston. As the campaign proceeded, additional Democratic liberals were targeted by NCPAC and the Republicans. The same themes were reiterated in media appeals as those applicable to the House elections and the Presidency itself. Clearly, the unified party campaign (with PAC help) goes a long way to explain the defeat of the Senate liberals. An aspect of that is the Reagan-as-Republican sweep of electoral votes across the nation, which we shall investigate shortly.[7]

Before considering the coattail relationship, two other factors present in the Senate defeats should be noted. First, there is the matter of the weight of great seniority. Donald Matthews, in a classic study of the Senate, perceived a senatorial life cycle.[8] Once elected, a senator, unlike his counterpart in the House, has a six-year hold on office. During this time he may build on initial constituency support, applying all the advantages of incumbency. Given the substantial resources attending the office — publicity, allowances, and the ability to perform services for his state — along with relatively small leadership and initiative-taking responsibilities *within* the Senate, the freshman can concentrate on "nursing" his constituency. If he is successful in these areas, he may even overcome the disadvantage of a competitive party system in the state or negative circumstances in the larger political and economic environment over which he may have limited control. Still, surviving the first term is the crucial challenge. Once reelected, Matthews found that the opportunity for going on successfully to a third term is greatly enhanced.

The next stage of the cycle comes into focus. By the beginning of the third term, typically, the senator is compelled to assume more internal, institutional responsiblities, which seniority mandates in the Senate. He is a high-ranking member of several committees, possibly chairman. Surely he will chair one or more subcommittees. His relationships with the President and the executive branch become increasingly involved. He often pays less attention to his home base. Fences go unmended. Local opposition groups are encouraged. The result, Matthews found, was that upon approaching the fourth-term contest, a senator is less secure than at any time after his first term: "Beyond a third term, the senior senator has less chance of gaining reelection than a freshman!"[9] Thus it may be that "excessive" seniority provided an additional handicap for half the members on our defeated list.

Finally, though we seek regularities in explanation, there are always idiosyncratic factors, peculiarities of the individual case. For example, in 1980, not only did Herman Talmadge of Georgia come to the contest with 24 years of seniority weighing on him but he had been denounced by the Senate for financial misconduct, had undergone a highly contentious divorce action, had admitted to alcoholism, and had fought off a serious primary election opponent. In retrospect, it seems unsurprising that he was not returned to office. Another apparent instance of the importance of individual factors was age. Six-term, seventy-five-year-old Warren Magnuson was not helped by the contrast between his vitality and that of his opponent, who reminded the voters periodically of his zest for mountain climbing and bicycle racing.[10]

Coattails and Ticket Splitting

A factor that is always of interest in congressional elections that coincide with presidential elections is the relationship between the two. A persistent thesis of political science suggests that a coattail effect should appear. The theory rests on the strength of party identification, however, and this has clearly declined in recent years. It was once supposed that the presidential candidate, as the main attraction and the name appearing at the top of the ballot in any constituency, would help candidates of his party farther down the list. That is, the *partisan* choice at the outset would be crucially important to subsequent voter choices. This could be particularly true in jurisdictions that provided for voting the "straight ticket" in one act.[11]

But there is an antithesis to the coattail thesis: the phenomenon of ticket splitting, or voting for candidates of different parties in different offices. For present purposes, let us sample the relationship between presidential and congressional choices by looking more closely at the thirty-four senatorial elections that occurred across the country (see table 5.3).

TABLE 5.3
SENATE AND PRESIDENTIAL VICTORY MARGINS, 1980

State	Winning Senate Party Margin (in %)	Winning Presidential Party Margin (in %)
Alabama	3R	2R
Alaska	10R	29R
Arizona	1R	33R
Arkansas	18D	.01R
California	20D	17R
Colorado	2D	24R
Connecticut	14D	9R
Florida	2R	16R
Georgia	2R	15D
Hawaii	60D	2D
Idaho	1R	42R
Illinois	13D	8R
Indiana	8R	18R
Iowa	8R	12R
Kansas	28R	24R
Kentucky	30D	1R
Louisiana	D*	6R
Maryland	32D	3D
Missouri	4D	7R
Nevada	20R	37R
New Hampshire	4R	30R
New York	1R	3R
North Carolina	.1R	2R
North Dakota	42R	37R
Ohio	42D	11R
Oklahoma	10R	25R
Oregon	8R	9R
Pennsylvania	3R	7R
South Carolina	44D	2R
South Dakota	19R	29R
Utah	48R	52R
Vermont	2D	5R
Washington	8R	11R
Wisconsin	2R	4R

*No opponent.

SOURCE:*Congressional Quarterly Weekly Report* 38 (15 November 1980): 3371.

We can see that President Carter won in only three states (Georgia, Maryland, and Hawaii) that had Senate races. In the first, the Republican senatorial candidate won, and in the other two the Senate Democratic winners outpolled the President 10 to 1 and 30 to 1 respectively. Obviously, there were no presidential coattails.

Among the 21 Republican senatorial victors, 18 had smaller pluralities than did candidate Reagan, indicating that, if anything, Reagan at the head of the ticket may have helped many of these candidates. In a few cases the help may have been crucial to the Senate victor, as in Arizona where Barry Goldwater managed to achieve reelection by only one percentage point while Reagan carried the state by 33 percent. Likewise, Reagan, who won New York by a 3 percent plurality, probably helped Senator Alphonse D'Amato, who won by only 1 percent in a three-way race. The best case for the pulling power of the Reagan coattails is surely the North Carolina outcome where Republican senatorial candidate John East won the Senate seat by a mere 7,000 votes out of nearly 2 million, while Reagan carried the state by 2 percent of the two-party vote.

For some candidates, the macabre side of the coattail theory suggests a downward drag to defeat rather than a boost to victory. The summer of 1980 found a number of Democratic congressional candidates worried about the damage their association with the incumbent President, who was far behind candidate Reagan in the polls, might do to their own electoral chances. In August, the list of the vulnerable (those who had won their previous election by 55 percent or less) circulated among Democratic congressional campaign strategists, and many of them determined to support the "open convention" idea in the upcoming Democratic conclave.[12] This was a last-ditch attempt to unseat the incumbent President and replace him with a more popular ticket leader, Senator Edward Kennedy. The attempted *putsch* failed, but the vulnerable legislators were not decimated in any case. Of the nervous 44, 32 (or 73 percent) won reelection in a tribute to voter ticket splitting, thus overcoming the liability of an unpopular President.

THE NEW CONGRESS: BEHAVIORAL EXPECTATIONS

In examining the new Congress, one is interested in such things as its potential effectiveness as a legislative body, the ideological tendencies that are likely to predominate, and the nature of its relationships with the President in the enactment of public policies. This section looks at some relevant evidence in search of clues that might help to predict future directions.

Experience
Particularly in recent decades, the Congress has been characterized as a body of political professionals. That is, the great proportion of its members have been people who moved into national legislative office after a considerable apprenticeship in politics and public office at state and local levels. Moreover, upon

arriving in Congress — especially in the House of Representatives — members tended to stay on, making a career on Capitol Hill. Indeed, just a few years ago, the *average* tenure of members of the House was eleven years. The style of work in Congress has also taken on some of the qualities of a professional, bureaucratic organization. The geometric growth in congressional staff is symptomatic.[13] Stable tenure, along with other internal factors, gave rise to discussions about the institutionalization of the House of Representatives.[14] The fact that a near majority of the House has come to office since 1976, however, suggests that the reign of stability is likely to continue to be challenged, as it has been during recent Congresses. This countertrend is also evident in the Senate, where a combination of retirements and incumbent defeats in 1980 resulted in nearly one-fifth of that body being newcomers.

But what of the political experience of these new members of Congress? Background information on these freshmen indicates that the path to Washington remains marked by stopovers at the statehouse, mayor's office, or city council chamber, though this is more true of senators, as might be expected, than of freshmen representatives.

Two-thirds of House freshmen and nearly 90 percent of the freshmen senators have been engaged in politics prior to election to their present offices. The partisan breakdown suggests that Democratic freshmen are somewhat more professional than their Republican counterparts. The two Senate Democratic freshmen were both practiced politicians, Christopher Dodd of Connecticut having promoted himself after serving three terms in the House and Alan Dixon of Illinois having spent nearly all his adult life in state-level positions, both legislative and executive. Two of the Republican freshmen senators stand out as newcomers to political life: Senator Jeremiah Denton of Alabama is a former admiral and prisoner of war in Vietnam, and Senator John East was a professor of political science at East Carolina University. The experience of the rest of the Republican freshmen senators ranges from service in the House shared by six (Quayle of Indiana, Grassley of Iowa, Abdnor of South Dakota, Andrews of North Dakota, Symms of Idaho, and Kasten of Wisconsin) to the local experience of the former supervisor of the Town of Hempstead, New York Senator Alphonse D'Amato.[15]

Let us suppose that effectiveness in Congress is partly related to an acquaintance with the political skills of bargaining and negotiation and a familiarity with complex institutional structure that provides a sense of place. Then one would anticipate that the freshmen Democrats of the House would be at somewhat of an advantage, an edge that may come in handy given their diminished numbers.

Liberalism and Conservatism in the New Senate

Positions on the great issues of American politics are conventionally polarized between traditional tendencies toward liberalism or conservatism. To be sure, these ideological labels are not exact. Much philosophical debate about what really *is* the liberal or conservative position on particular issues is a commonplace of political diaglogue. Yet the distinctions are useful; more important, most political figures think of themselves as predominately one or the other, and this self-designation has much to do with their actual behavior.

In Congress, granting the exceptions that always exist, liberals *tend* to be more open to social and political experimentation than their conservative counterparts do. They *tend* to favor domestic social welfare and economically redistributive programs as against the normal conservative suspicion of such thrusts. They *tend* to tolerate a larger role for the federal government and freer government spending. Conservatives have an ingrained skepticism about big government and advocate a tighter rein on the public treasury.

Unable to examine in necessary depth the liberal or conservative behavior of every congressman and senator, the political analyst seeks shortcuts, indicators of ideological placement. The most common of these shortcuts is an examination of the evaluations of legislative behavior made by groups that define themselves as standard-bearers of ideological positions. Several such groups routinely monitor the voting records of every legislator each year. Among them are the chief liberal groups—Americans for Democratic Action (ADA) and the Committee on Political Education of the American Federation of Labor-Congress of Industrial Organizations (COPE); and the chief conservative groups—Americans for Constitutional Action (ACA) and the Chamber of Commerce of the United States (CCUS). Each year these groups select about twenty major issues before Congress, define the "correct" ideological position on the issue, and score the legislators on whether they conform to the liberal or conservative position.

The 1979 scores awarded for liberalism by ADA–COPE (averaged) will be examined for those members of the Senate who resigned, retired, or were defeated in 1980. Fourteen Democrats and 4 Republicans fell into this category. They were replaced by 16 freshmen Republicans and 2 freshmen Democrats. The purpose is to find the extent of ideological change independent of partisanship and therefore to make an inference about the ideological quality of the new freshman class in the Senate.

There is a difficulty in comparison, however. Most of the freshmen senators do *not* have ADA–COPE scores because most of them did not hold positions rated by ADA before entering the Senate. We shall try to surmount this difficulty by reference to another indicator of ideology: the evidence of support

TABLE 5.4
IDEOLOGY AND SUCCESSION IN THE SENATE

State	Defeated Incumbent	ADA-COPE Rating	Winner	Support Groups
Georgia	Talmadge (D)	37	Mattingly (R)	C, 1
Idaho	Church (D)	54	Symms (R)	C, 2
Indiana	Bayh (D)	82	Quayle (R)	C, 2
Iowa	Culver (D)	87	Grassley (R)	C, 2
New Hampshire	Durkin (D)	57	Rudman (R)	—
North Carolina	Morgan (D)	35	East (R)	C, 3
South Dakota	McGovern (D)	97	Abdnor (R)	C, 2
Washington	Magnuson (D)	74	Gorton (R)	—
Wisconsin	Nelson (D)	86	Kasten (R)	C, 1
	Retired		Successor	
Alabama	Stewart (D)*	56	Denton (R)	C, 3
Alaska	Gravel (D)*	74	Murkowski (R)	C, 1
Connecticut	Ribicoff (D)	77	Dodd (D)	L, 3
Florida	Stone (D)*	22	Hawkins (R)	C, 2
Illinois	Stevenson (D)	71	Dixon (D)	L, 3
North Dakota	Young (R)	16	Andrews (R)	C, 1
Oklahoma	Bellmon (R)	23	Nickles (R)	C, 2
New York	Javits (R)*	71	D'Amato (R)	C, 1
Pennsylvania	Schweiker (R)	32	Specter (R)	C, 1

*Defeated in primary contest.

SOURCES: *Congressional Quarterly Weekly Report* 38 (26 April 1980): 1117; idem (8 November 1980): 3329-34.

given by several ideological groups to the campaigns of the senatorial candidates. This support took the form of endorsements, financial contributions, and general electioneering. There are seven such groups, four liberal and three conservative. ADA and COPE are represented among the four liberal support groups, and ACA is represented among conservative support groups. In addition, on the liberal side, the National Committee for an Effective Congress and the United Auto Workers were active. On the conservative side, the two additional rating groups were the Business-Industry Political Action Committee and the National Conservative Political Action Committee.[16] Table 5.4 reports the nature of support, liberal or conservative, and the number of groups supporting each freshman elected.

The inference made about ideological support being comparable to ideological ratings is lent additional confidence based upon experience. Four years ago, in speculating about the future behavior of the newly elected lawmakers, the same support group–liberal/conservative tendencies were hypothesized.[17] We are now in a position to look at the record to determine validity. On checking the ADA–COPE and ACA scores for 1979 of those Democrats elected in

1976 with liberal support and Republicans elected in 1976 with conservative support we find the following relationship:

Republican-conservatives: ACA (1979) 72.5%
Democratic-liberals: ADA (1979) 64.4%

The contrasts disclosed in table 5.4 are revealing. At bottom, we are looking at a Republican sweep that is also a conservative sweep. Every freshman Republican (except for two who rejected PAC suport) was endorsed by one or more conservative groups in 1980. Moreover, those sponsored Republicans elected to the Senate from seats in the House, and who therefore brought with them conservative records, had 1979 ACA scores as follows: Symms, 100 percent; Quayle, 91 percent; Grassley, 88 percent; Abdnor, 96 percent; and Andrews, 88 percent.[18] On the other hand, the Democratic incumbent losers, except for the four Deep Southerners, were liberal stalwarts for many years. Indeed, in the face of the concerted NCPAC assault begun against several of them a year before the election, some Senate liberal leaders moderated their positions throughout 1979, thus appearing less fully liberal than normally. *Congressional Quarterly* reported in 1980 that nine liberal Democratic senators (some of whom would be reelected in the fall) received ADA scores on average ten points below the previous year's tally.[19] In sum, political behavior in the Senate of the 97th Congress should be markedly more conservative than it has been in many years, due to the sweep of conservative Republicans. One detects no Javitses, Mathiases, or Weickers in this freshman contingent.[20]

Liberalism and Conservatism in the New House
Of the 74 incumbents of the House who either retired (43) or were defeated (31), exactly half, or 37, supported the liberal ADA position more than 50 percent of the time. As might be expected, these were all Democrats. In any case, only half of those who departed could be considered liberal by any reasonable standard.[21] The 97th Congress has 74 freshmen (52 Republicans, 22 Democrats) about whose ideological tendencies we can only speculate. Yet, if we can once again apply the maxim that a person is known by the friends he or she keeps, campaign group support levels for these freshmen may serve as an indicator. The same 4 liberal and 3 conservative groups surveyed in the case of Senate freshmen endorsed and supported House candidates. Table 5.5 reflects the sentiments of these groups in 1980.

In the case of House freshmen, 92 percent of Republicans elected had conservative group support, the average candidate having had the support of two such groups. Among freshmen Democrats, 91 percent had liberal group sup-

TABLE 5.5
GROUP SUPPORT FOR HOUSE FRESHMEN

All Candidates	N	%	Republican Groups	N	%	Democrat Groups	N	%
Group support								
Four groups	1	1				L, 4	1	5
Three groups	20	27	C, 3	13	25	L, 3	7	32
Two groups	31	42	C, 2	23	44	L, 2	8	36
One group	16	22	C, 1	12	23	L, 1	4	18
No groups	6	8		4	8		2	9
Total	74	100		52	100		22	100

SOURCE: *Congressional Quarterly Weekly Report* 38 (8 November 1980): 3329-3334.

port, again the average member garnering the support of two such groups. It is, of course, impossible to infer that the expectations of group supporters will be proportionately rewarded by approved ideological behavior on the part of the new lawmakers. Yet, in only 8 percent of the candidacies were ideological interest groups unwilling to place their bets. One conclusion that seems plausible in terms of net effect rests upon the shattering, better than two-to-one, superiority of freshmen Republican numbers. If the law of chance ordains that the conservatively supported Republican is likely to behave conservatively in Congress about as often as the liberally supported Democrat behaves as a liberal, then these freshmen will, as a body, tilt in a conservative direction.

In the House of Representatives, in particular, an additional factor that influences the ideological direction of the chamber's work beyond the partisan differences is the phenomenon known as the "conservative coalition." Indeed, it throws into bold relief the distinction between partisan polarities and ideological polarities. Since the early days of the Roosevelt New Deal, conservative northern Republicans and conservative southern Democrats have made common cause in opposing the policy direction of the generally liberal, northern Democratic leadership and its supporters. In truth, this has often resulted in a virtual three-party system in Congress.

The conservative coalition comes together only on votes that clearly pose conservative principles at odds with liberal principles, but these constitute most *major* issues. For individual legislators, voting records can be summarized by arithmetic measures. The sum of any congressman's votes in accord with the coalition alignment produces a conservative coalition support score. Reverse behavior produces a coalition opposition score.[22] In any given year, the conservative coalition may appear on about one-fourth of the votes and, on average, will win on two of three such roll calls. In looking at members' individual 1979 scores, it is clear that greater support of the coalition was prompted from several legislators who were under electoral attack for being "too liberal." A further

observation of interest that can be made after looking at individual scores is to
report that of the 32 top scorers in the House who voted with the coalition more
than two times out of three (23 of them being supportive more than 90 percent
of the time) only *one* was defeated in the November elections.[23] And that one
defeat was entirely idiosyncratic: Representative Bauman, Republican of
Maryland, lost his secure hold on his seat *only* after an allegation of homosex-
ual activity was publicized.

It seems clear, then, that the conservative Republicans elected in large
numbers to the 97th Congress will be supported not only by their co-partisans
but by 30 to 40 fairly regular participants in the conservative coalition. On important issues freighted with ideological implications, the possibility for a
working conservative majority in the House is at hand.

THE NEW CONGRESS AND
THE NEW PRESIDENT

Directions in the new Congress — whether it is effective or ineffective, whether
its work is touched by liberal or conservative impulses, whether it strengthens
or weakens support for the entire political system — will be shaped in large
measure by the body's symbiotic relationship with the President. For in contemporary American politics, the legislative process is one shared by 535 legislators
and the President. Modern Congresses demand legislative leadership from
Presidents, and Presidents must work for support from Congresses. A productive relationship depends upon the skill of the President in applying the arts of
persuasion[24] and the ability and will of the legislators to respond. The interplay
of partisan support, legislative institutional arrangements, and issue priorities
on both sides is crucial to a rewarding consummation of public policy.

The Legislative Parties
A major measurement of the stature of any Presidency is the extent to which the
chief executive succeeds in convincing Congress to enact his policies. In the
attempt, Presidents must rely primarily on legislative support from among their
partisans and secondarily on support from the opposition party. Logic would
suggest that the greater the size of the majority of the President's party in Congress, the better are his chances of success. Reciprocally, it would seem that
when the President's party is in the minority in Congress, his programs will
suffer. Success is determined by the extent to which Congress agrees with the
presidential position on policy matters coming before the lawmakers.[25]

If we look back on the record of the post–World War II administrations, Congress by Congress, the most striking conclusion is that even when the President is beleaguered by the minority status of his party in Congress, he will always succeed more than half the time, and might generally expect to succeed in seeing two out of every three of his policy preferences favored. When the President's party controls Congress – even narrowly, as in the first Eisenhower term – he can expect legislative support more than four times out of five.

The data further suggest that the *size* of congressional majorities has some bearing on presidential success. Thus, when the size of the Democratic majority shrank significantly in 1967, Lyndon Johnson's success rate declined. On the other hand, when the President's party is already in the minority, modest shifts in size do not seem to affect presidential success greatly, as in the Nixon years. Cataclysmic events seem to have an impact on presidential success that transcends congressional majorities. Lyndon Johnson's low point (1967–68) coincided with the agony of Vietnam; Nixon's low point (1973–74) reflected the crisis of Watergate.

One piece of recent research reinforces, by a different mode of analysis, the expectation that partisan and ideological distributions of legislative seats are crucial to the determination of presidential success. Hammond and Fraser examined the distribution of legislative seats among Democrats and Republicans, North and South (in order to capture the influence of the conservative coalition) over the past five Presidencies. They determined that faction size in relation to the President's own partisan-ideological persuasion was the best predictor of the extent to which the lawmakers would come into agreement with the chief executive. In other words, a conservative Republican President could expect maximum support when the contingent of northern Republicans and southern Democrats (i.e., the very definition of the conservative coalition) was at its height.[26]

Considering only the partisan configuration of the 97th Congress, the prospects for congenial executive-legislative relations in the early years of the Reagan administration are promising. The loss of many veteran House committee chairmen and party leaders and the infusion of a Republican-conservative stimulus to the already conservative proclivities of the lower house edges that body more rightward. In the Senate, of course, the Republican majority should reinforce the conservative White House leadership. Whether Mr. Reagan can exploit these advantages to maximum benefit depends in part on the ways the lawmakers are organized and incentives are structured within Congress.

Structures of Power

In his relationships with Congress, the President must influence and treat with two foci of internal power: the party legislative leadership and a collectivity of chairmen of the standing committees.[27] In the House, the degree of cooperation Mr. Reagan can expect from the O'Neill-Wright Democratic leadership (after the usual honeymoon period has run its course) will probably depend less on his own charisma than on the leadership's reading of the implications and impact of administraton proposals on the well-being of future Democratic candidacies. In short, soon the Democratic leadership will see its role as gearing up for the 1982 congressional contest. In the Senate, the President should anticipate a more pliant leadership, which corresponds to partisan fraternalism. That the President will not be reluctant to take positions on leadership questions was indicated immediately on his election. At Mr. Reagan's first press conference after the election, he was asked about the possible result of a move by some Republicans to deny the majority leader position to the heir-apparent, Howard Baker of Tennessee. After making a brief supportive statement about Senator Baker, the President-elect concluded with the line: "He will be the majority leader of the Senate."[28] This presents an interesting contrast to another conservative President, Dwight Eisenhower, who declared strict neutrality when urged to take a position on the House leadership struggle among his own partisans and the effort to oust Republican Speaker Joseph Martin.[29]

Dealing with the feudal barons of Congress, the committee chairmen, will be still more challenging to the new administration. In the House, though there were many new Democratic chairmen as a result of the electoral assault of November, they are Democrats who have been around for a while. For example, Representative Dan Rostenkowski, who succeeded Al Ullman as chairman of the powerful Ways and Means Committee, has served eleven terms in the House and that long an apprenticeship on the committee. He will not be reluctant to exercise the independent judgment and personal power that accord with his position. Reagan revenue proposals will receive the usual scrutinizing and deliberate reception in Ways and Means.

In the Senate, of course, the picture is very different. Functional leadership has passed to the conservatives in the aggregate, but the ideological shift *varies* from committee·to committee in significant ways. Consider the implications of table 5.6.

Overall, Senate leadership, like the entire body, is more conservative in the 97th Congress than it was in the 96th and many previous sessions. Democratic chairmen whose *liberalism* scores in the aggregate averaged 62 percent have been replaced by Republican chairmen whose *conservatism* scores averaged 67 percent. And surely the shift from a Kennedy to a Thurmond, or from a Williams to a Hatch, or from a Ribicoff to a Roth suggests the drama of revolution. And yet, as we inspect these transfers of power more closely, it becomes

TABLE 5.6

CHANGING COMMITTEE LEADERSHIP IN THE SENATE

Committee	Chairman 96th Congress	ADA-COPE	ACA	Chairman 97th Congress	ADA-COPE	ACA
Agriculture	Talmadge (D)	37	22	Helms (R)	5	100
Appropriations	Magnuson (D)	74	15	Hatfield (R)	61	40
Armed Services	Stennis (D)	23	46	Tower (R)	6	88
Banking	Proxmire (D)	48	59	Garn (R)	8	100
Budget	Muskie (D)	71	8	Domenici (R)	34	64
Commerce	Cannon (D)	41	24	Packwood (R)	40	38
Energy	Jackson (D)	82	11	McLure (R)	0	85
Environment	Randolph (D)	55	29	Stafford (R)	61	9
Finance	Long (D)	37	32	Dole (R)	21	64
Foreign Relations	Church (D)	54	24	Percy (R)	47	19
Govt. Affairs	Ribicoff (D)	77	6	Roth (R)	21	70
Judiciary	Kennedy (D)	87	5	Thurmond (R)	5	83
Labor	Williams (D)	85	0	Hatch (R)	8	96
Veteran Affairs	Cranston (D)	84	4	Simpson (R)	6	81

SOURCE: *Congressional Quarterly Weekly Report* 38 (26 April 1980): 1117 and *Congressional Quarterly Weekly Report* 38 (8 November 1980): 3305.

apparent that conservative euphoria cannot be untainted. For seniority does work in ways wondrous to behold. In 1981, Republican moderates elected in earlier times and earlier political climes made legitimate claims on some important leadership positions. Thus Senator Hatfield of Oregon is not likely to preside over the appropriations process in a way dramatically different from his Democratic predecessor. No one would suggest that Senator Percy, chairman of Foreign Relations, is a cold warrior of the radical right. (He voted against production of the neutron bomb and for the Panama Canal treaty.[30]) Senator Stafford of Vermont and Senator Packwood of Oregon—chairs of Environment and Commerce, respectively—have moderate-to-liberal records in the Senate.

Beyond obstacles to presidential dominance that may arise from ideological and policy differences, the spirit of the Congress as an institution that has developed over the past decade could result in rebuffs to executive leadership. After a considerable period during which Congress was regarded, and regarded itself, as a rather weak adjunct to executive policy making, the lawmakers increasingly are recapturing a fuller measure of their historic prerogatives. This has come about in two ways.

Congress, having realized that a large measure of its weakness was its own responsibility, engaged in a series of internal institutional reforms and self-evaluations. Was it undemocratic? It proceeded to make assaults on the seniority system in the House, and in 1975 the Democratic caucus actually deposed three committee chairmen. Was it overly secretive? It opened up its committee hearings to public scrutiny and introduced recorded teller voting in the House. Was it inefficient — most egregiously in the handling of its most important responsibility, money matters? It responded in 1974 by establishing congressional budget committees with the power to present a systematic and authoritative *congressional* budget. Did it fail to exercise proper administrative oversight? It began more zealously to employ its investigating committees and its own watchdog agency, the General Accounting Office. In short, Congress has taken significant steps in recent years to get its houses in order.

The other wellspring of a revivified Congress has resulted from its executive target of opportunity. Perhaps it took the excesses of the Nixon Presidency to prompt a retaliatory spirit in Congress. In any case, the imposition of controls on executive impoundments of appropriated funds is a case of Congress striking back, as is the War Powers Act, intended to harness presidential foreign policy adventurism. So, too, is the increased resort to a "legislative veto," whereby the lawmakers write an act with particular provisions that can be implemented only on condition of additional legislative approval.[31] In each of these ways, Congress of the mid-1970s began reasserting itself. And each mode of reassertion has been fueled by large turnovers in membership, bringing to its ranks young, active lawmakers unsocialized to the traditional, conservative norms of the chambers.[32]

President, Congress, and the Future

Considerable emphasis has been given in the preceding pages to the shift toward conservatism that seems to have taken place as a result of the elections of 1980. A presidential candidate who proclaimed *both* his conservatism and his Republicanism was sent to the Presidency on an avalanche of votes. In the process, he carried with him many conservative Republican cohorts. Is the prescription for the years ahead one of conservative realignment in the policy process and conservative retrenchment in the policy product? For several reasons, a somewhat less sweeping verdict seems likely.

First, the concrete meaning and definition of the spirit of conservatism is not unambiguous. Rhetoric is one thing; action is often another. To be sure, for some time now many Americans have been agitated by the demands of bureaucracy, the threats seen in certain aspects of social reform, a decline in personal prosperity, and a sense of loss of international dominance. And the call to return to simpler and more secure, and even allegedly more moral, times is beguiling. Some of those elected to Congress and some of those holding leadership positions in the Senate are anxious to respond to those public frustrations. During his campaign, the newly elected thirty-one-year-old Republican Senator Don Nickles of Oklahoma often repeated a litany of contempt for big gov-

ernment: "I'm against the DOE, HEW, HUD, EPA, and OSHA. . . ."[33] Mr.
Nickles is now, however, part of big government and doubtless will find that
the dismemberment of the machine is not easily carried out.

A week had barely passed since the elections when several of the new
Senate Republican leaders began to speak the language of caution and even
moderation. Senator Thurmond observed that he did not intend to use the anti-
abortion "litmus test" in evaluating judicial nominees. The words "pragmatic"
and "responsible" were frequently exchanged among the new centurions of the
Senate.[34] To be sure, one expects that domestic spending will decline incre-
mentally; (or, perhaps more likely, be stabilized) and that the defense sector of
the budget will increase proportionately. Moreover, there may well be some incremental adjustments made in various public assistance and insurance systems
— fine-tuning rightward. Yet, the very conservatism of the legislative institution itself — as institution — should serve as a brake on drastic change impulses.
The new President and the new Senate are likely to encounter the same persistent institutional obstacles to change that their predecessors experienced. For
generations, Congress has been reluctant, seemingly unable, to destabilize existing relationships among executive branch agencies, clientele groups, and
congressional committee empires.[35]

Dedication to the idea of ideological purity may come to be a bedeviling
problem for the President. It seems clear that Ronald Reagan is no ideologue
himself. Both his gubernatorial record and his campaign issue-adjustments
have the scent of pragmatism (see chapter 6). Nonetheless, some of his "follow-
ers" in the Senate and the party (and such related support groups as NCPAC)
may well end up denouncing the administration. The radical right — as Moral
Majority or in similar incarnations — may be more obstreperous than political
"enemies" on occasion. Dwight Eisenhower had his McCarthy cross and his
Bricker cross to bear. The former senator questioned Eisenhower's very patriotism, and the latter Senator fought to deny him basic constitutional, treaty-
making prerogatives. A scenario that suggests similar harassments in a Reagan
administration is not implausible.

Ideological tensions may prove to be a source of conflict in another way.
As noted earlier, there is considerable ideological variation among Senate
chairmen. The practical lessons of governance, when in power rather than
opposition, will need to be learned: the practices of mutual respect and mutual
adjustment. If they are not, at an extreme, the Senate could be absorbed in in-
ternecine ideological struggle.

One area in which both the President and the Senate will participate, and
one that is bound to result in portentous, long-term influences on the course of
political history, is the capacity for shaping the Judiciary. At the time of the

presidential inauguration, five of the justices of the Supreme Court were over seventy years of age. It is nearly inevitable, then, that President Reagan will be able to shape the general political orientation of the High Court. This was seen in potential before the elections; with the advent of a Senate Republican majority, it seemed assured.

ON TO 1982

In an inquiry devoted primarily to an understanding of elections and their consequences, it seems fitting to conclude with a consideration of future elections. To be sure, this is a matter which, if not already weighing on the minds of the lawmakers we have been discussing, soon will be. At this early stage, what can be said about the prospect for 1982? Three harbingers may be called to account. One concerns elections in the Senate and two are hints about prospects in the House.

The first observation about the 1982 Senate election cites an advantage for the Republicans, the arithmetical advantage that comes from long years in the wilderness of minority status. The 1982 contest will challenge the seats of 33 Senate incumbents, but only 12 of them will be Republicans. Thus, nearly twice as many Democratic as Republican Senate incumbents will be called upon to surmount the challenge of reelection. Unless the Reagan administration has produced unmitigated disaster, Republicans should have a certain sense of security.

The second observation concerns a consummation devoutly wished, but denied to the Republicans. The hope – and the carefully planned strategy of support – in 1980 was to bring about many shifts in state legislative majorities so that the redistricting process in the states, following the 1980 census, would give gerrymandered advantages to Republicans in terms of the redrawing of congressional districts. As the hope of state legislative takeovers dimmed, the idea of "protection" as a strategy followed. That is, if you can't control the redistricting process, try to impose a veto on the other side. Thus, the object became to arrange (especially in those large states where substantial representational changes would take place) to end up with either (1) the governorship in hand (veto potential) or (2) *one* of the legislative chambers dominated by Republicans. Success at the national level did not extend to the states. In the terse phraseology of the *Congressional Quarterly*: "Of the 41 states where partisan legislatures will draw the new congressional district lines, Republicans will be protected in 22 and have complete control in only three."[36] The conclusion is promising for the Democrats in 1982, other things being equal.

The third variable encountered rests partly on empirical data and partly on the faith that there is a regularity in political behavior. As such, it is of little comfort to the Republicans. We return to the experience which teaches that the party of the presidential incumbent loses seats in the House at midterm elections. To justify this judgment, let us consider the national elections of the past score years (see table 5.7).

TABLE 5.7
LOSSES OF SEATS IN THE HOUSE IN MIDTERM ELECTIONS, 1962-78

Date	Presidential Winning Margin (percent)	Date	Net Loss of House Seats Succeeding Election
1960	0.1 (D)	1962	17 (D)
1964	23 (D)	1966	47 (D)
1968	0.7 (R)	1970	12 (R)
1972	23 (R)	1974	48 (R)
1976	2 (D)	1978	16 (D)
1980	10 (R)	1982	? (R)

SOURCE: *Congressional Quarterly Weekly Report* 38 (11 October 1980): 3090, 3087.

At least in recent decades, the larger the winning margin of the presidential victor, the larger the number of House seats lost in the midterm congressional elections two years later. Should this tendency continue into 1982, Republicans might expect to lose thirty to forty seats, other things being equal.

Of course, other things are not always equal.

NOTES

1. *Congressional Quarterly Weekly Report* 38 (8 November 1980): 3317.
2. See especially David R. Mayhew, *Congress: The Electoral Connection* (New Haven:Yale University Press, 1974); Morris P. Fiorina, *Congress: The Keystone of the Washington Establishment* (New Haven: Yale University Press, 1977); and Richard F. Fenno, Jr., *Home Style: House Members in Their Districts* (Boston: Little, Brown, 1978).
3. *Congressional Quarterly Weekly Report* 38 (8 November 1980): 3318.
4. *Congressional Quarterly Weekly Report* 38 (11 October 1980): 2984.
5. *Congressional Quarterly Weekly Report* 38 (8 November 1980): 3300.
6. *Washington Post*, 17 August 1979.
7. Moreover, a further bit of information that suggests the importance of party over ideology in these elections has been produced by Professor Howard Reiter. He correlated ADA–ACA ideology ratings with the 6 percent vote shift from Democratic to Republican in the Senate races and found a statis-

tical relationship of .008 – or nothing. Howard Reiter, oral presentation, annual meeting, Northeast Political Science Association, New Haven, Connecticut, 20 November 1980.

8. Donald S. Matthews, *U. S. Senators and Their World* (New York: Norton, 1973).

9. Ibid., p. 242.

10. *Congressional Quarterly Weekly Report* 38 (11 October 1980): 3005, 3080.

11. See V. O. Key, *Politics, Parties and Pressure Groups* (4th ed.; New York: Crowell, 1958), pp. 615-16; and Warren E. Miller, "Presidential Coattails: A Study of Political Myth and Methodology," *Public Opinion Quarterly* 19 (Winter 1955-56): 26-39.

12. *New York Times*, 3 August 1980.

13. See, for example, Harrison W. Fox, Jr., and Susan Webb Hammond, *Congressional Staffs: The Invisible Force in American Law Making* (New York: Free Press, 1977).

14. The seminal study is Nelson W. Polsby, "The Institutionalization of the House of Representatives," *American Political Science Review* 62 (March 1968): 144-68.

15. *Congressional Quarterly Weekly Report* 38 (11 October 1980): passim.

16. *Congressional Quarterly Weekly Report* 38 (8 November 1980): 3329-34.

17. See Gerald Pomper, ed., *The Election of 1976* (New York: McKay, 1977), p. 96.

18. *Congressional Quarterly Weekly Report* 38 (26 April 1980): 1117. Although he had previously served in the House, Kasten was not a member in 1979.

19. Ibid., p. 1111.

20. An examination of the voting records of Senate Republican incumbents turned up only 8 who supported the conservative coalition less than half the time. *Congressional Quarterly Weekly Report* 38 (15 November 1980): 3366.

21. *Congressional Quarterly Weekly Report* 38 (26 April 1980): 1118-19.

22. *Congressional Quarterly Weekly Report* 38 (26 January 1980): 193.

23. Ibid., p. 195.

24. See Richard Neustadt, *Presidential Power: The Politics of Leadership* (New York: Wiley, 1980).

25. The Congressional Quarterly Service analyzes presidential messages, remarks at press conferences, and other presidential documents and statements to isolate the presidential positon on issues before Congress. Congressional votes are then tabulated in terms of whether the President's position has been sustained or defeated. At the end of the year a percentage

score reflecting the proportion of presidential victories is posted. See *Congressional Quarterly Weekly Report* 34 (30 October 1976): 3094.

26. Thomas H. Hammond and Jane Fraser, "Faction Size, the Conservative Coalition, and the Determinants of Presidential 'Success' in Congress," (paper delivered to the 1980 annual meeting of the American Political Science Association, Washington, D.C., 28-30 August 1980).

27. The best analysis of legislative party leadership in the House is Robert L. Peabody, *Leadership in Congress* (Boston: Little, Brown, 1973), chaps. 1 and 2.

28. *New York Times*, 6 November 1980.

29. See Joe Martin, *My First Fifty Years in Poltics* (New York: McGraw-Hill, 1960).

30. Michael Barone, Grant Ujifusa, and Douglas Matthews, *The Almanac of American Politics, 1980* (New York: Dutton, 1979), p. 238.

31. By February 1980 Congress had passed 167 laws (most of them in recent years) with one or more veto provisions. See *Congressional Quarterly Weekly Report* 38 (8 March 1980): 661.

32. On congressional norms, see Matthews, *U. S. Senators*; see also Richard F. Fenno, Jr., *The Power of the Purse: Appropriations Politics in Congress* (Boston: Little, Brown, 1966); and Roger H. Davidson, *The Role of the Congressman* (New York: Pegasus, 1969).

33. *New York Times*, 14 October 1980.

34. *New York Times*, 16 November 1980.

35. On the "subsystem" or "subgovernments," see Randall Ripley and Grace A. Franklin, *Congress, the Bureaucracy and Public Policy* (Homewood, Ill.: Dorsey, 1976). See also the earlier study, J. Lieper Freeman, *The Political Process: Executive Bureau-Legislative Committee Relations* (New York: Random House, 1955).

36. *Congressional Quarterly Weekly Report* 38 (15 November 1980): 3374.

6

Outlook for the Reagan Administration

R O S S K . B A K E R

Looking back on his two decades of active political life, there is a strong tempta-
tion to speak of two Ronald Reagans: Ronald the Radical and Ronald the Reasonable. The former Reagan is the doctrinaire true believer and conservative
zealot who stokes up right-wing audiences with generous helpings of red meat,
whose ideology has a sharp and well-defined edge, and who has longed for the
day when the principles he has espoused can be brought to fruition in the Presidency.

The second Reagan came through in his two terms as governor of California, but most notably in the second term, and his general election campaign in
1980. This Reagan is the thoroughgoing pragmatist who dwells in the realm of
the practical and achievable rather than the ideal and optimal. The first is the
blunt-spoken, shoot-from-the-hip ideologue; the second is the recognizable
half-loaf politician who practices the arts of compromise and builds a consensus
around essentially centrist programs and incrementalist policies.

It is not the case that Ronald the Radical is a historical figure relegated to
his bygone days of cowboy conservatism who has been replaced by a totally
new persona in Ronald the Reasonable. Reagan is, and probably always will be,
two people who coexist. His instincts and his hard-core following are to be
found on the right. His distinctive qualities have been shaped by these elements
and remain constant. His pragmatic side comes into play as a product of the
situations he encounters, situations in which deep-dyed conservative principles
run up against political realities that call for adaptability rather than rigidity.

By political instinct, Reagan is a conservative; he has been guided over the
years by a number of fundamental beliefs about the nature of government, the
economy, foreign policy, and social concerns. Briefly stated, they are as follows:

1. The greatness of America is the result of the vitality of the forces of the market. Free enterprise is, in most cases, superior to governmental intervention in the economy. The domain of government is best limited to providing a strong line of defense behind which the American economy may flourish and in acting as a kind of referee that prevents Americans from victimizing one another. Governmental regulation tends to create a drag on the forces of the marketplace, which creates inefficiency, low productivity, and even inflation. Large and expensive government, moreover, goes into debt to pay its bills. This tends to drive up interest rates, thereby worsening the plight of the individual citizen.

2. The communist world in general and the Soviet Union in particular are bent on extending their influence and control to areas of the world that are at present noncommunist. To further these ends, the USSR, as the premier socialist state, has launched a major strategic buildup in long-range weapons, enabling it to hold the United States and its allies at bay while extending its domain through wars of national liberation, subversion, or outright invasion, as in the recent case of Afghanistan.

Reagan faulted the Carter administration for policies that failed to render support to friendly governments simply because they were dictatorial. He chided Carter for failure to support the Shah of Iran, for abetting the takeover of Nicaragua by a left-of-center coalition, for failure to support anticommunist factions in the Angolan civil war, and for putting pressure on South Korea to institute domestic reforms. Anticommunism, then, seems to be a sufficient test for whether a foreign government merits American support. The Carter human rights policy had the effect of coercing friendly states upon whom leverage could be applied and leaving unaffected those states of the socialist world whose human rights transgressions were equally flagrant, but upon whom we could exert no pressure.

3. Reagan's social policy is profoundly influenced by his aversion to the domination of the federal government. Apart from social security and Medicare, which he now concedes are worthy of being maintained in their present state, albeit on a firmer financial footing, he sees the states as being better able to shoulder this burden. He believes that social needs vary from state to state and that welfare policy ought to reflect this diversity. In this conviction, he is on the opposite side of the Carter administration and of most liberal Democrats, who favored a national standard that would reduce the disparities in welfare payments prevailing among the fifty states.

The practice of channeling money to the states through programs of categorical grants, each of which is targeted on a particular problem and contains very specific sets of mandates and guidelines, is one that Reagan has vigorously challenged. He favors the use of bloc grants that give local officials a greater degree of latitude as to how they may use federal money. The assumption here is the same one that underlies his thinking on social policy generally: rigid federal formulas and standards fail to take local conditions into account; states and localities are the best judges of their own needs.

Reagan's faith in the remedial powers of private initiative to deal with problems that have resisted solution is reflected in his view of the cities. He maintains that jobs can best be provided through tax incentives to industries to locate in low-income areas and to provide jobs rather than in creating federal jobs programs such as those under the Comprehensive Employment and Training Act (CETA). Such public-sector approaches, he asserts, not only burden the federal treasury but also ignore the promise of the most reliable source of long-term employment, which lies in the private sector.

What emerges, then, is a comprehensive view of the relationship between the private and public sectors and between the federal government and the states that is taken *verbatim* from sacred conservative writ. It teaches that when one is confronted with choices between federal action and private initiative and between national or state-level solutions, the latter pair is preferable every time.

The most tantalizing question about President Reagan is the extent to which he will apply these conservative principles in particular situations. In his acceptance speech at the Republican National Convention, he referred to "our crusade" and asked for the silent prayers of his listeners to sanctify it. To conceive of a political campaign in terms of the church militant was to give heart to conservatives everywhere. For one of their own to have achieved the Presidency would seem to confirm the belief that dramatic changes are in the offing, that fifty years of power devolving upon Washington will be reversed, that the expanding domain of federal power will be arrested, that restrictions on private industry will be lifted, and that the traditional virtues of American life — family, neighborhood, thrift, patriotism, and individual initiative — will be exalted. There is much in the record that suggests that this will be so.

T W O   M O D E L S

The Reagan Presidency: A "Radical" Model

After the ideological indeterminacy of the Carter administration, it will be bracing to have a President who does not shrink from a philosophical label. The intriguing question, however, is what kind of conservative he will be: for as there are two Reagans, there are also two conservatisms.

The first conservatism has often been styled as "populist." In fiscal policy it expresses itself as "supply-side economics." It is based on the controversial premise that massive tax cuts would be an economic panacea that would, simultaneously, create a surge of purchasing power that would reinvigorate industry by providing individuals with the money needed to buy goods and services. Conventionally, such massive individual tax cuts have been seen as worsening the problems of the federal deficit by cutting off the government revenues that taxes provide. The unconventional response to this, provided by University of Southern California economist Arthur Laffer, is that all this economic activity will produce more revenue for government than was lost to the tax cut. It is further argued by the supply-side economists that high taxes discourage productivity and savings and that freeing up money that would otherwise have been paid in taxes would induce people to be more productive and to save, spend, and invest. This theory was made flesh in the form of the Kemp-Roth bill, which had the objective of reducing taxes by 10 percent a year for three years and which Reagan endorsed.[1]

The populist radicals also favor a return to the the gold standard and were able to place in the Republican platform a plank that, while not mentioning gold by name, called for "the restoration of a dependable monetary standard." Reagan, once an apostle of the return to the gold standard, mentioned this controversial proposal less and less as the primary campaign went on and ultimately referred to it only as a matter that was being discussed by his advisers.[2]

In the area of foreign policy as well, there is a well-defined group that espouses a very hard line vis-à-vis the Soviet Union. Members of this group are exceedingly pessimistic about Soviet intentions and feel that only through massive increases in American weaponry can the United States deal effectively with a state that is expansionistic by its very nature. Soviet expansionism, moreover, has its accomplices in the nonaligned states that act as regional staging areas for attacks on pro-Western nations.

Not only do these hardliners dissent, as a general rule, from Carter's defense and foreign policies, but from those of the Kissinger era in Republican foreign policy as well. They are suspicious of détente, wary about strategic arms negotiations with the Soviets, and believe that the USSR must be dealt with only from a position of unequivocal strength. It is a group in which members of the post–World War II foreign policy establishment do not loom large. A number of the more senior advisers have been sailing against the wind since the days of the Kennedy administration.[3]

The Reagan Presidency: A "Reasonable" Model

In major areas of domestic and foreign policy, there is another model that might inform us about the future conduct of the Reagan administration. This is the recognizably Republican administration in which more or less familiar players orchestrate more or less temperate themes in a more or less conventional style. This would be an administration that feels comfortable with big business, that draws upon the talent of major corporations, and that frames public policy with the welfare of major industries in mind.

This administration would be dominated by individuals who feel uncomfortable with such novelties as supply-side economics. As for radical notions such as a return to the gold standard, the attitude of these long-time pillars of Republican economics was best summed up by Herbert Stein, who served as chairman of the Council of Economic Advisers under Nixon, and who once quipped, "This not an idea with much support among my friends."[4]

One of the reasons why supply-side economics has so little allure is that these moderate Republican economists fear, above all else, an uncontrollable inflationary result from massive tax cuts not accompanied by considerable reductions in government expenditures. Inflation is their major preoccupation, and their main weapons for controlling it are through the money supply, through reductions in the cost of government that will bring the budget into balance, and, parenthetically, by tolerating moderately high rates of unemployment.

Their second concern is overproductivity, and on both counts their apprehensions are warranted. The country has seen its basic rate of inflation — apart from such "shock" inflation as OPEC price rises bring about — climb from 6 percent a year to about 10 percent annually. Projected over the next four years, such an increase would bring the annual rate to almost 17 percent. The effect of this, especially on people living on fixed incomes, amounts, in the view of these moderate Republicans, to a form of confiscation.

The productivity picture Reagan will face is equally grim. When Jimmy Carter entered office in 1976, productivity — that is, real output per hour of work — was increasing by about 1 percent annually. Historically, this was not a spectacular growth compared to the 3 percent for the years between the end of World War II and the end of the Vietnam war. Carter, however, presided over an annual decline in productivity of about .5 percent. When worker output declines, each unit produced is more expensive. This makes low productivity a major contributor to inflation.[5]

This group is also profoundly influenced by monetarist thinking. They see the control of the money supply, as defined in the policies of the Federal Reserve

Board, as having a major impact on inflation. In this conviction, they are not too far removed from the thinking of Paul Volcker, whom President Carter appointed to head the Federal Reserve.

A tight money supply can serve to bank the fires of inflation, but it has some unfortunate side effects. It tends to drive up the cost of borrowing money. It inhibits the purchase of major consumer items such as homes and cars. On the bright side, it also tends to strengthen the dollar because overseas investors, in particular, seek out the highest interest rates for their money. Monetary stability ranks high on the wish list of large corporations. It is not, however, in much favor with radical economists who opt for stimulating the economy and enhancing productivity through massive tax cuts and deregulation. Indeed, the case can be made that the two techniques—fiscal stimulation and a stable money supply—would merely result in higher interest rates and more "stagflation."[6]

A moderate Reagan foreign policy would differ more in degree and emphasis than in kind and essence from a more radical one. For one thing, there is a virtual consensus that defense spending must increase. While moderates are more inclined to favor arms control agreements based on present levels of forces than are the foreign policy radicals, there is broad agreement that no treaty that resembles the SALT II agreement will see the light of day.

Moderates would be inclined to go along with the present style of American participation in international organizations. They would be disposed to continue the "North-South" dialogue between the industrial countries and the developing world. They make all of the standard pledges in support of Israel, but favor a course that does not preclude targets of opportunity in the Arab world, especially where oil supplies are concerned.

Alliance relationships are of particular importance to Republican moderates. These are people who prefer to act in concert with our major European allies, Canada, and Japan in any major initiative. They have grown tolerant of NATO members who do not always repond to Soviet moves with the alacrity that has sometimes characterized the United States. These are people who feel quite at home at conferences in Brussels or Geneva and are well socialized into the norms of diplomacy. They are free-trade advocates, supporters of foreign economic assistance, and have come to appreciate the subtlety of dealing with nonaligned countries that do not always see the world the same way we do.

These also tend to be people who feel comfortable in corporate board rooms, in the company of international financial figures, and in the bosom of such nongovernmental institutions as the Council on Foreign Relations and even that *bête noire* of the far right, the Trilateral Commission. These are international managers, people such as the Secretary of State, General Alexander Haig, and Secretary of the Treasury Donald Regan. Vice-President George Bush fits comfortably into this group.

These people would favor a recognizable Republican foreign policy: defense-minded but essentially cautious; committed to the maintenance of the alliance structure but disinclined to get tough with allies who part company with us; eager to win firm friends in the developing world but with a decent tolerance for the ambiguities that govern our relationships with those states; and, above all, reverential of old-style spheres-of-inflence politics that makes the United States and USSR sovereign in their immediate domains.

These two models of the future of the Reagan administration are, of course, ideal types. They suggest approaches to broad areas of domestic economic and foreign policies that presuppose a consistency that is unlikely to develop. Even with a President who is unique in his long-term association with an ideological faction of his party, one must be quick to recognize that his two terms as governor of California were not all that conservatives might have wished. Nonetheless, California, which Reagan repeatedly reminded us during the 1980 campaign has the world's seventh largest economy, is not the United States of America. The national stakes are immeasureably higher, the political forces vastly more complex, the interests considerably more varied, and the constraints much more imposing. Recognizing this, let us now turn to those institutions with which Reagan must deal and those areas of policy with which Reagan must come to grips over the next four years and attempt to discern which model — the ideological or the pragmatic — will be dominant. We will first consider the policies he is likely to pursue and then the institutions that he will need to deal with to bring those policies to fruition.

D O M E S T I C   E C O N O M I C   P O L I C Y

Let us begin the outlook for the Reagan domestic economic policy with an assumption: Reagan sees his principal economic task as providing financial relief for the American middle class. A success here would have long-term beneficial effect on the fortunes of the Republican party. What are the economic ailments of the middle class and what can Reagan do to alleviate them in the policies he pursues?

The first affliction is clearly inflation. Both fiscal (taxing and spending) and monetary (money supply) medications could be administered. Reagan tended to dwell almost exclusively on the fiscal prescriptions in the course of the campaign. His close friend and long-time adviser, California car dealer Holmes P.

Tuttle, put the case for fiscal remedy in a characteristically blunt fashion. De-emphasizing the monetary nostrums, Tuttle said,

> Every politician knows you've got to stop this deficit spending [by the federal government]. . . .
>
> As long as you have a $60 billion or $70 billion deficit, there's not much the Federal Reserve can do [with the money supply]. . . . It's as simple as that.[7]

In economic terms, Tuttle is correct in arguing that nothing could be simpler. In political terms, however, it is a challenge not only in terms of what candidate Reagan promised during the election but a challenge to his own conservative principles. Reagan's decision to press for a substantial tax cut — clearly a gesture to the beleaguered middle class — would cut the Treasury off from a significant amount of revenue unless this action has such a tonic effect on economic activity (as the supply-side theorists argue) that more will be gained in revenues than is lost. Other inflationary aspects of this proposal cannot be dismissed lightly.

An equal or even greater challenge are the cuts in federal spending. Where can they be made? In practical terms, about three-quarters of the federal budget is composed of items referred to as "uncontrollables," such as interest payments on the national debt and the so-called entitlement programs like Medicare, social security, and federal retirement payments that have the additional feature of being indexed (i.e., they rise automatically as inflation rises). Congress indexed these payments in 1974 to keep people on fixed incomes, principally retired persons, abreast of inflation.[8]

A broad-scale attack on entitlement programs is unlikely. Having recanted his old vow of making the Social Security System voluntary, Reagan pledged in his acceptance speech to the GOP convention that "the integrity of all aspects of the Social Security System [must] be preserved."[9] This message has particular resonance in an aging population. New census figures show that the percentage of Americans above the age of sixty-five has increased from 9.9 percent in 1970 to 11.2 percent in 1980. Within a few years, those over sixty-five will outnumber teen-agers; the number of those active workers contributing to the Social Security Trust Fund will continue to shrink, and the number of retirees drawing benefits will inexorably rise.[10]

Other entitlement programs include such sacred cows as veterans benefits, farm price supports, and revenue sharing for states and cities. Reagan will not tamper with veterans benefits because of his personal conviction that they are the least that a grateful nation can do for those who served honorably. He seemed to rule out any move against price supports for farmers in a speech in Nevada, Iowa, on September 30, 1980, saying, "We will not turn our backs on programs that assure the farmer a reasonable income."[11] Revenue-sharing cuts to states and localities would be inconsistent with Reagan's pledge to transfer responsibility for some programs back to the states. The only way in which states could assume these burdens would be through a system of grants or from some taxing authority currently held by the federal government.[12]

But even if Reagan were disposed to take his budgetary hatchet to these programs, he would quickly realize the limits of his power to cut them. These are, after all, programs authorized by Congress and for which the House and Senate have appropriated funds and devised such formulas as indexing. Whatever political problems Reagan would personally incur here, they would pale beside the agonies suffered by members of Congress.

The congressional process of authorization and appropriation of money for programs is highly decentralized. This has continued despite the existence of the 1974 Budget Act, which attempted to put some overall logic into the process and to keep the authorizing and spending committees mindful of the revenues within whose limits they would have to work. The overall product, however, is the sum of a number of individual committee decisions; and it is in this fragmented environment that interest groups can apply the maximum of pressure to have their favorite programs retained or even increased in funding.

The new Congress may be different in many respects from its predecessor, but there is little evidence to suggest that the 535 men and women of the 97th Congress will be any less sensitive to the entreaties of interest groups than any other recent Congress. Ideology, party loyalty, or fidelity to the goals of a new President cannot be wholly dismissed, but it is political survival that dictates to members that they not ignore the messages of those organized interests whose political and financial resources help them retain their jobs. The new President, moreover, has his own electoral debts that must be discharged.

With this in mind, and with the recognition that the main push against inflation will be in the area of federal spending, which of the nondefense budget items seem most vulnerable and which will suffer the least?

An all-out attack on government programs by a radical Reagan administration would have considerable support from conservative intellectuals and activists. They have hungered for the day that would inaugurate the repeal of the New Deal. Many of the newly elected members of Congress share this passionate commitment to drastic cuts in some programs and the virtual elimination of others. The disadvantage that these ultraconservatives suffer from is that they are either outside the new administration or are so junior in Congress that their influence is limited. One of the few at the core of power in the Congress, Senator Jesse Helms (R.-N.C.) is a long-time foe of the food stamp program. As the new chairman of the Senate Agriculture Committee he is in a position to move against the program. Another influential chairman, Robert Dole (R.-Kan.) is a staunch advocate of the program and is unlikely to stand idly by while it is dismembered.

Other conservative members of Congress wasted little time after the election was over in making moderate noises. Senator Robert T. Stafford (R.-Vt.), chairman of the Senate Committee on Environment and Public Works, rejected the idea of a wholesale curtailment of clean air and water programs. Republican National Chairman Bill Brock dismissed the idea that environmental and workplace safety and health regulations will be on the chopping block, saying instead that these worthwhile safeguards "could be achieved better with less bureaucracy."[13]

Sensing this resistance to radical approaches by influential Republicans well schooled in the give and take of politics, Reagan the Reasonable will probably concentrate on eliminating "waste, extravagance, abuse and outright fraud in federal agencies and programs . . ."[14] rather than expend political capital on outright abolition.

How much money can be saved by an attack on these problems is an open question. Certainly, the number of auditors, accountants, lawyers, and investigators required to ferret out waste and mismanagement in a $630 billion government with 2 million civilian employees would be staggering. It is doubtful that much could be saved by better management alone; the cuts will have to come in the substance of these programs if they are to be significant.

One illustration of this problem is the estimated $175 billion owed to the Treasury in the form of outstanding loans, delinquent taxes, and overpayments to social security recipients and grantees. The inability of federal agencies to pursue these delinquent accounts can be traced to a 10 percent decline in available manpower between 1975 and the present. A substantial increase in the federal work force would be needed to collect these debts, but this seems inconsistent with candidate Reagan's pledge to reduce the size of government.[15]

Reagan will probably want to make controversial cuts sooner than later. Deferring them would risk jeopardizing the Republicans' 1980 gains in the 1982 congressional elections. This seemed to be the logic behind the reported recommendations of the economic task force headed by former Health, Education, and Welfare Secretary Caspar Weinberger, which dealt with the possibility of deindexing federal pension programs.[16]

Cutting loose such programs as Old Age and Survivors Insurance, military retirement programs, and even veterans pensions from the index that ties compensation to rate of inflation would indeed save a great deal of money and please ultraconservatives. Politically, it would be dynamite. If Reagan can use his persuasive powers to convince those on fixed incomes that deindexing will create an antiinflationary dividend, which would offset the automatic increases in benefits, it will be an important first step in controlling inflation.

One program almost certain to survive, however, is revenue sharing. The augmented and increasingly vocal group of Republican governors insists upon this, and Reagan's pledge to allow the states to assume functions that are now performed by the federal government seems to dictate that the states receive the wherewithal to do the job. What is likely to happen, however, is that the dollar amounts of revenue-sharing funds will not keep pace with the new obligations of the states, and the poorer states may find that this new lease on life for federalism is a mixed blessing at best. In domestic economic policy, then, Ronald the Radical must keep his reasonable guise close at hand.

DEFENSE AND FOREIGN POLICY

Part of the urgency behind the likely cuts in domestic spending is the state of the nation's defense and the perception that the prestige of the United States, in the eyes of the world, has diminished over the past four years. In his acceptance of the GOP nomination, Reagan reminded his listeners that "war comes not when the forces of freedom are strong, but when they are weak. It is then that tyrants are tempted."[17] He said in a subsequent interview that in the area of armaments, "the Soviets have been racing but with no competition. No one else is racing. They know the difference between their industrial power and ours. And so I think that we'd get a lot farther at the [negotiating] table if they know, as they continue, they're faced with our industrial capacity and all that we can do."[18] There is a clear linkage between what Reagan can do to augment American defenses and the basic health of the economy.

Reagan enters office with American industry working at three-quarters capacity. The national output of goods and services (the gross national product) turned up by a modest 1 percent in the third quarter of 1980, after having sagged to −9.6 percent in the second quarter. High interest rates, which may act as a check on inflation, also serve to inhibit investment in new plant and equipment. Unless he can reverse these trends, Reagan could not hope to deliver on the plank contained in the party platform which promised that "we will build toward a sustained defense expenditure sufficient to close the gap with the Soviets, and ultimately to reach the position of military superiority that the American people demand."[19]

The Radical Reagan would be tempted to make a big splash in the defense area by initiating or reviving a number of expensive and controversial weapons systems programs. He would accelerate production of naval cruisers, main battle tanks, and F-16 fighters. He would resurrect the B-1 bomber killed by the Carter administration, deploy antiballistic missiles around the existing Titan and Minuteman missile sites to secure them from Soviet attack, and go on an unprecedented spending binge directed at new military hardware. In such an effort he would have the support of the vast bulk of his senior defense advisers and such strong congressional backers of increased defense expenditures as Senators John Tower, Henry Jackson, and Sam Nunn. The fact that Jackson and Nunn are Democrats indicates strong bipartisan support for a major buildup.

Ronald the Reasonable would look at the problems of America's defenses in a different way. While making the required gestures in the direction of new and improved weapons systems, he would pay equal attention to such necessary, but less spectactular, problems as training troops and maintaining equipment. He would look at the problems that came to the surface during the abortive hostage rescue mission and the disappointing performance of the Rapid Deployment Force in its maneuvers in Egypt. He would attempt to improve the quality of military personnel by raising military salaries and benefits and even reconsider his opposition to draft registration—a move that would win him support from such influential defense-minded Democrats as Sam Nunn. He would bring all ten army combat divisions stationed in the United States up to a level of full readiness and provide the spare parts for the estimated one-half of all combat aircraft that have been grounded because parts are unavailable.

Rather than break ground for new strategic weapons systems, he would adapt and modify existing systems for new roles. He would reconfigure the Strategic Air Command's aging fleet of B-52s to enable them to fire the Cruise missile, deploy the Minuteman and Titan missiles in mobile form, and opt for a series of technological "quick fixes" while studying the best long-term improvements to the strategic arsenal.

Given the broad range of support for a massive and immediate buildup, and the fact that Reagan is in earnest about the priority he gave to defense improvements during the campaign, the radical approach seems likely. Ronald the Reasonable will, however, put in a later appearance when it becomes clear that the resources of the United States will simply not allow a major augmentation of American forces across the board. By that time he will have learned about the disposition of the military to cry wolf, and the fact that throwing money at defense problems is no more effective than throwing it at social problems.

He will learn that there is as much villainy and ineptitude among defense contractors as is found in welfare programs, except that in the former case the stakes are much higher. When he contemplates the daunting problems of the Trident submarine program, he may well give voice to some of the lamentations uttered by President Eisenhower. At this point, the Reasonable Reagan will assert himself and take a hard look at America's defenses in the light of the limited resources at its disposal.

Will SALT Be on the Table?
One alternative to a costly and dangerous buildup in strategic weapons would be the negotiation of a major arms limitation agreement. For Reagan, however, a buildup would be a prelude to an arms control agreement, not an alternative. He believes that the Soviets will be induced to negotiate an agreement that significantly reduces the military weapons of both sides only when they sense that the United States has the ability to match them militarily. At that point, it is reasoned, the leadership of the USSR will seek to avoid the sharp increase in military spending and diversion of resources away from sorely needed consumer goods and will come to the table to negotiate, not merely limitations, but actual reductions in their strategic forces.[20]

In no event will strategic arms limitations agreements loom as large in the Reagan administration as they did during the Carter Presidency. SALT, after all, does not cover conventional forces, and there is a considerable suspicion here that even if agreements on strategic missiles and bombers are concluded, the Soviets will continue to be a threat to Western Europe and the developing world.

In the latter case, Reagan has made the point, that "there has to be linkage between arms control and other areas of difference. . . . You cannot sit there and negotiate [strategic] arms and pretend that the Soviet Union is not in Afghanistan."[21] He was even more blunt in his assertion that "their overall policy of aggression must be a part of what is going on at the negotiating table."[22] This is vintage Reagan radicalism, which has tended to see strategic arms agreements as giving the Soviets license to indulge in mischief in areas of the world where the use of strategic weapons is not appropriate.

It is a tall order indeed to accept the argument that the Soviet Union will accede to a "SALT III" agreement in the train of a major American strategic buildup and that they will agree to a linkage between strategic arms talks and a promise of good behavior elsewhere in the world. It is unimaginable that the USSR would look with composure on turmoil or power vacuums on their borders, any more than the United States would ignore similar situations in contiguous or nearby countries. As to the more remote areas of the world, the Reagan administration must ponder how far it is willing to go in countering arms shipments and the dispatch of communist military personnel to areas in Asia and Africa. There are limits to the unilateral exercise of military force across the spectrum from conventional to strategic weapons and throughout the expanse of world trouble spots. Some concept of what constitutes truly vital national interests must be formulated; we cannot be everywhere at once, brandishing all manner of weapons with equal effect.

The Alliance Structure

Given the finiteness of American wealth, we cannot, simultaneously, achieve strategic superiority, offset the Soviet advantage in conventional forces in Western Europe, and be prepared to fight limited wars in peripheral areas of the world. We were unable to accomplish this even in our palmiest days. What other resources, then, can we draw upon? A natural place to turn would be to our allies in Western Europe and Asia, who share our values and many of our vulnerabilities.

The North Atlantic Treaty Organization (NATO), our senior alliance, is in its chronic state of disarray. If it were only a question of the size and readiness of the armed forces of the Western European states, the problem would not be so great. There are, however, outstanding political differences between the United States and its alliance partners. The strictly military problems are, in large measure, an outgrowth of the differences over American and Western European perceptions of the seriousness of the Soviet threat to the NATO area, the relative importance of détente, and problems that lie outside the immediate zone of contact between Eastern and Western Europe — notably the Middle East.

On the simplest level, the Europeans are not now, nor have they ever been, convinced that the United States would involve itself in a nuclear war with the USSR if communist forces intruded into Western Europe; and they have doubted the deterrent effect of the American "nuclear umbrella" in dissuading the USSR from taking such a fateful step. So profound were French doubts on this count that President de Gaulle pulled his forces out of NATO in 1967. Efforts by the United States and its Western European partners to share nuclear weapons have borne little fruit and contribute to European suspicions that the United States would not imperil its own safety to keep the Soviets out of Western Europe.

One of the Europeans' principal apprehensions about the determination of the United States stems from the American tendency — most notable in the Carter years — to fluctuate between rapprochement and belligerence in its relations with the USSR. They resent bilateral American-Soviet relationships taking precedence over European interests and reason that they might be better served by striking their own deals with the USSR. In regard to NATO, there is little difference between the radical and reasonable Reagans. A tiny fringe of isolationist conservatives is not likely to be influential in their arguments for a fortress America. Mending fences with our European allies is likely to be high on the agenda.

What Reagan promises them in return for an almost-certain request for higher military expenditures and troop contributions for NATO is a greater consistency in American foreign policy. He will also make the standard pledge of recent Presidents for more consultation with our NATO allies. This consultation will also have to embrace Japan, which is moving to expand its own defense role to counter increased Soviet activity in Asia. Japan might expand its armed forces to approximate its economic role in the world. This could relieve the United States of the burden of defending Japan, which it has borne since 1945.

Increases in military expenditures and harsher rhetoric coming out of the Reagan administration invite speculation on what the Soviet response might be. In a peculiar way, the Soviet Union might be inclined to adopt a measured response. They are aware that a good deal of saber rattling in American political campaigns is for domestic consumption. The USSR, moreover, has tended to feel more comfortable with Republicans in the White House if they are of the "reasonable" stripe. They avoid talking about human rights and steer clear of social democratic rhetoric, which the conservative leaders of the Kremlin find unsettling. They also shun the threats of the conservative radicals to challenge the USSR within its own immediate sphere of influence in Eastern Europe. The reasonable Republican is the recognizable pillar of big business in their eyes, and this is a known quantity. The silk-hatted capitalists with dollars stuffed in their vests so often caricatured in *Krokodil* and other Soviet publications are predictable figures. The Soviets seem willing to write off much of Reagan's confrontational language as the understandable excess of a politician hankering for office. "Expediency," wrote one Soviet journalist during the election, "is setting the tone in the present election campaign. It often determines political life in Washington."[23]

What seems to suggest the dominance of the Radical Reagan in foreign policy is that, unlike his more evenly balanced group of domestic advisers, his foreign policy aides are overwhelmingly hard-liners. Almost uniformly, they reject the Kissinger-era efforts at détente with the Soviet Union. Reagan himself often alludes to the success of John F. Kennedy in standing up to the Soviet Union during the Cuban missile crisis of 1962. While disposed to get tough with the USSR, Reagan will have to acknowledge that the United States does not possess the strategic advantages it enjoyed in 1962. This realization alone would tend to warn him away from a policy based on confrontation with the USSR. Proving that the United States cannot be pushed around is a dangerous game if it is with the Soviet Union that Reagan attempts to make the point.

Reagan and the Third World

It may well not be the Soviet Union whose feet Reagan will attempt to hold to the fire, but lesser antagonists. This is in keeping with Reagan's radical side. He will tend to use the test of a Third World government's attitude to the United States to grant or withhold support. We may see a good deal more covert action by the Central Intelligence Agency in the developing world. Specifically, this might involve stepped-up aid to Afghan rebels; a move to lift the controls on military aid to the UNITA forces fighting the Marxist government in Angola — which was attempted by conservative Republicans in the Senate spearheaded by Senator Jesse Helms on November 19, 1980 — and a much harsher attitude toward the Sandinista government in Nicaragua. It might take the form of increased aid to the conservative government in Guatemala and the centrist coalition in El Salvador.

In Africa, the strong disposition will be to put much less pressure on South Africa to dismantle the *apartheid* system of racial discrimination. There will also be a less hostile attitude toward the so-called territorial solution of dividing the territory of South Africa into a white republic and a dozen small black independent states. The threat of Nigeria, our second-largest supplier of oil, to use the oil weapon on this country if there is a tilt toward South Africa cannot be dismissed casually. Nonetheless, there is some feeling among Reagan advisers that the strategic location of South Africa athwart the world tanker routes and its possession of a number of important minerals more than offsets the Nigerians' vow of retaliation. Energy supply realities, however, may force Reagan to reconsider this impulse to ease up too conspicuously on South Africa.

REAGAN AND ENERGY

The energy problems of the United States are simultaneously in the realms of domestic and foreign policy. Reagan the candidate placed an exceedingly heavy emphasis on increasing domestic production of oil. While some Republicans in Congress maintain the old Nixonian belief in energy independence for this country, and of deemphasizing foreign policy as a device for insuring reliable supplies, the assumptions underlying these convictions have been increasingly called into question.[24]

While increased domestic production will continue to be the goal of the new administration, it will become clear to the new President that our reliance on foreign suppliers will continue into the indefinite future. This realization will give further impetus to increases in conventional forces to protect sources and lines of supply. As Senator Henry M. Jackson, a member of the Reagan advisory team on energy and the ranking Democrat on the Senate Committee on Energy and Natural Resources, observed, "Our access to oil imports will rest in no small part on the strength and credibility of our defenses."[25]

America's oil problems are of both a short-run and long-term nature. The short-term need is to buffer this country from a dramatic loss of foreign supplies such as occurred in 1973 and 1979; the long-term need is to ensure supplies of oil sufficient to maintain enduring growth in the economy.

Reagan can deal more readily with the short-run problem by accelerating the storage of oil in the Strategic Petroleum Reserve. With only 100 million gallons currently in reserve, this country has only a few weeks of stored oil to offset a catastrophic loss of imports. There is strong support for the reserve in Congress and a goal of a million gallons a day pumped into the salt caverns in Louisiana would not be unrealistic. The most sensible immediate device would be to maintain and expand the conservation measures instituted by the Carter administration.[26]

Conservation measures such as the national 55-mile-per-hour speed limit have never been terribly popular with conservatives. The thrust of their energy policy has clearly been aimed at removing obstacles to domestic production by price deregulation on all fuels, easing environmental restrictions on coal and oil shale operations, and speeding up the leasing process for drilling and mining on federal lands. Reagan ridiculed such proposals as the John Anderson plan for a 50-cent-a-gallon tax on gasoline to be used to offset other federal taxes. Reagan cited this as another example of government's assertion that it can use the people's money more wisely than the people can. We are unlikely to see this tax as part of any legislative proposal from the Reagan White House.

An intriguing question is what Reagan will do with the Synthetic Fuels Corporation, which was the centerpiece of the Carter energy program. The objective of this program is to produce, by 1992, 2 million barrels of synthetic fuel a day, principally from coal and oil shale. Reagan may allow the SFC to proceed on its first phase, which is a $20 billion, seven-year effort to provide incentives for industry to develop synthetic alternatives to petroleum. After a few years, he may review the accomplishments of the public corporation and if he finds that progress has been made, he may go to Congress to seek the additional $68 billion to carry the program through to 1992.[27] The likelihood is that by the time such a review is made, so many companies will have invested in synthetics that termination will be politically impossible.

There will probably not be a great expansion in nuclear power plants, even though Reagan favors them. There is a mixed feeling about them among utility executives, although some already on the drawing boards might find the licensing process less rigorous. State action is involved here, and local pressures against new atomic plants can be more than utility companies want to take on. Coal, by contrast, should receive a major boost as an alternative to oil. Reagan favors a softening of environmental restrictions on the mining and burning of coal, and Congress may well comply by modifying laws and regulatory authority relating to clean air and strip-mining.

The windfall profits tax, although it was assailed by Reagan, will probably be kept on the books. The public sense that oil company profits are unwarranted will limit any attempts to tinker very much with this tax. The Reagan administration will also need the revenues that this tax yields to support the synthetic fuel program. There may be an attempt to get Congress to write in exemptions for low-ouput stripper wells or a proposal for plowback provisions that will exempt from taxation those profits devoted to additional exploration, but the Treasury will need the proceeds from these profits if other taxes are to be cut and alternative fuels are to be developed.

The much-maligned Department of Energy will probably wither rather than be abolished. The latter attempt might bring on a fight with Congress, which approved DOE. It may be stripped of its authority over nuclear power, may lose its price and allocation functions, and may be allowed to fall into a state of "innocuous desuetude." This is in keeping with a basically reasonable approach to energy problems that may come to resemble the policy of the Carter administration.

THE REAGAN WHITE HOUSE AND CONGRESS

So much of what Reagan, or any President, proposes is contingent upon congressional action. The Congress that Reagan will go to for legislative authorizations and appropriations is a strange creature indeed. Not since the 72nd Congress in 1931 has a President faced a Congress whose two houses were split along partisan lines. Both houses of the Congress may be vastly more conservative (see chapter 5) than the Democratic 96th, but the institutional forces that have always shaped executive-legislative relationships will probably be more powerful than ideological compatibility.

Reagan must necessarily take a broader, national view of the problems confronting him; members of Congress by their very nature have a more parochial outlook. Left to his own devices, Reagan would probably prefer to avoid some of the bruising battles over busing, abortion, school prayer, voting rights, and open housing and concentrate on economic issues that dominate his agenda and that of the American people, but he may find himself dragged into such battles and risk expending his political capital on controversial issues that he would probably rather avoid. Republican strength is not so great (53–47 in their favor in the Senate and 243–192 in the Democrats' favor in the House) as to force great social innovations on such slender majorities. For the Congress to fall into bitter wrangles over highly emotional moral issues will jeopardize the economic core of the Reagan program. The Reasonable Reagan may soon find himself at odds with radicals of his own party in Congress.

Reagan will find a number of fixed points in the Washington firmament.

> In the triangular relationship among members of the presidency, the bureaucracy, and Congress, the President often confronts a preexisting, entrenched relationship between bureaus and congressional committees and subcommittees. If the President's policy preferences differ from those held by members of the entrenched relationship, and if he feels intensely enough about his preferences to want to pursue them and impose them, then it is inevitable that the White House and . . . officials acting under his direction, are going to be viewed as disturbing influences by members of the entrenched relationship — committee and subcommittee members in Congress, their staff, and members of the affected agency.[28]

Reagan must also take into account the fact that the regulations and bureaucratic discretion against which he railed during the campaign usually have their champions in Congress. A primitive regulatory structure or an excessively simple bureaucracy would not provide an opportunity for members of Congress to intervene on behalf of their constituents and then claim credit for having hacked through the bureaucratic wilderness on their behalf.[29]

Bureaucrats are not without powerful political friends; the friendless do not endure and prosper in Washington. It is here where Reagan's vow to "get government off the backs of people" runs into trouble. Bureaucrats do not climb onto the people's backs without a boost from interest groups and members of Congress. They do not write regulations because they are malevolent but because someone wants those rules on the books. The style of these regulations is not legalistic and impenetrable because that is their preference but because it enables the legions of Washington lawyers to charge clients for the use of their Rosetta Stones to decipher the regulations.

Congress, in the interest of appearing responsive to public revulsion with large and complicated government, may tinker a little here and streamline a little there, but the basic structure of alliances will remain intact. What may compel this Congress to be more cooperative with Reagan's plans for unhorsing the bureaucracy is the temper of a public that wants results. It is, however, doubtful whether the number of cuts that Reagan and a more cooperative Congress can effect in government spending can really have much impact on inflation.[30]

As for federal programs — most notably the entitlements — Americans have shown themselves, in the words of Lloyd Free and Hadley Cantril, to be philosophical conservatives and operational liberals."[31] They applaud government frugality, but when cuts are proposed in programs that benefit them personally, it becomes a case of whose ox is being gored. What is praiseworthy as a principle is odious in application, and members of Congress know this.

Reagan will succeed with Congress until his proposed reductions in federal spending begin to threaten politically popular programs. At that point, the first law of congressional survival comes into force: vote your constituency. The hallowed response of Presidents when this occurs is to take their case to the people over the heads of Congress. Few Presidents have really succeeded at this but if anyone can bring it off, it is Reagan.

THE REAGAN CABINET: MANAGERS AND SELF-MADE MEN

Long-time observers of the Presidency must be forgiven their skepticism when they hear a President-elect promise to fill his Cabinet with the best minds in the country, give Cabinet members unprecedented managerial authority, and have them act as a collective advisory body. Pledges of this kind go back at least as far as Warren Harding. Of more recent vintage are those vows to cut the White House staff down to size and to entrust them only with staff, and not administrative, functions. Cabinet departments, so the standard promise goes, will not be run from the White House. No stern-visaged chief of staff housed adjacent to the Oval Office will guard the access routes to the President. Such pronouncements were made by Ford in 1974 and Carter in 1976. It remains to be seen whether the tough and ambitious James A. Baker 3rd will content himself with routine staff work or will evolve into a *major domo* such as his predecessors Hamilton Jordan, Richard Cheney, and H. R. Haldeman. Precedent argues strongly for the latter.

The Reagan Cabinet listed below is replete with first-rate minds and broad governmental and business experience, but there has been a built-in tension between Cabinet and White House that springs from the inescapable fact that they deal with fragments of policy of particular importance to powerful interests and that he is the President of all the people who must necessarily take the more comprehensive view of the public good. As Charles Peters has written, "Even [those cabinet members] who would theoretically like to cooperate are often persuaded by their subordinates and by their departments' constituencies to see the world more in terms of departmental interests."[32]

TABLE 6.1
THE REAGAN ADMINISTRATION

Position	Name	Age	Residence	Religion	Occupation	Previous Experience	Education
President	Ronald W. Reagan	69	California	Christian Church		Sportscaster; film actor; Governor of California	B.S., Eureka College
Vice-President	George W. Bush	56	Texas	Episcopalian		Oilman; congressman; U.S. Representative to UN; Chairman, Republican National Committee; Director of CIA	B.A., Yale
Secretary of State	Alexander M. Haig	56	Connecticut	Roman Catholic	Business Executive	NATO Commander; Deputy Chief of Staff, U.S. Army; White Chief of Staff	B.S., U.S. Military Academy
Secretary of the Treasury	Donald T. Regan	62	New Jersey	Roman Catholic	Chairman of brokerage firm	Stockbroker	B.A., Harvard
Secretary of Defense	Caspar W. Weinberger	63	California	Episcopalian	Columnist	State legislator; state Republican chairman; Chairman, FTC; Director, OMB; Secretary of HEW	B.A., Harvard
Attorney-General	William French Smith	63	California	Episcopalian	Attorney	Bank director; Chairman, U. of California Regents	B.A., U. of California; LL.B., Harvard
Secretary of the Interior	James G. Watt	42	Colorado	Assembly of God	Attorney	Deputy Assistant Secretary of Interior; member, Federal Power Commission	B.S., Wyoming; LL.B. Wyoming
Secretary of Agriculture	John R. Block	45	Illinois	Lutheran	Farmer	Director, Illinois Dept. of Agriculture	B.S., U.S. Military Academy
Secretary of Commerce	Malcolm Baldridge	58	Connecticut	Congregational	Business executive	State Republican finance chairman	B.A., Yale
Secretary of Health and Human Services	Richard S. Schweiker	54	Pennsylvania	Schwenkfelder	U.S. senator	Business executive	B.A., Penn State

Position	Name	Age	State	Religion	Occupation	Government Position	Education
Secretary of Labor	Raymond J. Donovan	50	New Jersey	Roman Catholic	Construction company executive	Republican fundraiser; labor relations specialist	B.A., Notre Dame Seminary (New Orleans)
Secretary of Housing and Urban Development	Samuel R. Pierce	58	New York	Methodist	Attorney	Judge; General Counsel to U.S. Treasury	A.B., Cornell; LL.B., Cornell
Secretary of Transportation	Andrew (Drew) Lewis	49	Pennsylvania	Schwenkfelder	President of management consulting firm	Deputy Chairman, Republican National Committee	B.A., Haverford; M.B.A., Harvard
Secretary of Energy	James B. Edwards	53	South Carolina	Methodist	Oral surgeon	Governor of South Carolina	A.B., Coll. of Charleston; D.D.S., Louisville
Secretary of Education	Terrel H. Bell	59	Utah	Mormon	Utah Commissioner of Higher Education	U.S. Commissioner of Higher Education	B.A., Albion State (Idaho); Ed.D., Utah
Director, Office of Management and Budget	David A. Stockman	34	Michigan	Methodist	Congressman	Congressional staff member	B.A., Michigan State
United States Ambassador to UN	Jeane J. Kirkpatrick	54	Maryland	Baptist	Political Scientist	Consultant, Dept. of Defense	B.A., Barnard; Ph.D., Columbia
Special Assistant to the President for National Security Affairs	Richard V. Allen	44	District of Columbia	Roman Catholic	Business consultant	Deputy National Security Adviser	A.B, Notre Dame; M.A., Notre Dame
Director of Central Intelligence	William J. Casey	67	New York	Roman Catholic	Attorney	Chairman, SEC; Under-Secretary of State; President, Export-Import Bank	B.A., Fordham; LL.B., St. John's (New York)
Chairman, President's Council of Economic Advisers	Murray L. Weidenbaum	53	Missouri	Jewish	Professor of economics	Corporate and government economist	B.S., CCNY Ph.D., Princeton

President Reagan's Cabinet, like that of recent Presidents, is a collection of cronies and strangers, technicians and politicians, obscure state officials and people whose names are household words. More to the radical-reasonable point, it is a Cabinet divided between those who, in the words of Taylor Branch, "deliver the mail" and those who seek the "Holy Grail." The "mailmen" include such management-oriented moderates as Treasury Secretary Regan, HUD Secretary Pierce, Baldridge of Commerce, Donovan of Labor, and Lewis of Transportation. The "Grail seekers" are Watt of Interior, Edwards of South Carolina, Block of Agriculture, and Special Assistant for National Security affairs Richard V. Allen.

It is a Cabinet that reflects Reagan's electoral constituencies. Environmentalists, liberal labor unions, and low-income groups that did not support Reagan have little to cheer about. Farmers, developers, and representatives of energy interests, who did favor his candidacy, have every reason to feel elated. At the same time it is not a conservative's dream Cabinet. Secretary of State Haig is seen by some on the Right as a disciple of the mistrusted Henry Kissinger; Secretary of the Treasury Regan admitted to having made contributions to Democratic candidates; and OMB Director David Stockman, for all his impeccable supply-side credentials, was an antiwar activist in his youth. If this disparate collection of individuals, representing as they do a broad range of clienteles, can be yoked together for a common presidential purpose, it will be a great tribute to Presidential Counselor Edwin Meese, to whom falls the task of being wagonmaster.

Reagan may be more successful in cutting down to size one White House appendage that has enraged the professional diplomats at the State Department: the Special Assistant to the President for National Security Affairs. Reducing the importance of this job is somewhat easier than limiting the role of the head of the Domestic Policy Staff. There are fewer special interests with high economic stakes riding on foreign policy. Both Reagan and Richard Allen, his senior defense and foreign policy adviser, have asserted that no Kissinger or Zbigniew Brzezinski will arise in the Reagan White House and that the Secretary of State will be preeminent in diplomacy and national security policy.

This structure might be established if the new Secretary of State is forceful and decisive and if the National Security Adviser is willing to hide his light under a bushel. Reagan may also starve the security adviser for staff assistance and force this key aide to run a leaner operation. The world of the Presidency, however, is a little like the world of war; he who commands the high ground has a tactical advantage. So long as it is the National Security Adviser who is housed in the White House and it is the Secretary of State who is a mile away in Foggy Bottom, the former has the high ground. It is he who gets the first shot at the President with his early morning briefing and who tends to set the agenda.

One Reagan innovation that will be interesting to watch will be the Executive Committee of the Cabinet, or the "Inner Cabinet" of hand-picked advisers to aid him with major policy decisions. This may operate in conjunction with a "kitchen cabinet" of personal advisers, which will be composed of old friends who may or may not have official titles. Executive committees of the Cabinet may function as task forces in particular policy areas with their membership determined by the nature of the problem.

A Footnote on Bush
Ronald Reagan is the oldest man ever inaugurated President. This makes us mindful of the importance of his vice-president. Traditionally, those in the second spot on the ballot are ticket balancers or those who bring to the ticket qualities that the standard-bearer may not possess. This was certainly the case with George Bush, who reassured moderate Republicans and proved a great asset.

Bush is not beloved of conservatives. Indeed, in what was an unprecedented challenge to a newly elected vice-president, Paul Weyrich of the conservative Committee for the Survival of a Free Congress admonished Bush to get in line with the conservative policies of the Reagan administration or face the wrath of the right. George Bush is not a man easily intimidated, but he also is a good soldier who is not likely to air any differences that he might have in a public fashion.

Bush's own experience, which he somewhat immodestly referred to as "these fantastic credentials," which include U. S. representative to the UN (1971–72), Republican national chairman (1973–74), envoy to China (1974–75), and director of the Central Intelligence Agency (1975–76), make him the most broadly experienced vice-president since Nelson Rockefeller.

Bush will probably be used most extensively in the area of foreign affairs and also as an important liaison to the small but influential eastern wing of the party. Issue for issue, he was not so different from Reagan in the Republican primaries. It is principally on social issues where the two men differ, and these are elements that Reagan will try to deemphasize. The model of what a vice-president can do is, paradoxically, that of Bush's immediate predecessor. If he were to be used to such good advantage as was Mondale, it might be a sign that the office was getting a new lease on life.

THE WORLD OF RONALD REAGAN

Ronald Reagan feels at home in the world of self-made men. His ideas and instincts have been shaped by the hard-driving studio executives he worked with in Hollywood and by the half-dozen wealthy septuagenarians such as Holmes

P. Tuttle, Justin Dart, Theodore Cummings, and Earle M. Jorgensen, who are his closest friends and are certain to be his informal advisers. For the most part, these are men who began with little, but who rose, in the best Horatio Alger style, to positions of considerable wealth. They are, in short, very much like Reagan himself, whose father was a shoe salesman. With so much confirmation around him of the value of hard work and canny investment, it is not surprising that Reagan sees the world in terms of the power of individual initiative.

Reagan, who is by all accounts a genuinely decent man, sees his friends as the proper model for the path to the prosperity that he wishes for all Americans. He is profoundly concerned about the impoverishment of the American middle class by the ravages of inflation and likens it to the economic depression that cost his father his job. Ironically, the government that gave Jack Reagan a job is the same government Reagan now sees as the author of the misery of the middle class. Reagan identifies personally with their struggle.

While he is assuredly no racist, Reagan bridles at the thought of providing compensatory help to people strictly on account of their race. He is perfectly happy to welcome to the ranks of the middle class those blacks and Hispanics who made it through the opportunity window between 1965 and the present. As for the minority poor, he sees their best hope for prospering in the private sector, which was the locale for his success and that of his friends. That competitive factors have changed in the years since his friends' fortunes were made is an argument that Reagan would turn around and use to make the case that those older and more auspicious conditions ought to be restored.

The restoration of those conditions, a long-shot prospect at best, may depend more upon the energy and determination of those around Reagan than upon the President himself. It has been said of Reagan:

> [For] all of his fiery rhetoric he is essentially passive in his personality. He lets his staff dominate him; indeed, he encourages it to do so. . . . [H]e is more inclined to let things happen than to work doggedly at reshaping the world the way he wants it to be.[33]

People tend to attribute magical qualities to the staffs of candidates who win the Presidency, even those who win it as narrowly as Carter did in 1976. The ultimate success of the Reagan campaign must be judged in the light of the fact that it was not a seamless and flawless operation. Conflict among top Reagan staffers did exist, and there were predictable clashes among ambitious campaign officials. Translated to a Presidency presided over by a man who abhors strife but who, in the opinion of his own press secretary "doesn't kick ass enough," this passivity could spell trouble.

If Reagan finds that the domestic revolution he promised and the economic turnaround he vowed to engineer do not meet public expectations or comport with the most sanguine hopes of conservatives, he may quickly direct his energies to that area in which Presidents are more sovereign: foreign policy. This is Reagan's own preferred area of public policy. It is, in the words of a Senate staff member who has long watched senators struggling to secure seats on the Foreign Relations Committee, "the big boys' playpen." Here the President enjoys greater latitude but also courts the ultimate hazards of life in a dangerous world. We may hope that Reagan, a secure and self-confident man, will not project those frustrations he will almost surely suffer on a world in which the United States is no longer perceived with awe.

The Reagan Future: Ideology and Incrementalism

Will President Reagan play the radical that his philosophical yearnings dictate, or will he affect the sweet reasonableness that his nature and disposition ordain? The answer is that he will go with his ideology but only up to the point where he encounters the cold steel of opposition. He will set a conservative tone and bridle at being labeled a pragmatist. He will not meet the exacting standards of those who are, paradoxically, called "Reaganites." His own words suggest the manner in which he will operate:

> There are some people who think that you should, on principle, jump off the cliff with the flag flying if you can't have everything you want. . . .

> If I found when I was governor that I could not get 100 percent of what I asked for, I took 80 percent.[34]

If Reagan succeeds in getting 80 percent of what he wants, he will have simultaneously validated the principle of pragmatism and vindicated the precepts of conservatism. In a mature system such as ours, that feat would place Reagan in the select circle of great Presidents.

More than any single program cut or increased, and more than any individual policy emphasized or abandoned, the overall tone and theme of the Reagan administration will have the greatest impact on American society. Governmental action in areas of social policy that we have taken for granted for twenty years will slacken. We will see far less official support for busing as a tool of desegregation, affirmative action programs, legal services for the poor, public housing projects in middle-class neighborhoods, and rigorous application of environmental safeguards.

More generally, we will see a congenial environment for the reassertion of institutional authority, a decline in the tolerance of unorthodox and unconventional styles of life, a return to an era in which "standards" and norms are emphasized, and an atmosphere in which "deviant" behavior receives less tolerance. Some of this new tone will be set by federal legislation, but most will be expressed in the attitude of a public bewildered and threatened by the rapid social change of the past two decades.

Viewed in the most favorable light, it will be just one more example of the swing of the pendulum from left to right. Less auspiciously viewed, it provides an estimable setting for demagogues, self-appointed guardians of public morality, and an inquisitional and accusatory mentality. These are not developments that President Reagan would personally favor, but his election has been interpreted by a reinvigorated political right as a license for these impulses. Once unleashed, these forces would be very difficult to control — especially by a man of Reagan's relaxed and easygoing temperament.

N O T E S

1. Steven Rattner, "Ronald Reagan's Economic Policy," *New York Times*, 13 April 1980; and Joseph Kraft, "Can Reagan Control His Own Right?" *Washington Post*, 17 June 1980.

2. David Rosenbaum, "On the Issues: Ronald Reagan," *New York Times*, 22 March 1980.

3. Don Oberdorfer, "Reagan Names 67 Foreign, Defense Policy Advisers," *Washington Post*, 22 April 1980; and "Reagan's Foreign Policy — From Someone Who Knows," *New York Times*, 29 June 1980.

4. Rattner, "Ronald Reagan's Economic Policy."

5. Herbert Stein, "The Economic Issue," *Wall Street Journal*, 31 October 1980.

6. Leonard Silk, "A Tough Terrain for Mr. Reagan," *New York Times*, 9 November 1980.

7. Quoted in Robert A. Bennett, "Trying to Guess Reagan's Policy," *New York Times*, 7 November 1980.

8. Steven Rattner, "The Budget: Missiles, Rockets, and 'Uncontrollables,'" *New York Times*, 20 January 1980.

9. *New York Times*, 18 July 1980.

10. David L. Kaplan and Cheryl Russell, "What the 1980 Census Will Show," *American Demographics* 2, no. 4 (April 1980): 2.

11. *New York Times*, 1 October 1980.

12. Sara Fritz, "What Reagan Will Do as President," *U. S. News and World Report*, 17 November 1980, p. 25.

13. Philip Shabecoff, "Reagan Group Seeks Shift in Pollution Law," *New York Times*, 14 November 1980; and Adam Clymer, "A Chance to Govern," *New York Times*, 6 November 1980.

14. *Washington Post*, 10 October 1980.

15. Charles R. Babcock, "Of $175 Billion Owed U. S., Much Is Uncollected," *Washington Post*, 16 November 1980.
16. Peter Behr, "Economic Advisers Urge Reagan to Cut Some Retiree Plans," *Washington Post*, 16 November 1980.
17. *New York Times*, 18 July 1980.
18. Associated Press interview with Ronald Reagan, excerpted in the *New York Times*, 2 October 1980.
19. George C. Wilson, "Reagan Advisers Urge Military Buildup," *Washington Post*, 16 June 1980.
20. Interview with Fred C. Iklé in *U. S. News and World Report*, 24 November 1980, p. 55.
21. Interview with Ronald Reagan, *Time*, 17 November 1980, pp. 36-37.
22. Ibid.
23. Yuri Gudkov, "Ronald Reagan's Stake," *Novoye Vremya*, no. 38 (September 1980): 27-30, trans. Foreign Broadcast Information Service, 30 September 1980.
24. See Robert D. Hershey, Jr., "Senate Report Doubtful of Energy Independence," *New York Times*, 21 November 1980.
25. Ibid.
26. "Can a Conservative Conserve Oil?" *New York Times* editorial, 14 November 1980.
27. See Rich Jaroslavsky, "Reagan Is Easing Stand on Energy Plans He May Not Be Able to Scuttle if Elected," *Wall Street Journal*, 6 October 1980; and Bill Paul, "Energy Executives Are Elated, Expecting Unfettered Growth With Reagan Tenure," *Wall Street Journal*, 6 November 1980.
28. Randall B. Ripley and Grace A. Franklin, *Congress, The Bureaucracy and Public Policy* (rev. ed.; Homewood, Ill.: Dorsey, 1980), p. 57.
29. See David Mayhew, *Congress: The Electoral Connection* (New Haven: Yale University Press, 1974), pp. 55-57; and Morris P. Fiorina, *Congress: Keystone of the Washington Establishment* (New Haven: Yale University Press, 1977), pp. 42-43.
30. See "The Balanced Budget Is a Placebo," *Challenge*, May/June 1980, p. 3.
31. *The Political Beliefs of Americans* (New York: Simon and Schuster, 1968), pp. 23-40
32. Charles Peters, *How Washington Really Works* (Reading, Mass.: Addison-Wesley, 1980), p. 125.
33. Martin Smith, "Lessons from the California Experience," *Change* 12, no. 6 (September 1980): 33.
34. Interview with Ronald Reagan, *U. S. News and World Report*, 5 May 1980, p. 33.

7

The Meaning of the Election

WILSON CAREY MCWILLIAMS

It didn't mean much. The election of 1980 did not try our souls; it tried our patience. Matthew Josephson's description of the election of 1880 applied a century later: "the indifference of the public seems as marked as the excitement of the professionals seems feigned."[1]

Reagan had a zealous following and there were some Carter loyalists, but most voters saw little to recommend either. Carter was a humorless bungler and Reagan was an amiable simpleton, "the Ted Baxter of American politics."[2] Even the enthusiasm for John Anderson was negative, deriving from distaste for the major-party nominees. A good many voters marked their ballots in a mood of revulsion, and masses of citizens stayed home. The majority of voters finally decided, probably on the basis of the presidential debate, that Reagan was not so kooky as to keep them from gratifying their desire to be rid of Carter. Reagan will have four years to try his hand, but Americans stopped believing in progress in 1980, and few of them feel any confidence in the new experiment. That is the central meaning of the election of 1980.

The election does have other things to tell us. In the first place, the election of 1980 made it clear that the primary-dominated system of nomination is an unqualified disaster. Second, among Democrats, the old Roosevelt coalition is yielding to something we can call the Kennedy coalition. Third, conservative Republicanism is experiencing its own, analogous change, and conservatism may find victory more painful than defeat. The election may, of course, prove to have far more profound and far-reaching consequences for American politics, but no such portents are visible. We will have to wait and see.

THE FAILURE OF THE PRIMARIES

In 1980, there were more primaries than ever and a record number of voters participated in choosing the candidates. Yet, in a seeming paradox, the result was radically unpopular. By any standard, the primaries failed as a method of choosing presidential candidates.

Primaries have been around since the Progressive era, but until the last decade, nominations resulted from a mixed system in which most delegates were chosen by state conventions but candidates tried to show popular appeal in a few, carefully selected contests. In 1948, for example, Thomas E. Dewey was able to offset Harold Stassen's string of primary victories by defeating him in Oregon after a debate, heard nationwide, in which Dewey opposed and Stassen advocated outlawing the Communist party.[3] Similarly, when John F. Kennedy defeated Hubert Humphrey in West Virginia in 1960, he dispelled the fear that his Catholicism would be a fatal liability in Protestant areas, or at least, lessened such anxieties enough to let him win the nomination. But primaries, if often decisive, were only one part of the nominating process. Adlai Stevenson was drafted at the 1952 Democratic convention, and as late as 1968, Hubert Humphrey was nominated without seriously contesting, let alone winning, any primaries. Humphrey's victory, however, was *finis*: the disastrous Chicago convention of 1968 set in motion the torrent of reform. Since 1968, the number of primaries has roughly doubled, and about three-fourths of the delegates are now chosen in primary elections.

The record of the new, primary-dominated system is not impressive. Since the election of 1968, not one first-rate person has been nominated for President. It could easily be argued that Richard Nixon was the most able of the major-party nominees. Of course, the old system sometimes selected mediocrities. The choice between Harding and Cox in 1920 was at least as limited as our options in 1980. Yet in the eighteen presidential elections between 1900 and 1968, only ten nominations went to candidates who are even arguably second-rate.[4] Twenty-six major-party nominations went to evidently first-rate people. For the "smoke-filled room," mediocrity was the *exception*; for the primary-dominated system, it has been the *rule*.

The primaries fail because they are based on the assumption that voting in elections is the essence of democracy. At most, however, voting is the *final* act of the democratic process, deciding between alternatives that have been defined by some sort of deliberation.

Voting forces a decision. Our choices are limited, *and the more limited they are*, the more clearly we know the consequences of our choice. If there are two candidates, by voting for one I am voting against the other. But if there are three serious candidates (as it briefly seemed there might be in 1980), if I vote for Anderson, it is not at all clear that I am voting against Reagan and Carter. If I hate Carter and would prefer Reagan, then I am helping Carter by voting for Anderson. Added alternatives make voting complicated and confusing.

This is especially true since my vote is *irrevocable.* I cannot take it back once I see which way the wind is blowing or after I have second thoughts. If I could change my vote, third candidates would not be so confusing; I could vote for a third-party candidate and wait to see if he or she could make a race of it. If not, I could fall back on one of the front-runners. As it is, however, voting encourages us to narrow our alternatives, concentrating on the two leading candidates so that the meaning of our vote is clear: for A, against B. Even with a more or less proportional distribution of delegates, so that one does not "throw away" a vote for a third candidate, this narrowing tendency is evident in the primaries. In the last stages of this year's campaign, only two candidates remained in each party. An election aims at a clear and irrevocable decision and encourages voters to limit their alternatives.

Deliberation, by contrast, attempts to define the terms of choice rather than decide between them. In deliberating, we value all the complications and flexibilities that elections aim to rule out. We want to avoid limiting our choices prematurely. We want to consider all possible alternatives — all the candidates who might run, for example, not merely those who have announced so far. Similarly, deliberation encourages the exchange of views; it values second thoughts, changed minds, and modified opinions. It is not enough to express our opinions; we need a chance to respond to other opinions. This response is more than "compromise"; it involves the chance for considered judgment, rendered after weighing (and counting) the opinions of others. We want the best chance to refine our thinking before decision; hence, *Robert's Rules of Order* allows a minority to keep debate open. And even after we decide, *Robert's Rules* allows us, with appropriate constraints, the chance to reconsider. Finally, deliberation aims at agreement or broad consensus, hoping that discussion will obviate the need for decision. Deliberation, then, puts off decisions, multiplies alternatives, permits considered judgment, and strives for consensus.

In nominating a candidate for President, only one vote is *necessary,* the final ballot of the party's convention. All the rest of the process, although it involves decisions to select delegates in the several states, is or ought to be deliberative. Evidently, the party's most authoritative decision only establishes an alternative for the voters in the general election. The nomination is the last step in a process of deliberation and the first step of a contest leading to an electoral decision.

The primary-dominated system, by contrast, all but displaces deliberation. In the first place, primary elections limit us because they demand *early* decisions by candidates. It is quite possible that a majority of Democrats in 1980 would have preferred some candidate other than President Carter or Senator Kennedy. "The voters don't want us," a Carter loyalist told me on the eve of the Florida primary, "but they don't want *them* even more." A great many Republican voters would have preferred President Ford to Ronald Reagan, including a great many who preferred Reagan to George Bush. Ford himself was eager to prevent Reagan's nomination, and when it became likely, Ford offered to run himself. Ford, however, had delayed too long; he would not have been able to enter enough primaries to change the result. Possibly Ford was genuinely unwilling to run unless a Reagan nomination threatened; possibly he secretly hoped, all along, that the party would turn to him. In either case, Ford's experience in 1980 (and Senator Humphrey's in 1976) indicates that our primaries demand that candidates decide early. They cannot respond to events or change their minds.

The primaries thus deprive us of the most powerful argument for persuading excellent people to seek office: the fear that they will otherwise be ruled by second-raters or worse.[5] By the time that such a threat has become credible, it is likely to be too advanced to be evitable.

Similarly, early support matters much more than considered support. Since voters tend to choose between candidates they feel have a "real chance" of winning, a tide runs in favor of candidates who establish themselves as front-runners. Voters in early primaries have a disproportionate influence on events. Several big states (with about 20 percent of the convention delegates) voted on "Super Tuesday," June 3, after the nominations were effectively decided. It would take away this advantage, of course, if we all voted on the same day, but then *only* early support would matter because voters would have no chance to react to or learn from the elections in other states.

In becoming a front-runner, established celebrities have an edge. Carter won as a dark horse in 1976, but he ran against a field of unknowns. It also helps to have an enthusiastic, ideological following. Even if you don't win, your zealots may keep you among the leaders. And you will have a good chance to win; primary voters are not representative of the party as a whole, and highly committed voters are likely to have disproportionate influence.[6] In the early primaries, moreover, against a fragmented opposition, an ideological following may enable a candidate to win with less than a majority, as Ronald Reagan often did in 1980. Senator George McGovern in 1972 won a similar victory by establishing himself as the candidate of the Democratic Left. Senator Edmund Muskie, an acceptable second choice for almost all factions, was driven from the race. The primaries have small place for second choices, even though, like second thoughts such selections are more likely to reflect a concern for the good of the whole.

The media, of course, play an enormous role in selecting front-runners. In the first place, media predictions tell voters where their "real choice" lies. More importantly, the media can create an important candidacy by coverage alone, as they certainly did with Congressman Anderson in 1980. The problem does not lie with the supposed ideological biases of the media; the worst distortions result from the desire to make political news exciting. Anderson was noteworthy in early Republican gatherings because he said strikingly different things. In 1972, by contrast, the press severely damaged Senator Muskie by focusing on his crying during a speech in Manchester, New Hampshire. Moreover, while it is important to win primaries, a victor must do "as well as expected" by the media and a losing candidate who fares better than the polls predict may establish himself as a serious contender. A "good" loss inspires supporters in subsequent states, just as a "bad" victory dispirits them. Muskie lost ground by winning New Hampshire in 1972 and Senator Henry Jackson's candidacy could not survive his victory in New York in 1976. As James Ceaser writes, "The media love the story, which is to say that they tend to look for, and overplay, new and unexpected developments. Thus they turn politics into drama, rather than reporting on the drama of politics."[7] At their best, the media encourage us to react to more or less accurate images, which we have no means of checking.

In short, the primaries give special weight to initial support for candidates who enter early, they advantage ideological followings, and they emphasize media images. They discourage considered judgment and place no particular value on party coalitions. They violate all the requirements of deliberation in precisely that aspect of our electoral process — the choosing of nominees — where deliberateness is most needed.

The older system of precinct and ward caucuses, leading to county and state conventions, was, even at its worst, based on discussion and personal knowledge of the candidates. The deliberation that occurred was often crass, ungrammatical, and parochial, but it *was* deliberation for all of that. It was based on local, face-to-face groups where real discussion and participation was possible and where people could select representatives who reflected the gamut of their views. The fault of the old system was simple: it shut people out. Party organizations were too often closed and unresponsive, denying citizens (and partisans) a role in an essential democratic process. But this shortcoming did not reflect on the convention system; it militated against excluding people *from* that system.

The logical reform would have been a more or less open caucus, similar to the present system in Iowa. Instead, the reform tradition insisted on a mass election where citizens cannot deliberate and in which control of such discussion as there is passes to the mass media.[8] Local party organizations and elites may have been discomfited, but at the cost of increasing the sway of far more powerful and less accessible elites, as Henry Jones Ford forecast long ago.[9] More of us vote in primaries, but our voices are not heard, and our vote says little about what we think, feel, and revere. Adding insult to injury, the primary system produces candidates who are unworthy. In 1980, voters made clear their distaste for the result; it is now up to their leaders to scrap the process.

Unfortunately, the primaries are probably here to stay. They are suited to liberal political theory, the "irrational Lockeanism" that dominates our thinking about public matters.[10] In liberal theory, human beings are not naturally political animals. They are isolated individuals, concerned to protect themselves and advance their essentially private interests. In this view, we have an interest in deciding who rules us, but no interest in ruling, since rule requires that we take time away from our private concerns. Self-government becomes government we *choose* rather than government in which we *participate*, and democracy is defined by elections, not deliberation. The primary system, which derives from liberal individualism, is compatible with all the forces that are fragmenting our communities, our political parties, and our public life. At best, we will try to "improve" the primaries, an endeavor that can inspire no confidence. These sadly limited efforts ignore the signs, evident in 1980, of a demand for politics and party government.

THE DEMOCRATS: THE NECESSITY OF PARTY

For the Democrats, the election of 1980 was their worst defeat in a quarter century. The returns seem unambiguous; the Democratic party was repudiated by an electorate that decided to "Vote Republican, For a Change." Yet even that statement must be qualified, given the peculiarities of the election.

Toward the end of his campaign, Jimmy Carter appealed more and more to party loyalties and the Democratic pantheon. A Democratic advertisement featured clips of Franklin Roosevelt, Harry Truman, and Jack Kennedy; Lady Bird Johnson and Muriel Humphrey said a few words. It was a celebration of tradition and an appeal to allegiance — and it came entirely too late.

For four years, Carter disdained the party and its organizations. He recognized that party loyalties — and especially, loyalties to party organizations — seemed to be attenuating, and he had no interest in reversing the decline. As Carter apparently saw it, the Democratic party apparatus was simply a collection of more or less parochial interest groups, committed to inflationary policies and the expansion of the federal bureaucracy and tied to outdated patronage politics. It was part of the "establishment" Carter had opposed in 1976, which for the most part had opposed his nomination. He saw little to hope from it, and he preferred to build a personal coalition devoted to policies deemed in the public interest, especially as defined by "good management" rather than politics. The personal note was ubiquitous; even the membership organization of the Democratic National Committee called itself "The President's Club."

In the first few months of his administration, Carter initiated a number of highly publicized ventures in direct contact with citizens designed to end the isolation of the Nixon years. He attended a "town meeting"; he answered telephone calls from voters, took notes on their questions, and called back with answers. It was undeniably good politics; the programs were popular, and they enlisted support. Yet they were allowed to lapse. The President evidently thought of them as symbolic gestures, a sort of political fluff to be sacrificed to the real, administrative demands of the Presidency. He did not return to the town meeting, for example, until late in his administration.

The President thus scorned party, the traditional basis of support in Congress and the country, but he did not appeal to voters directly in any way sufficiently consistent and compelling to move reluctant members of Congress to his side. Rather half-heartedly, he did invoke the public on behalf of the "windfall profits tax" against the oil lobby, and even that lukewarm appeal contributed to one of the infrequent cases in which his program succeeded. Carter seemed to realize that one cannot successfully appeal to the public very often. He did not recognize, as great Presidents always did, that this implies that recourse to the general public is most effective as the exception to a strategy of party government. Party, for all its faults, sometimes *may* move a member of Congress beyond immediate self-interest, which alone is enough to make it invaluable.

We need no encouragement, after all, to be self-interested and parochial. In a country as vast and diverse as the United States, the public interest is a distant abstraction. It may be that it is in my interest to help workers in Youngstown, but the connections that tie my interest to theirs are indirect, impalpable and subtle. I know, by contrast, that it helps me to pay lower taxes.[11] If you tell me that it is in my interest to pay taxes to support those Ohio workers, I will need persuading. I know, too, that America is a changing, complexly interdependent society that no one fully understands. Even if your reasoning is ingenious, you might be wrong; it might make matters worse to try to help the workers in Youngstown. Moreover, you may not have my best interests at heart. Even presuming that you mean well, you may not understand or care about what matters to me.[12] Surely, I have done all I can be asked to do if I take care of my own. That, at least, is the way all of us are tempted to reason, and many of us submit. Allegiance, public spirit, and support for the common good are in perennial short supply.

Politics — participation and partisanship — are indispensable means for developing civic spirit. My participation in deliberation enlists my support because it makes me feel less helpless: I contribute to the shaping of decisions instead of simply reacting to events. Political participation involves us in, and teaches us to see, the life of a larger society. For most of us, participation can only be local. But even close to home, we can come to know — and possibly, to trust — the local leaders who carry our voice to larger tribunals. These days, of course, even local participation is the exception, although it could be encouraged, and local party organizations are in disarray. But, for most of us, party still gives us some sort of political identity and defines leaders we can trust, "men like ourselves," who can at least be relied on to share more of our basic values than their opponents. Party is still the safest source of trust between rulers and ruled.[13]

Jimmy Carter did more than spurn party; he seemed to violate that trust. Historically, the Democratic party has stood for compassion and sympathy, for the refusal to allow human relations to be governed by the requirements of "efficiency" or "sound currency." The party's great rhetoric speaks to that commitment, from Bryan's "Cross of Gold" to Roosevelt's credo that "divine justice weighs the sins of the cold-blooded and the sins of the warm-hearted in different scales."[14] Carter's emphasis on management and quasi-monetarist fiscal policies were, at least, a new departure. In 1976, William Shannon wrote, Carter was "saying that government can be compassionate but also skeptical."[15] By 1980, the compassion seemed to have vanished.

On the face of it, Carter had broken with Democratic tradition, and he needed politics and party in the *conduct of government*, not merely in campaigns, to persuade voters that he acted out of necessity and with fidelity to the party's heritage. By campaign time, it was too late, especially since Ronald Reagan was clearly a man of warm sympathies. Thomas Jefferson taught that "sentiment, not science" was the source of justice, and whatever else may be said about his argument, it speaks to democratic politics in general and the politics of the Democratic party in particular.[16] Carter, neglecting Jefferson's maxim, helped seal his political doom.

For its part, Congress magnified all of Carter's faults. The horde of neophytes swept into office by Watergate were not elected by party organization, and most of them had run ahead of Carter in 1976. They owed the party little, and the President less. Carter's failures as a party and legislative leader left all too many members of Congress disposed to play a lone hand, insisting — with fervor greater than that of the Moral Majority — on pure liberal ideology or following their favorite interest groups. It was an exceptionally unproductive Congress, especially given the energy crisis and our economic troubles. Of course, politically, it is easier to give than to take away, and social justice is a difficult goal in times of relative scarcity.[17] Even if we are generous on that account, however, Congress's record was barren.

A great many voters detested this Congress, not so much because it was liberal as because it was obstructive. If only the Congress had been Republican, Jimmy Carter could have tried to repeat Harry Truman's campaign against the "obstructionists" of the "do-nothing" Eightieth Congress.[18] In this, at least, Carter and the congressional Democrats were united: Carter could not denounce them effectively. What the voters rejected, however, was not the Democratic party. It was *government without party*, the combination of Carter's managerialism and the Congress's indiscipline. That makes it harder than it ought to be to read the party currents in 1980.

THE NEW DEAL COALITION
AND THE NEW DEAL FAMILY

Political parties are not ad hoc coalitions of interest groups for and against particular policies, going out of being as quickly as they appear. Parties make deeper claims on our memories, our identities, and our hopes. In many ways, a party is like a family. New members are added; some old members are lost to new connections; some kinsmen become distant, while others, who have been out of touch, come back into the family circle. With those rare exceptions called "critical elections," parties undergo "slow, all but unconscious transformation."[19] The election of 1980 suggests that the New Deal coalition is no longer with us; but, to this moment at least, the New Deal family is still alive, its relationships strained and altered but still intact.

In 1932, Franklin Roosevelt inherited a political party in which the southern (and western) wing, Protestant and rural, had lost control to an urban, industrial wing, heavily Catholic and rooted in the Northeast.[20] The change was formally ratified in 1936 with the repeal of the "two-thirds" rule that had allowed the South to block any unacceptable candidate. The New Deal coalition picked up support as it went along — notably from Jews and blacks — but its center of gravity continued to lie with the northern white working class, increasingly unionized and composed of predominantly Catholic ethnic communities. John Kennedy's nomination and victory in 1960 relied on those voters, and it reaffirmed their Democratic allegiance.

Nevertheless, two gradual processes were changing the Democratic coalition. The first was obvious: Those who profited from the New Deal developed new economic interests. Protected by trade unions, contracts, seniority and pension rights, established workers had less to fear from unemployment and more to fear from inflation. Given the entitlements of this expanding "contract society," old anxieties were pushed into the background. Established workers became homeowners worried about property taxes and parents concerned with the costs of higher education. Moving into middle-class styles of life, sometimes at great cost, they felt menaced by affirmative action programs that seemed to threaten their own — and even more, their children's — ascent and which undermined the neighborhood school. A variety of new economic and social interests strained the old ties of established workers to the Democratic party.

On the whole, however, white ethnic workers remained loyal to the party. Their memories of the past ran too strong, and Republican hostility to their gains was too apparent. The "right to work" crusade by Republican hard-liners in 1958, for example, revitalized Democratic loyalties that had begun to waver in the 1950s. The white working-class communities stayed in the Democratic coalition, but they became increasingly exposed to cross-pressures, propertied proletarians who were vulnerable to issues like "communism in government" or, more recently, the "social issue."[21]

These ethnic working-class communities, the backbone of "regular" Democratic party organizations, became increasingly unreliable. The regulars became irregular, undependable voters; "safe" districts, in state or national elections, changed into the arenas of interparty competition. It has been years since the Democratic party could take these voters for granted, and holding them in the coalition requires increasing attention to their dignity, their particular concerns, and their sense of neglect.[22]

As white working-class Democrats ceased to be the core of the party's support, blacks replaced them. Increasingly, blacks are the "new Irish," the party regulars and the heart of Democratic straight-ticket support. Carter held black voters in 1980 and may even have increased his support marginally. In fact, Carter's achievement, in 1976, in bringing the South back into the Democratic fold was possible only because of monolithic support from southern blacks. The relatively high Democratic totals in the South in 1980 reflect Carter's own residual regional popularity, but they also reflect the comparatively large number of black voters. It is not merely a quixotic passion that made Senator Strom Thurmond speak, in the aftermath of Reagan's victory, of "reexamining" the Voting Rights Act of 1965. As long as that act remains in effect, a Democratic South is likely whenever the region's interests and feelings are reasonably reflected in the Democratic platform and nominee.[23]

The fact that blacks have displaced the white working class as the party's regulars, however, is an indication of shifts that have taken place in the Democratic coalition. The blacks have moved to the core; the white ethnics have moved to the periphery; the pattern of urban residence is replicated in party loyalty. This, by any standard, is a change from the old relationships of the New Deal.

In that sense, the Roosevelt coalition has come to an end, as it was bound to. There are middle-aged voters today who were not born when Franklin Roosevelt died, and the youngest voters in 1980 were only a year old when John Kennedy was shot. We will remember Roosevelt and the Great Depression less and less, and — just as Truman has suddenly acquired cachet — Kennedy will increasingly be the symbol whose memory excites Democratic partisans.

There are strong tactical reasons for that change of symbols. Democrats need to give unmistakable evidence, as Kennedy's campaign did in 1960, of their concern for white workers and ethnic Americans. Notably, no Catholic has received the Democratic nomination since Kennedy, despite a sharp rise in ethnic consciousness. Senator Edward Kennedy might have won the nomination in 1980, in fact, if he had been less identified with liberalism and more identified with his ethnic heritage. Attending to the dignity and the concerns of working-class, ethnic audiences must be a Democratic priority. In 1976, William Shannon thought that Carter was "tacitly repositioning his party" to achieve that goal, especially through his concern for "patriotism, a strengthening of families and neighborhoods, and the work ethic."[24] Carter's failure to develop these themes ranks high among the political failures of his administration.

Certainly, Democrats need to be concerned that working-class America be better represented in party councils and that the party give less attention, by contrast, to advocates of abortion rights, gay liberation, and similar movements, who have — given the logic of American politics — nowhere else to go except into third-party impotence. The Democrats have one tactical advantage. When they lose an election, the defeated candidates tend to be drawn from the party's extreme liberal wing, as were so many of this year's losers. Defeat can contain its own corrective, driving the party back to more pragmatic bastions. But that remains to be seen.

A final note is needed. Foreign policy strained the Democratic coalition as severely, in 1980, as the tensions inherent in the "contract society." Even among those voters who remember FDR, memories of the Second World War, the common experience of older and middle-aged voters, have grown more important as recollections of the depression wane. The war years created a deep sense of American power, and everything in the early postwar years strengthened that impression. For all but the youngest voters, American power and independence are basic expectations and fundamental assumptions rooted deep in the emotions. The "decline" of American power has, correspondingly, been both painful and fundamentally incomprehensible.

Since American postwar power depended, in part, on the prostrate condition of Europe and Japan, the decline of our position was predictable. Moreover, declining or no, America is still a colossus. Nevertheless, one does not "reason" with basic feelings. We grew up with the sense that America did not depend on anyone. We were genuinely independent, an "arsenal of democracy" capable, if the need arose, of going it alone. In large measure, these feelings were justified at the time: our only major shortage during World War II was rubber, and we rationed gasoline to save tires. Even during the Arab oil boycott of 1973, we were relatively unaffected and could have taken a high tone if we wished. In recent years, by contrast, we have been forced to deal with the reality of our dependence on others. We need the Saudis to keep the oil flowing at premium prices; we need the Germans to support the dollar; we must listen to both hector us about the need to control inflation. And so on. It does not help much to remind ourselves that other countries need us as much as we need them. The experience of dependence is painful, even if it is shared. In 1980, Steven Roberts observed, we were brought face-to-face with "America, the vulnerable."[25]

The prolonged conflict of America and Iran over the hostages reminded us of all the things we could *not* do, all the constraints and reasons for inaction. Reagan touched a deep chord when he said that, if elected, he would not "do nothing," as Carter had done. Raised in an activist culture, we believe that man can master nature and that civilization can rise above barbarism. Yet our helicopters broke down in the Iranian desert, and there was the Ayatollah, barbarism incarnate, and the crowds chanting, "Khomeini fights, Carter trembles." We *felt* it as a "humiliation," the word Reagan used, and Iran, along with any number of slights and setbacks, readied us for heroic measures in foreign policy. As Richard Betts wrote,

> In the 1970s . . . "No more Vietnams" became as misleading and confining a principle as "no more Munichs.". . . Today, the pendulum is swinging back. Soviet advances in Ethiopia, Afghanistan and Yemen and the collapse of the regime in Teheran, raise the specter of falling dominos. Hysterical reaffirmation of containment by large-scale intervention will be no improvement over adamant abstention.[26]

Betts is probably right, but the mood is unmistakable.

I suspect that we are ready for similarly drastic remedies in domestic affairs, where they may be more clearly needed. The voters do not want a nine-to-five regime that leaves them alone. They selected Reagan partly in the hope that he would prove a "strong leader," and a majority would probably welcome declaration of an "economic state of emergency." Of course, Americans are not eager for constraint and sacrifice. They may be ready for policies that suggest strong action and to which citizens can *contribute.*

President Carter's policies relied on indirect government controls, such as the effort to curb inflation through rising interest rates or the more successful attempt to limit gasoline consumption by allowing prices to rise. Such policies, however, make citizens feel helpless, whether or not they are successful. We are allowed only to react to events. Even when such policies work, we feel we are being manipulated, and all too often we suspect that these policies distribute sacrifice unfairly. Direct controls — gas rationing, for example — are more compatible with our dignity and with our concern for justice. They ask for conscious sacrifice for a public purpose, with the burden distributed on the basis of public criteria. And whatever their other problems, direct controls are more likely to make us feel that our problems can be solved by political action.

Certainly, there is no need for the Democrats to retreat from their commitment to "big government." They should, of course, suggest that they would manage government efficiently, and they need to demonstrate an increased concern for local community. But there is a good deal of reason to believe that, in foreign and domestic policy, many voters who defected to Reagan wanted *more* government, not less, and that they chose him hoping for a regime that would be less hesitant and ambivalent about the use of power. The Roosevelt coalition is passing, and the Kennedy coalition may be succeeding it within the New Deal family. That ought to hint, at least, at nostalgia for Camelot; imperial government may be on the verge of a new wave of popularity.

THE REPUBLICANS AND THE NEW CONSERVATIVES

It was surely a sign of the times that the Republican candidate, by his own admission, voted for Roosevelt all four times he ran.[27] One of Reagan's undoubted advantages was his freedom from the baggage of old-line Republicanism. He quoted Roosevelt happily; he paraded his admittedly peculiar trade-union past and his lifetime membership in the Screen Actors Guild. Even his attacks on the cherished gains of labor — his criticism of the minimum wage, for example — were couched in language designed to make them acceptable. Reagan argued for a "two-tier" wage system, with a lower minimum wage for teen-agers and the hard-core unemployed. Whatever else may be said of this proposal, it was tailored to allay the fears of established white workers. Reagan preferred to run as a New Dealer grown conservative, and that stance persuaded millions of voters that he was safe enough to afford them the luxury of dumping Carter.

Reagan's campaign, in other words, signals changes in conservatism more striking than any change in the Democratic majority. Not so long ago, Reagan's rhetorical fondness for organized labor would have been high treason in Republican circles. The "supply-side" economics symbolized by the Kemp-Roth tax proposal, moreover, indicates the change even more clearly. Traditional Republican doctrine always worried about inflation. True to laissez-faire, it wanted to let the market alone and relied heavily on the "bourgeois virtues" of the independent middle class. The cure for inflation, in this doctrine, was less consumption and more saving, self-discipline, and frugality. Asked the cure for rising food prices in 1947, Senator Robert A. Taft responded, "We should eat less."[28] Nothing could have been more alien to the style and substance of Reagan's campaign, and Reagan made much, scornfully, of Carter's suggestion that inflation resulted from the fact that we have lived "too well." Rectitude and self-denial were themes of Congressman Anderson's campaign, but Anderson's old style, middle-class individualism is now peripheral in Republican politics.

Reagan's proposals turn on the notion that less restraint — a massive tax cut — can stimulate investment and productivity enough to offset inflation. Self-indulgence takes the place of self-denial. After years of learning that "you don't shoot Santa Claus," the Republicans decided to nominate him. Even if Reagan's proposals work as well as he hopes, they make a mockery of middle-class virtues. Ants are only grim, ill-humored folks who eat badly; grasshoppers are good citizens who fight inflation too. Supply-side economics is self-consciously modeled on the Kennedy tax cut of 1963, and it clearly involves government planning, though planning of a decidedly conservative sort.

In fact, a good many of Reagan's promises suggest more government intervention, not less. During the campaign, for example, he argued for "enterprise zones" to stimulate growth in the industrial cities, and his transition team circulated a paper that would deny federal aid to any locality that persisted in rent control. These are conservative plans, but they call for a good deal of government involvement on behalf of the "private sector." And all this says nothing about Reagan's proposals for stronger defense and federal policies to defend the family.

In fact, the term "private sector" is a talisman. In the first place, it suggests that there is a legitimate *public* sector, an inescapable component of government input into and regulation of our economic life. In the second place, referring to the "private sector" allows Reagan to scrap "free enterprise" with its laissez-faire connotations. Like quoting Roosevelt, referring to the "private sector" is a way of disowning the past, abandoning the world of the independent, small-town bourgeoisie for the new world of tax shelters, multinationals, and computer programs, where planning is the rule.

Reagan suggests that the private sector, assisted by a sympathetic government, can make sacrifice unnecessary. We are an "energy-rich" country, and the energy companies will prove it. Taxing ourselves less will still enable us to balance the budget and provide for a bigger military, and at the same time interest rates will come down. Reagan, in other words, presents himself as the defender of the American "fifth freedom," the *right to consume,* and he assures us that we will enjoy that liberty in his term of office.

It is hard to say how much of this the voters believed. Carter took a more somber tone, but he also shied away from any call for self-denial, promising "careful" and "balanced" tax cuts and the like. Voters, in other words, were neither asked nor permitted to choose between austerity and extravagance. Anderson's "new realism" seems the exception to this rule, since he did not hesitate to call for restraint. With few exceptions, however, Anderson's supporters knew he would not win; they knew, in other words, that in practice they would not be required to *make* the sacrifices he urged. His candidacy, therefore, had a secret attraction for well-to-do liberals. Since in practice, a vote for Anderson helped elect Reagan, his supporters could affirm their anti-inflationary *principles* at the same time that they forwarded their inflationary *desires.* In any case, it seems likely that a great many of Reagan's supporters took their candidate's economics with a grain of salt.

It is hard to believe, for example, that a great many voters did not notice that Reagan's faith in the private sector was contradicted by Detroit's dramatic, dismal failure to anticipate the demand for small, fuel-economical cars. In reality, the auto industry showed all the rigidity and lack of imagination that, in conservative doctrine, is supposed to characterize government. The auto industry underrated the need to economize and our willingness to do so; the federal government, by contrast, had been urging the change on a recalcitrant Detroit for some time. The example of the auto industry does not augur well for a policy of "getting the government off the backs of the American.people." Detroit will need more help, not less, and the new conservatives will probably provide it. The private sector does not want to be let alone; it wants government to help it and, where necessary, to pick up the tab. In economics, that is likely to be the direction of the new regime.

A good many Democrats who defected to Reagan ignored his economics. They voted for him in the hope that he will do something about the "social issue," introducing government into the world of the family and the other traditional refuges of private life. Clearly, this calls for "big government" with a vengeance, and while the social issue was bound to hurt any Democratic regime, the new Republican administration is not likely to find it much more congenial.

Americans continued to feel society crumbling around them in 1980. Carter had promised to make the American family a major concern of his administration, but the Democrats only damaged themselves when they tried to address the issue. Civil libertarians and partisans of new, "liberated" arrangements protested against making the traditional family the norm of policy, and the administration yielded, although it ought to have been possible to advocate stronger and more stable relationships whether or not these are "traditional." Fundamentalists expected more from Carter than Sunday pieties, and they did not get it. And while Carter himself was against providing federal funds for abortion — little enough to ask, as "right-to-lifers" saw it — the Democratic convention in New York decidedly did not share the President's view.

Reagan made every effort to appeal to social conservatives, especially since the social issue lies at the hiatus between the liberals and working-class Democrats. There is little doubt that Reagan's administration will continue this strategy, and the new President can be relied on to oppose the ERA and abortion, to look for ways to permit prayer in the schools, and possibly to support aid to denominational education.

There is every reason, however, to think that Reagan's social conservatism, though sincere, is also superficial. The forces that are weakening local communities and families are bound up with our individualism, mobility, and commitment to growth. Change, "unsteady, irregular and hard to predict" makes yesterday's certainties into today's follies.[29] We cannot commit ourselves very deeply to the institutions that are so prone to change; and people, like everything else, are only too likely to be different tomorrow.[30] Children, uprooted from homes and neighborhoods, learn through loss to be more reserved in making their commitments. People who are left behind — so often the old — frequently suffer even more than those who leave, and become still more guarded in consequence. Long-distance may be "the next best thing to being there," but AT&T is only reminding us that we will probably *not* live close to our families or old friends. Our communities, as Scott Greer wrote years ago, are "limited liability communities" where we learn to commit ourselves only superficially, retaining the freedom to cut our losses or move up as the social market dictates.[31]

Family relationships are bound to reflect these currents. We have learned more and more to regard divorce as a normal event of life. The election of Reagan, the first divorced person to become President, will probably do more to legitimate divorce than his conservatism will do to stabilize families. Yet the more normal divorce seems, the more we are reminded that we can and do make mistakes in judging others, even in our most important commitments and in our strongest feelings. And thus the more we are likely to limit our subsequent commitments. Herbert Hendin writes that affection and harmony are growing scarcer, "in and out of families." We are drawing more and more into ourselves and away from family, country, and community.[32]

Reagan is not likely to lend federal power to the quest for stability in personal relationships. To do so, however indirectly, would require a willingness to curb individual freedom, change, and economic growth; but both Republican ideology and the corporate economy regard such restraint as anathema. To make family, community, and morality the goals of public policy would require that we subordinate private liberty to civil order, something neither Reagan nor his party is likely to consider. As Reagan's ambassador to the United Nations, Jeane Kirkpatrick, wrote in 1979,

> Republican spokesmen have consistently emphasized private concerns such as profit and taxes, and private virtues such as self-discipline and self-reliance, and either have not had, or have not communicated, a persuasive conception of the public good.[33]

The reason is simple: The tradition of liberal individualism, which shapes Republican ideology, acknowledges no public good that is not simply an aggregate of private goods and liberties. Reagan will give social conservatives the symbols, but he will leave the substance to the forces that are making for privatism and social disintegration. If there is light and hope in the future of the Republic, it is not visible in the election of 1980.

NOTES

1. Matthew Josephson, *The Politicos* (New York: Harcourt, Brace, 1938), p. 287. There are other suggestive similarities between the elections of 1980 and 1880. In 1880, the minority Democrats nominated their closest equivalent of a movie star, a handsome Union general, Winfield Scott Hancock, a hero of Gettysburg famed for his copious and wide-ranging profanity. General Hancock's economics were also as weirdly imaginative as Ronald Reagan's: he once described the tariff as a "local question." E. E. Robinson, *The Evolution of Political Parties* (New York: Harcourt, Brace, 1924), pp. 198-99.
2. This wonderful description of Reagan was coined by Mike Royko, "Maybe It's Better to Know Nothing," *Newark Star Ledger*, 8 November 1980.
3. Irwin Ross, *The Loneliest Campaign* (New York: New American Library, 1969), pp. 35-57.

4. I have tried to make my list inclusive: I count Coolidge, Cox, Davis, Goldwater, Harding, Landon, McKinley, Nixon, and Parker, although Professor Harry Jaffa is engaged in the attempt to rehabilitate Coolidge, and others on this list — like Landon and Goldwater — are men of parts by our contemporary standards.

5. Plato, *Republic*, Book I, 347B-D.

6. Austin Ranney, "The Representativeness of Primary Electorates," *Midwest Journal of Political Science* 12 (1968): 224-38.

7. James Ceaser, "America's Primaries: Part of the Problem or Part of the Solution?" *Los Angeles Times*, 8 June 1980.

8. Walter Nicgorski, "The New Federalism and Direct Popular Election," *Review of Politics* 34 (1972): 3-15.

9. Henry Jones Ford, "The Direct Primary," *North American Review* 190 (1909): 1-14.

10. Louis Hartz, *The Liberal Tradition in America* (New York: Harcourt, Brace, 1955).

11. Mancur Olson, *The Logic of Collective Action* (Cambridge, Mass.: Harvard University Press, 1965).

12. I have vivid memories of McGovern supporters explaining to devout Catholics that opposition to abortion was not, after all, in their "real" interest.

13. Otto Kirchheimer, "The Party in Mass Society," *World Politics* 10 (1958): 289-94; see also John L. Sullivan and Robert O'Connor, "Electoral Choice and Popular Control of Public Policy," *American Political Science Review* 66 (1972): 1256-68.

14. The quotation is from Roosevelt's acceptance speech, 27 June 1936: *The Public Papers and Addresses of Franklin D. Roosevelt* (New York: Random House, 1938), 5:235.

15. William V. Shannon, "Liberalism, Old and New," *New York Times*, 2 October 1976, p. 25.

16. Adrienne Koch and William Peden, eds., *The Life and Selected Writings of Thomas Jefferson* (New York: Modern Library, 1944), p. 404.

17. Otto Eckstein, "The Economics of the Sixties," *Public Interest* 19 (Spring 1970): 86-97.

18. Ross, *Loneliest Campaign*, pp. 176-80.

19. Josephson, *Politicos*, p. 287.

20. David Burner, *The Politics of Provincialism: The Democratic Party in Transition, 1918-1932* (New York: Knopf, 1967); see also Arthur N. Holcombe, *The New Party Politics* (New York: Norton, 1933).

21. Samuel Lubell, *The Revolt of the Moderates* (New York: Harper & Row, 1956).

22. Daniel P. Moynihan, "Bosses and Reformers," *Commentary* 31 (June 1961): 461-70.
23. An extraordinary amount of this is anticipated in V. O. Key, "The Future of the Democratic Party," *Virginia Quarterly* 28 (1952): 161-75; see also Donald Matthews and James Prothro, *Negroes and the New Southern Politics* (New York: Harcourt, Brace, Jovanovich, 1966).
24. Shannon, "Liberalism, Old and New."
25. Steven V. Roberts, "The Year of the Hostage," *New York Times Magazine*, 2 November 1980, pp. 26 ff.
26. Richard K. Betts, "From Vietnam to Yemen," *New York Times*, 25 March 1979.
27. Reagan also voted for Truman, apparently; John Connally, of course, voted Democratic as late as 1968, but he, evidently, is still regarded as a turncoat.
28. Ross, *Loneliest Campaign*, p. 42.
29. Alvin Toffler, "Law and Order," *Encounter* 41 (July 1973): 19.
30. I find it illustrative that in our tax code, *six months* is a "long term" for the purpose of assessing capital gains.
31. Scott Greer, *The Emerging City* (New York: Free Press, 1962).
32. Herbert Hendin, *The Age of Sensation* (New York: Norton, 1975); see also Christopher Lasch, *The Culture of Narcissism* (New York: Norton, 1979).
33. Jeane J. Kirkpatrick, "Why We Don't Become Republicans," *Commonsense*, Fall 1979, cited in the *New York Times*, 23 December 1980, p. A13; see also J. Hitchcock, "The Uses of Tradition," *Review of Politics* 35 (1973): 3-16.

Inaugural Address of
President Ronald Reagan

Thank you. Senator Hatfield, Mr. Chief Justice, Mr. President, Vice President Bush, Vice President Mondale, Senator Baker, Speaker O'Neill, Reverend Moomaw, and my fellow citizens:

To a few of us here today this is a solemn and most momentous occasion. And, yet, in the history of our nation it is a commonplace occurrence.

The orderly transfer of authority as called for in the Constitution routinely takes place as it has for almost two centuries and few of us stop to think how unique we really are.

In the eyes of many in the world, this every-four-year ceremony we accept as normal is nothing less than a miracle.

Mr. President, I want our fellow citizens to know how much you did to carry on this tradition.

By your gracious cooperation in the transition process you have shown a watching world that we are a united people pledged to maintaining a political system which guarantees individual liberty to a greater degree than any other. And I thank you and your people for all your help in maintaining the continuity which is the bulwark of our republic.

The business of our nation goes forward.

These United States are confronted with an economic affliction of great proportions.

We suffer from the longest and one of the worst sustained inflations in our national history. It distorts our economic decisions, penalizes thrift and crushes the struggling young and the fixed-income elderly alike. It threatens to shatter the lives of millions of our people.

Idle industries have cast workers into unemployment, human misery and personal indignity.

Those who do work are denied a fair return for their labor by a tax system which penalizes successful achievement and keeps us from maintaining full productivity.

But great as our tax burden is, it has not kept pace with public spending. For decades we have piled deficit upon deficit, mortgaging our future and our children's future for the temporary convenience of the present.

To continue this long trend is to guarantee tremendous social, cultural, political and economic upheavals.

You and I, as individuals, can, by borrowing, live beyond our means, but for only a limited period of time. Why then should we think that collectively, as a nation, we are not bound by that same limitation?

We must act today in order to preserve tomorrow. And let there be no misunderstanding — we're going to begin to act beginning today.

The economic ills we suffer have come upon us over several decades.

They will not go away in days, weeks or months, but they will go away. They will go away because we as Americans have the capacity now, as we have had in the past, to do whatever needs to be done to preserve this last and greatest bastion of freedom.

In this present crisis, government is not the solution to our problem; government is the problem.

From time to time we've been tempted to believe that society has become too complex to be managed by self-rule, that government by an elite group is superior to government for, by and of the people.

But if no one among us is capable of governing himself, then who among us has the capacity to govern someone else?

All of us together — in and out of government — must bear the burden. The solutions we seek must be equitable with no one group singled out to pay a higher price.

We hear much of special interest groups. Well our concern must be for a special interest group that has been too long neglected.

It knows no sectional boundaries, or ethnic and racial divisions and it crosses political party lines. It is made up of men and women who raise our food, patrol our streets, man our mines and factories, teach our children, keep our homes and heal us when we're sick.

Professionals, industrialists, shopkeepers, clerks, cabbies and truck drivers. They are, in short, "We the people." This breed called Americans.

Well, this Administration's objective will be a healthy, vigorous, growing economy that provides equal opportunities for all Americans with no barriers born of bigotry or discrimination.

Putting America back to work means putting all Americans back to work. Ending inflation means freeing all Americans from the terror of runaway living costs.

All must share in the productive work of this "new beginning," and all must share in the bounty of a revived economy.

With the idealism and fair play which are the core of our system and our strength, we can have a strong, prosperous America at peace with itself and the world.

So as we begin, let us take inventory.

We are a nation that has a government — not the other way around. And this makes us special among the nations of the earth.

Our Government has no power except that granted it by the people. It is time to check and reverse the growth of government which shows signs of having grown beyond the consent of the governed.

It is my intention to curb the size and influence of the Federal establishment and to demand recognition of the distinction between the powers granted to the Federal Government and those reserved to the states or to the people.

All of us — all of us need to be reminded that the Federal Government did not create the states; the states created the Federal Government.

Now, so there will be no misunderstanding, it's not my intention to do away with government.

It is rather to make it work — work with us, not over us; to stand by our side, not ride on our back. Government can and must provide opportunity, not smother it; foster productivity, not stifle it.

If we look to the answer as to why for so many years we achieved so much, prospered as no other people on earth, it was because here in this land we unleashed the energy and individual genius of man to a greater extent than has ever been done before.

Freedom and the dignity of the individual have been more available and assured here than in any other place on earth. The price for this freedom at times has been high, but we have never been unwilling to pay that price.

It is no coincidence that our present troubles parallel and are proportionate to the intervention and intrusion in our lives that result from unnecessary and excessive growth of Government.

It is time for us to realize that we are too great a nation to limit ourselves to small dreams. We're not, as some would have us believe, doomed to an inevitable decline. I do not believe in a fate that will fall on us no matter what we do. I do believe in a fate that will fall on us if we do nothing.

So, with all the creative energy at our command let us begin an era of national renewal. Let us renew our determination, our courage and our strength. And let us renew our faith and our hope. We have every right to dream heroic dreams.

Those who say that we're in a time when there are no heroes — they just don't know where to look. You can see heroes every day going in and out of factory gates. Others, a handful in number, produce enough food to feed all of us and then the world beyond.

You meet heroes across a counter — and they're on both sides of that counter. There are entrepreneurs with faith in themselves and faith in an idea who create new jobs, new wealth and opportunity.

There are individuals and families whose taxes support the Government and whose voluntary gifts support church, charity, culture, art and education. Their patriotism is quiet but deep. Their values sustain our national life.

Now, I have used the words "they" and "their" in speaking of these heroes. I could say "you" and "your" because I'm addressing the heroes of whom I speak — you, the citizens of this blessed land.

Your dreams, your hopes, your goals are going to be the dreams, the hopes and the goals of this Administration, so help me God.

We shall reflect the compassion that is so much a part of your makeup.

How can we love our country and not love our countrymen? And loving them, reach out a hand when they fall, heal them when they're sick and provide opportunity to make them self-sufficient so they will be equal in fact and not just in theory?

Can we solve the problems confronting us? Well the answer is a unequivocal and emphatic yes.

To paraphrase Winston Churchill, I did not take the oath I've taken with the intention of presiding over the dissolution of the world's strongest economy.

In the days ahead I will propose removing the roadblocks that have slowed our economy and reduced productivity.

Steps will be taken aimed at restoring the balance between the various levels of government. Progress may be slow — measured in inches and feet, not miles — but we will progress.

It is time to reawaken this industrial giant, to get government back within its means and to lighten our punitive tax burden.

And these will be our first priorities, and on these principles there will be no compromise.

On the eve of our struggle for independence a man who might've been one of the greatest among the Founding Fathers, Dr. Joseph Warren, president of the Massachusetts Congress, said to his fellow Americans, "Our country is in danger, but not to be despaired of. On you depend the fortunes of America. You are to decide the important questions upon which rest the happiness and the liberty of millions yet unborn. Act worthy of yourselves."

Well I believe we the Americans of today are ready to act worthy of ourselves, ready to do what must be done to insure happiness and liberty for ourselves, our children and our children's children.

And as we renew ourselves here in our own land we will be seen as having greater strength throughout the world. We will again be the exemplar of freedom and a beacon of hope for those who do not now have freedom.

To those neighbors and allies who share our freedom, we will strengthen our historic ties and assure them of our support and firm commitment.

We will match loyalty with loyalty. We will strive for mutually beneficial relations. We will not use our friendship to impose on their sovereignty, for our own sovereignty is not for sale.

As for the enemies of freedom, those who are potential adversaries, they will be reminded that peace is the highest aspiration of the American people. We will negotiate for it, sacrifice for it; we will not surrender for it — now or ever.

Our forbearance should never be misunderstood. Our reluctance for conflict should not be misjudged as a failure of will.

When action is required to preserve our national security, we will act. We will maintain sufficient strength to prevail if need be, knowing that if we do so we have the best chance of never having to use that strength.

Above all we must realize that no arsenal or no weapon in the arsenals of the world is so formidable as the will and moral courage of free men and women.

It is a weapon our adversaries in today's world do not have.

It is a weapon that we as Americans do have.

Let that be understood by those who practice terrorism and prey upon their neighbors.

I am told that tens of thousands of prayer meetings are being held on this day; for that I am deeply grateful. We are a nation under God, and I believe God intended for us to be free. It would be fitting and good, I think, if on each inaugural day in future years it should be declared a day of prayer.

This is the first time in our history that this ceremony has been held, as you've been told, on this West Front of the Capitol.

Standing here, one faces a magnificent vista, opening up on this city's special beauty and history.

At the end of this open mall are those shrines to the giants on whose shoulders we stand.

Directly in front of me, the monument to a monumental man. George Washington, father of our country. A man of humility who came to greatness reluctantly. He led America out of revolutionary victory into infant nationhood.

Off to one side, the stately memorial to Thomas Jefferson. The Declaration of Independence flames with his eloquence.

And then beyond the Reflecting Pool, the dignified columns of the Lincoln Memorial. Whoever would understand in his heart the meaning of America will find it in the life of Abraham Lincoln.

Beyond those monuments to heroism is the Potomac River, and on the far shore the sloping hills of Arlington National Cemetery with its row upon row of simple white markers bearing crosses or Stars of David. They add up to only a tiny fraction of the price that has been paid for our freedom.

Each one of those markers is a monument to the kind of hero I spoke of earlier.

Their lives ended in places called Belleau Wood, the Argonne, Omaha Beach, Salerno and halfway around the world on Guadalcanal, Tarawa, Pork Chop Hill, the Chosin Reservoir, and in a hundred rice paddies and jungles of a place called Vietnam.

Under such a marker lies a young man, Martin Treptow, who left his job in a small town barber shop in 1917 to go to France with the famed Rainbow Divison.

There, on the Western front, he was killed trying to carry a message between battalions under heavy artillery fire.

We are told that on his body was found a diary.

On the flyleaf under the heading, "My Pledge," he had written these words: "America must win this war. Therefore I will work, I will save, I will sacrifice, I will endure, I will fight cheerfully and do my utmost, as if the issue of the whole struggle depended on me alone."

The crisis we are facing today does not require of us the kind of sacrifice that Martin Treptow and so many thousands of others were called upon to make.

It does require, however, our best effort, and our willingness to believe in ourselves and to believe in our capacity to perform great deeds; to believe that together with God's help we can and will resolve the problems which now confront us.

And after all, why shouldn't we believe that? We are Americans.

God bless you and thank you. Thank you very much.

Index